With Sai Baba by my Side

An unusual story

Publisher's note

The original material was published in Danish as two books. The first book was published in 1994. As the material for the second book was ready for publication in Danish in 2012, the first book was edited and published with the same cover look as the second book to make a pair.

The first book was initially translated to English by Preben P. Sorensen, as stated in Acknowledgements in 1993, but had not been published. The first part of this translation has been reworked by Karin Valentin and May Engel while the rest of book one and book two have been translated by Erik Istrup.

The translations of the two books, is here published as one, after final proofreading, but still presented as two books, named Part One and Part Two.

The author uses the terms, dream and vision. A dream is where you redraw from your usual state of consciousness to the dream state when you are sleeping. During a vision, you expand your consciousness to include the consciousness where the vision is experienced.

This edition of Marguerite Janving's story has a different title than the original, English edition. This is done to place the focus on the human journey and not the excitement for the master. The book is printed in black and white, but the colour pictures is presented on the inside of the cover. The rest of the pictures are pencil drawings and presented through part one.

Marguerite Jalving was born in 1931 and died in Denmark on february 15. 2015, 84 years old.

Thank you to Sai Baba, The Kryon, Kuthumi Lai Singh and others for participating in the creation of this book. You have been very present all through the process and urged me to move on.

- Erik Istrup

With Sai Baba by my Side
An unusual story

by Marguerite Jalving
Illustrated with Sai Baba's artwork via Jalving

Humanity ought to think itself lucky having Sai Baba among us today
and we should make an effort to live by His message: "There is only
one religion, the religion of love."

This book is dedicated to
Bhagavan Sri Sathya Sai Baba.

Then Jesus said onto him:
"Except ye see signs and wonders, ye will not believe."
John, .4:48.

There is only one religion,
the religion of love

Marguerite Jalving, December 1993
Aum Sai Ram

[With love Baba]

Erik Istrup Publishing
Jyllandsgade 16 stth, 9610 Nørager, Danmark
eip@erikistrup.dk
www.erikistrup.dk/publishing/

Contents

You must be a lotus unfolding its petals
when the sun rises in the sky, unaffected by
the slush where it is born or even
the water which sustains it
- *Sai Baba*

Aum Sai Ram

Acknowledgements (for Part One)

First and foremost, I would like to express my gratitude to Sai Baba, for all the beautiful dreams and visions; words fail me. Thank you, Swami for your guidance, without it, this book would not have come into existence.

I would also like to thank Gerda Nørgaard who has done a great job by typing and editing the manuscript.

Special thanks to Mrs. Maheswary Gopalasamy from Prasanthi Nilayam and all my friends, who encouraged me to write this book.

Finally, I would like to express my gratitude to Preben P. Sorensen from Australia, who translated the book from Danish to English, and to my friends who assisted in proofreading of the manuscript.

- Marguerite Jalving, December, 1993.

Aum Sai Ram

Foreword (for Part One)

The author of this book, Marguerite Jalving, is a person with both feet on the ground.

With her fashionable high heels and elegant style, she stands with her strong temperament, firm in her own opinions. She gives vent to spontaneous anger as well as enthusiasm and sometimes less humble thoughts to Sri Sathya Sai Baba, when she thinks, He goes too far. At the same time, she also feels the deepest affection and humble surrender for the divine, which is this book's paradox.

You will find the book both humorous and deeply devotional; a picture of a human being's dialogue with the divine, with its dreams and heavenly visions.

- Lise Jersing

Dreams and visions

I have had, and still have marvellous, beautiful visions and dreams with Sai Baba.

The reader may find it difficult to distinguish between a vision and a dream as both take place during sleep. However, there is a difference which is almost impossible to describe, but I shall try anyway.

In a dream, Baba comes and gives me a message, or shows me something I ought to learn; to put it simply: a lesson.

A vision is something quite different. Here I am with Baba, or alone, in beautiful celestial places full of light, and with a wonderful atmosphere. This adventure is Baba's gift to me. For a short moment, I am allowed to experience this wonderful atmosphere in different planes. It will be clear from the context of the book.

I would like to add that these are just words, words, words, which I try to use to express my experiences. Ultimately, these visions cannot be described as they are divine experiences.

One must have faith in higher powers, which are beyond our physical world and daily life, if we want to understand what the meaning of life is.

How I came to write my book

I started writing, "*With Sai Baba by my Side*" at the beginning of December 1992 after several people urged me to write this book.

In spite of the many requests, I did not feel sure that I should. The idea of writing a book seemed absurd to me as I am neither an author nor a journalist, and at the same time I felt it would be too big a task for me to manage. Nevertheless, one of my friends said to me, "At least you should write down your dreams, they are so fantastic and beautiful."

"No," I said, "I do not at all want to think along these lines. And besides that, the dreams are only meant for me."

Now and then I thought about the many beautiful dreams and visions in which Baba came to me. Especially one vision of islands, which I tried to interpret, that kept coming into my mind. Often it is difficult to grasp what Baba wants you to understand, and even if you think you have understood the message, there is still a long way from understanding to practice.

At that time, I had a colour brochure with pictures of the Maldives Islands, situated in the Indian Ocean. They are exotic islands far away from civilisation; I imagined the natural surroundings by the sea filled with a blessed peace. It was attractive. The brochure stated that you could learn to dive, deep down, to the virgin coral reef.

"This is something for me, to try to dive down to the bottom of the sea to the coral reef. That must be a fantastic experience," I said to a friend.

She said, "What are you going to do there? You are not supposed to dive down to the bottom of the sea, but to dive into your own inner being. What about all your beautiful dreams and visions?" We were somewhat amused about the whole thing.

Later, I thought about it. I began seriously pondering if I really should start to write a book! Was it Baba's idea?

Finally, I came to an agreement with myself. If there is anything worth doing, and meaningful, then it has to be to write down my dreams and visions. So, it was not to the depth of the Indian Ocean I had to dive, but deep down into my being, which I slowly started to do.

As soon as I had started, Baba came to me in several dreams. From the different dreams, I got the idea that it was Baba's wish that I should write the book. I will leave that for the reader to experience.

Please, bear in mind that these are only my experiences with Baba. Many other people have had great experiences with Him. And they are all different. He gives each and everyone what they need.

Baba is among us today. Everybody can travel to India to see and experience Him. The first time one travels to India to visit Sai Baba, it would be best not to expect anything. With this attitude, I believe, one will have the greatest experience.

It is always Baba who is the giver, and I am the humble receiver. I have learned to take what I get and be grateful. Baba knows best.

I was amused when I figured out how long it took me to write the book. It turned out that I had been writing for nine months, and I suppose you know what else takes nine months!

Meeting Sai Baba

It all started one summer day in 1978, when a friend of mine called and asked if I would like to go to see a film and listen to a lecture by Hagen Hasselbalch, about a holy man in India whose name was Sai Baba and who could do miracles. It sounded interesting to me, so we went along. Many people showed up, and it was really interesting, so interesting that I felt like going to India right away to see who this Sai Baba really was.

As days went by it receded in my mind, and I did not think about it till a few months later. On a sudden impulse, I went into a shop and bought a magazine, one which, by the way, I had never bought before. The first page I opened, contained a long article with many beautiful pictures of Sai Baba written by Hagen Hasselbalch.

I was very fascinated by Sai Baba so I bought the magazine again, the following week, when the article finished. Having read it a few times, Sai Baba had made such a great impression on me that I decided straight away to start saving for a trip to India to see and experience Him.

I wrote a letter to Him in which I told Him how much I admired His work and what He stood for. I was very anxious to know if I would get a reply, as I had written that I would see Him in November.

Five weeks passed without anything happening, but then one day, when I was sitting in my room reading the article about Sai Baba, a smell which I could not quite define suddenly appeared, but it made me think about something burning. The smell got stronger and stronger, and I got scared and went into the kitchen to find out if I had forgotten to turn off something. That was not the case, so I went into the room again and continued my reading when my glance fell on one of the pictures of Sai Baba on which holy ash, or "vibhuti", was spreading. Then it occurred to me that it was vibhuti, the holy ash, which was giving off the smell. Later, I have been told that this is one of Sai Baba's ways of showing His presence.

From that day on many different and strange things took place.

Each day while I was at home relaxing, I felt vibrations like electric currents through my body; at the beginning it scared me quite a lot. Little by little, I connected this strange phenomenon with Sai Baba. I thought a lot about Him, but nevertheless, I could not quite understand what was going on. The only thing now on my mind was to go to India as soon as possible to Sai Baba. As days went by the vibrations turned into exercises and then into what I later realized was yoga.

Baba now started to talk to me as an inner voice. He calmed me and said I should not be afraid. The yoga would benefit me and, at the same time, He said, "There is a reason for everything Baba teaches you. It is all something you will need in the future."

It now turned out to become a steady programme every morning during which Baba taught me yoga for about half an hour. After that I repeated a ritual after Him, and this I still do to this day. As a matter of fact, I would like to say that I have never ever in my life been interested in yoga. I had hardly any idea what it was all about, as I had never been interested in spiritual things like meditation and the like of which I had not experienced before. I now felt that I had a need to get greater knowledge about those subjects. I went to the library to borrow books about yoga. There I got hold of a book with illustrations and realised that it was Hatha Yoga, which Sai Baba was teaching me. I also understood the benefit of the different and very simple exercises. At the same time, I read a great deal about India and Hinduism.

My life changed slowly as I gradually lost interest in the material world. The experiences with Sai Baba fascinated me so much that they overshadowed everything else and my first trip to India was drawing closer.

Sai Baba taught me the Hindu greeting and brought the palms of my hands together each time He talked to me. He always said, "Remember, nothing is accidental. There is a reason for everything that happens to you. Baba develops and prepares you and has a task for you, which He knows you can do and which you will be happy about. You are going to help to spread my message, but remember all beginnings are difficult. The beginning is necessary in order to proceed."

The last fortnight before going, Sai Baba trained me in sitting cross-legged, the posture you sit in during darshan. He also made me stop smoking, because in Prasanthi Nilayam liquor and tobacco are not allowed. Finally, the day came when I, for the first time, was going to India to my Guru and Master, which Sai Baba indeed had become. From the other side of the world, He had changed my life.

India

My first journey to India in 1979 went via Bombay to Bangalore where I stayed overnight. The next day I took a taxi to Puttaparthi. I knew that Sai Baba was in Prasanthi Nilayam, He had said so to me. Prasanthi Nilayam, Sai Baba's ashram, means "The Abode of the Highest Peace".

Never in my life had I experienced anything as exciting as when I, the next morning, drove through the small Indian villages. Everything was so foreign to me with the holy cows which always gave way at the last moment. I had the feeling that I was taking part in the crowd scene for a film. This is the impression I got of India the first time I was there. The rain was pouring down and I asked the driver if the monsoon had started. He said "no" and told me that it did not start till June, but it rained so heavily that one could not see through the windows of the car. When we finally arrived at Prasanthi Nilayam, everything was drowned in the rain. This was the first disappointment; later, more was to come.

I was shocked when I saw where I was going to stay. As you know, I had never been in India and did not know what an ashram was; I was horrified. Everything was so different from what I had imagined. I pumped up my inflatable mattress and was on the verge of tears. My lodging gave me the impression that I was in a cell with bars in front of the windows. I did not see Sai Baba. But I saw all these strange people with stripes on their forehead who looked peculiar. I did not get any food. It was a devastating feeling.

Baba now said to me, "Relax, and remember now that all beginnings are difficult. Nothing is accidental. You need Baba and Baba needs you."

I went out into the rain, for I felt like seeing Sai Baba and His temple. I stood in front of it as the rain was pouring down, and finally, I went back soaking wet to try to get some sleep. The next morning the sun was shining but I did not get any breakfast. The only thing on my mind was to go to darshan and see Sai Baba. darshan means seeing the Lord and receiving His Blessing. Normally, Baba gives darshan twice a day during which everybody can see Him and perhaps have contact with Him. Of course, I expected that He would call me for an interview as I had travelled halfway across the world to meet Him.

The only long frock I had taken along had been drenched the night before, so I dressed in a short one, ignorant about the fact that one has to be "properly" dressed for darshan. Arms and legs must be covered, and a sari was the solution, but of course I did not have one. I arrived, as mentioned before, in my short dress and was lucky to get a seat in the front row. One of Baba's female disciples came up to me and said that I was not supposed to wear a short dress, and I had to take off my shoes as well, as I was on holy ground. She suggested that I should go and buy a sari and come back for the afternoon darshan. Then I went into hysterics and answered that I had travelled so far and had become soaking wet during the downpour the previous evening. Now finally I had the opportunity to see Sai Baba, and I was determined to stay and had no intention of leaving. She had to give up and shook her head at having to deal with such an ignorant Westerner.

However, a sweet Indian woman came to my rescue and lent me a shawl which could cover my arms. I thanked her and stayed where I was.

Finally, the moment came when Sai Baba arrived. He first went to the men's site. Note that in India, the sexes are separated so the men sit on one side and women on the other during darshan. Baba went slowly along the rows and received letters which were handed to Him. Now and then He stooped and blessed somebody, said a few words to others and came closer to the place where I sat. I felt as though I was going to faint, and now Baba stood just in front of me, but He did not address me. Instead, He spoke to an Indian woman behind me, after which He walked on without so much as giving me a glance.

What I felt cannot be expressed in words. My head was spinning. I was furious with Baba and just felt like going home immediately. I just could not understand that He had ignored me. But Baba continued with the darshan, after which He went into the temple.

The first thing I did, of course, was to go to buy a sari, which, by the way, I did not know how to drape, so I had to give up. Later, however, I learnt the art. The next thing was to find out when the canteen opened. I had had nothing to eat or drink for a whole day.

First, I had to buy some coupons, and I lined up in a long queue. Suddenly, someone said to me, "This queue is only for men." Then I had to go and line up in another queue. I had not thought about that. We Westerners do not think along those lines. Finally, it was my turn. I was standing with a plate on which I was served a lot of different things, all served in one go, with rice in the middle. The smell of the food with the strange spices made my stomach turn. Furthermore, I saw to my disgust that one ate with one's fingers. I decided I had to try if I was not to die of hunger. I tried with my fingers, but the smell alone made me sick. I left the canteen without having eaten anything. Instead, I went to buy some fruit. But deep inside I felt that I would never be able to eat that food and never with my fingers. (Today there is a canteen for Westerners, where you will also find cutlery). I then went back and tried to rest for a couple of hours until I had to go for darshan in the evening.

Baba spoke reassuringly to me and said, "You must be patient, and remember there is a meaning in everything, and everything is OK." I was thinking that Baba had purposely not asked me in for an interview at the first darshan, for I had of course to learn to be patient. During the darshan in the afternoon, I was sure that He would ask me in for an interview.

I had put on my long dress, which was dry now. I did not know how to wear the sari as mentioned before, but I felt that with my long dress, I was correctly dressed. I once again went to darshan but this time I sat in the second row. Everybody waited eagerly. Probably, about 2-3,000 people were gathered, and then it happened again. Baba appeared, and this time He went to the women first. Everything repeated itself. Baba received letters, blessed things which were handed to Him, stopped now and then and spoke to some and got closer to where I sat. I was so excited that my heart almost stopped beating, and Baba now came slowly towards me ... but passed.

I was hopping mad. My patience had come to an end, and in that moment, I lost all feelings for Baba. I did not understand at all what the meaning was. Sai Baba had guided me every single day, taught me the Indian greeting and how to sit cross-legged, taught me yoga and asked me to come. Had all this just happened in order to see Him walk past me? "No, Baba," I thought. "I am not going to stay one more night. I have nothing to do here. I am totally finished with You and Puttaparthi. I leave for Bangalore tonight."

Then Baba talked to me and said, "You stay; you are not going anywhere!"

I had planned to be there for eight days, but I ignored Baba's words and would have nothing to do with Him anymore. I was quite sure that I had been in Puttaparthi for the first and the last time. Everything had been one big disappointment. So I went to Bombay and moved into a luxury hotel costing 350 rupees per night, nothing less would do. I had not had proper food or anything to drink for two days. For a change, I now had all that the heart could desire, and I enjoyed it. The strange thing was that Baba did not let go of me. He spoke to me and said, "You will come back to Prasanthi Nilayam again. Remember, all beginnings are difficult, but the beginning is necessary in order to go on. It is at the beginning that we make mistakes, and we have to learn from them."

Everything was as before. In the morning, Baba taught me yoga after which I repeated the ritual after Him, and each time He talked to me, He brought my palms together in the Indian greeting. It only took place when I was alone. Baba can always see me. He knows what I think and do, and I must admit that the loving way in which Baba talks to me, teaches me yoga, etc. results in the fact that I cannot live my life without Baba, although I did not quite understand it at that time. I returned home eight days later still more confused than before I went. It happened as Baba had said. I once again went to Prasanthi Nilayam. Many other strange things happened before I left for India ten months later. Yes, when Baba calls, you go, regardless of whether you want to or not. One simply cannot do anything else.

The drawings

One evening, shortly after I had come back home, I attended a spiritual gathering with a few friends. It was my first meeting. The medium came up to me and said, "You should have a pencil and paper by your side when you are calm and at peace. I see it clearly."

She probably thought that I looked somewhat confused because she said once again, "I see it clearly. Please try to be a little open."

I made light of it and when we came out we made fun of it. I said to my friends, "Things start to become more and more interesting. First, Baba teaches me all sorts of things, for instance yoga, and now I am supposed to have a pencil and paper. What will the next be?"

As mentioned before, it was my first meeting, so the medium did not know me at all and had no idea about my relationship with Sai Baba, nor did she know about my journey to India. My friends thought, however, that I should give it a try; in fact, we found it exciting.

A few days later, when I sat in my living room and relaxed, I put a pencil and a pad next to me. And what happened? My hand took the pencil, and I started to draw circles. I was extremely surprised because, in fact, it was not me who was drawing, but it was as though my hand were guided. Little by little it got more and more shape, and suddenly it turned into Indian goddesses, fishes, flowers and birds.

I suppose I do not have to tell you that I have never been able to draw before. I do not have any artistic talents. I have not been so surprised as when I saw what my hand had created on the paper.

The drawings became more and more beautiful. I was also quite thrilled by them. Baba now started to intervene. He said to me, "What you are drawing is beautiful. One day, you are going to be Baba's great artist and disciple. Through your drawings, you are going to help spread my message, but remember, all beginnings are difficult."

I was now so fascinated by what I was drawing that everything else receded into the background. I was living my life completely with Sai Baba. As soon as I had finished a new drawing, He said to me, "Place it in a frame, so I can really look at it."

I framed it, and Baba and I looked at it together. Little by little it became quite natural for me to be guided by Baba, down to the smallest detail. He always said to me, "Take good care of your drawings, they will be of great importance one day. Put them in a briefcase with dates and numbers. Make sure they do not get soiled and do not give any away. And remember, everything takes place as it should. Everything I am teaching you, you will need. Nothing is accidental, everything has a deep significance."

The second trip I had planned for India was drawing closer. I was not sure whether I should or shouldn't go. My last journey, which had turned into a great disappointment, was still clear in my mind. However, my longing for Sai Baba was uppermost in my mind, although I did not understand how and why it happened, and I still do not quite understand what is happening to me. Baba then said to me, "This time you will arrive with your drawings."

I was immediately encouraged and felt I had a reason to travel the long distance to India.

Drawing no. 134 from 1981

Going to India again

Well, I was going to India for the second time in September 1980. I had set aside eight days for the journey, and this time everything worked out much better. Nothing surprised me. I was better prepared than last time, so I felt at ease. The sun was shining this time, and Baba received me in such a beautiful way, which I shall never forget. I arrived early in the afternoon, with plenty of time to take part in darshan. There were a few Westerners, but it was mostly Indians. I went there early, to get a good a seat.

Yes, I was sitting here again! Understand it whoever can, and this time dressed in a sari! I could not understand it myself, but I had to be here, whether I liked it or not. Finally, the moment came, that I had spent ten months waiting for. Sai Baba appeared and went slowly towards a devotee who was sitting in front of the pillars of the temple. He spoke a few words to him and then went back again. There were many that afternoon who did not manage to see Baba, and some thought that He had not given darshan at all, but He had to me. I had seen Baba at a distance, the sight I had spend so much time waiting for, and I felt at peace. If Baba this time had passed me without even giving me a glance, or if He eventually had stopped and not addressed me, I do not know how I would have reacted. But He did neither of those things, and I felt happy.

A little later Bhajans, which are holy Indian hymns, were chanted, and now Baba did something which I shall never forget in my life. While the Bhajans were sung in Prasanthi Nilayam, Baba came out and faced me and gently put my palms together, the greeting Baba had taught me, and said, "Welcome to Prasanthi Nilayam, this is your true home. In these eight days, you will experience Prasanthi Nilayam as your home."

"Thank you Baba, my beloved."

These eight days became the turning point in my life. Everything was upside down. Nothing was as before and never will be again: A more beautiful welcome than the one Baba gave me, nobody could have.

In all the eight days I was at Prasanthi Nilayam, Baba did something to make me feel at home. The first day during darshan in the morning Baba just appeared and then drove to the college. Baba has colleges and schools in different places in India. He is reviving the Indian culture and spirituality in education.

There was no darshan, so when Baba had driven off, people got up and walked away. I felt a little unsure, and did not quite know if I should stay or leave the temple area. Then Baba said to me, "Just be quiet and remain where you are. Relax, in no time I shall be back." As I was used to receiving instructions from Baba, I of course remained seated. Baba returned twenty minutes later, and you could hear the people shout, "He is coming, He is coming."

Sure enough, Baba got out of His car and came walking slowly into the square. When He was about two metres away from me, He stopped abruptly, turned slowly around and looked directly at me. It was so direct and personal that an Indian woman, who was sitting almost next to me, exclaimed, "Baba looked at you, He knows you are here."

"Yes, indeed, I do hope He does," I answered.

Yet again Baba did not just walk past me, and I felt more and more at home, because I felt I was gradually beginning to understand Baba's doing. Every day when Baba approached me, He talked to me and looked lovingly at me and then walked on. Not one single day during the eight days I stayed there, did He pass me by. After darshan He went into His room in the temple. Even though He was in the temple, I felt His presence, when He talked to me.

Baba said, "You have now arrived home, home after a long journey, Prasanthi Nilayam is your true home. But remember, all beginnings are difficult, and there is a meaning to everything. Nothing I teach you is accidental; all of it you will need later, but everything takes place in a certain sequence. I am preparing and developing you for a task. In this way, you will take part in spreading my message. Your drawings will be of great importance. Look after them well. When you are at home, we will both count the days until you are here again. You know what you have to do when you arrive at home."

I knew that for sure.

When the eight days had passed, Baba said, "All doubts will have left your mind when you leave Prasanthi Nilayam this time."

And so it was. When I was leaving, I stopped for a moment and observed silence when I passed Baba's temple and He said, "Did I not tell you that when you leave Prasanthi Nilayam all doubts will have left your mind?"

I decided to go back home to sell my flat and to settle my affairs; it took me about three months. I left Denmark in Christmas 1980 together with my sixteen-year-old son, Kenneth to start a new life in India with Sai Baba at Prasanthi Nilayam. I took my drawings along. The drawings which Sai Baba had said again and again were so important. There were now 125 drawings, each one more beautiful than the others.

Prasanthi Nilayam

We arrived at Prasanthi Nilayam on December 25, Christmas Day, 1980 and managed to take part in the beautiful Christmas celebration, which Baba arranges for both Easterners and Westerners. Many thousands of people of all nationalities gather there to celebrate Christmas every year. I guess there were between seven and eight thousand people that Christmas.

Everything was very confusing for me as there were thousands of people. The first fortnight we spent in a big hall with a lot of others, as it was impossible to get a flat for ourselves. It was quite trying when Baba then said to me, "Now, remember all beginnings are difficult. We shall now start all over again in a new way. You have to get used to seeing Me in person and to calm down and understand that Prasanthi Nilayam is now your home."

It was difficult for me to understand and to calm down under such conditions, which I felt were so foreign. I had the feeling that I probably would have to go through quite a lot in order to learn. After some time, we got a flat with a toilet and bath, which cost three rupees a day, which was about US$0.25. The bathroom had a tap, a bucket and a scoop, but it was okay. However, today the flats are more modern, and in 1997 it costs about US$0.50 per person.

Baba talked to me every day and said, "You must be patient and remember that there is a meaning to everything and things follow a certain path. The way Baba does things is correct. Do not try to understand, but just accept it."

Well, that was what I was trying to do. On one of the first days, two young Danes moved in close to us. They introduced themselves as Boye and Poul Erik. They were travelling around India and had now reached Prasanthi Nilayam. I was happy as I hardly knew anybody in Denmark who knew Sai Baba at that time. They both were of great help to me.

At the beginning of January, a group of Swedes arrived at Prasanthi Nilayam, Boye and Poul Erik took Kenneth by the hand and joined the Swedish group to attend darshan. The Swedish group was called in for an interview and Kenneth, Boye and Poul Erik followed suit. Baba materialised a medallion for my son, Boye got a similar one and Poul Erik was given a ring. I was quite furious with Sai Baba that He only called the men in for an interview, but of course, I was happy on behalf of my son. And I had to remember what Baba had said to me, "Remember, there is a meaning in what I do, and the way I do it," but I was furious nevertheless.

Boye told me later that during the interview Baba had asked, "What is the matter with this boy?"

Baba referred to my son. Someone answered that they thought he was retarded. "No, no," Baba said. "There is nothing wrong with him mentally, but he is deeply depressed and something is wrong with his legs."

I did not have a clue that anything was wrong with his legs.

I would like you to know that my son does not say much, but manages with a few words. On the other hand, he manages so well with these that he is not that keen to learn to speak. During his life, he has been examined by several doctors, partly at the Rigshospital, Denmark's main hospital, and at other hospitals, and nobody has been able to diagnose his condition, why he only says what is necessary.

I do not understand why Baba talked about depression as Kenneth is a very happy, outgoing (but with only a few words) and calm child. But Baba tells me that time will develop him, and that I must not put pressure on him. As it does not seem to be a problem for Kenneth, I am not going to make it so. At one point, I thought that it was because of Kenneth that Baba had called me to Him, but this was not the case.

Sai Baba was going to go to Whitefield near Bangalore. He has a university at Puttaparthi and one at Whitefield where He stays part of the year. Here, too, He gives darshan both morning and afternoon. From Whitefield Baba went on to Madras to consecrate a temple. We went along and had a very beautiful experience. Thousands of people were gathered there. Here Baba again did something to make me happy. We were sitting close together in rows, the men to the left and the women on the right. From where I was sitting, I could see that Kenneth, Boye and Poul Erik were sitting in the front row. Finally, Baba appeared. He stooped and materialised vibhuti and also gave some to my son, but Kenneth pushed Baba's hands away, which amused Baba. It was probably the first time somebody had pushed Baba's hand and said 'no thank you' to vibhuti. Later, Kenneth started to take a little vibhuti every morning. From Madras, Baba went back to Whitefield, and we followed.

Drawing no. 112 from 1980

I had a problem as my visa had to be renewed. It reminded me of the fact that I had not done anything to improve my English. Baba said to me, "Do not worry. Your visa will be renewed. Nothing that happens to you and around you is accidental, so you need not to worry."

So I did not, and my visa was indeed renewed for a whole year. Boye took care of everything without even me asking for help. It was the most natural thing in the world for Boye to help. At the same time, Poul Erik said to me that he had thought it might be a good idea for him to teach me a little English. We could practice an hour every day. I thought that was a good idea too, so we started the next day. It was not a small task, to say the least. Poul Erik taught me for the next two months while we were at Prasanthi Nilayam. When they left sometime later, I got along much better on my own.

Baba can do anything.

Goodbye to Boye and Poul Erik

After a while Boye and Poul Erik realised that it was not a coincidence that we were at Baba's ashram at the same time, and that our paths had crossed. They did everything to support me. I think that I can say for sure that if they had not been there, I would have returned to Denmark in a rage. Baba kept on saying that I had to be patient, that the way He did things was right, that even if I did not understand it I should accept it. And He repeated what He had said so often, that all beginnings are difficult, and that everything happens in a particular way. And I should continue to draw. These drawings would later be of great importance, as I would play a part in spreading His message. He told me that I was not there to have an interview, as my background was different. I was there because I needed Baba, and Baba needed me. And everything He taught me I would need later, and I had to remember that there was a deep meaning in everything.

This I had to listen to every day. Finally, I realised that all Baba said was true. So I drew and drew and drew, and my drawings became more and more beautiful, which I was happy about. But what was it all about? This was not revealed to me at that time and resulted in the fact that, now and then, I was angry with Baba. Well, I thought that He should have called me for an interview and told me what it was all about, but He did not do so. I just had to draw and draw and understand that what He was doing was always the right thing. Patience and faith were two things I simply had to learn, whether I liked it or not. Being patient was the most difficult thing for me, and I was tested severely. Deep inside me, I realised, that I could not leave Baba.

When I really got angry with Baba and more than anything felt like leaving Baba immediately, Boye and Poul Erik said to me, "You must do as Baba says and understand that there has to be a meaning in all this." Then I pulled myself together and continued to draw. Baba praised my drawings and said that they had become very beautiful, and that I should make sure to take good care of them. Of course, my spirits rose again, but I was still subject to a great psychic and physical pressure and what I had to endure was necessary, I just did not understand it at that time.

The funny thing was, that every time I thought that Boye and Poul Erik were going to leave, I felt that I should leave too as Baba did not give me a clear directive. I did not really think that it was proper for me to leave before them, as long as they were there. They were of such great assistance to me and extremely helpful. When I was in that mood, Baba said, "You are not going anywhere." Nor did I, for each time they just 'happened' to postpone going home. I think I said goodbye to them three times, I had to stay where I was, and Baba said to me, "Everything that happens to you and around you is not accidental." And probably it was not.

Drawing no. 113 from 1980

Back to Denmark

It was the month of May and the heat was unbearable. Boye and Poul Erik had just left so Kenneth and I were on our own. We were at Prasanthi Nilayam. I drew every day. I had only a few pages left in my sketch book, which worried me a little as it is impossible to get that kind of paper in India. But Baba said, "Do not worry. When there are no pages left in your sketchbook, you will get a new one."

I was eager to see if that was going to happen. I drew every day and my drawings became still more beautiful. Baba now said to me, "Now you can return home and go on to draw, draw and draw. You are going home to complete the task I have trained you for over a long period of time. Your drawings will hang in many homes and through these, you will help to spread Baba's message. You can go home without any worries and meet the future bravely. You must tread the path Baba has shown you, and remember, nothing is accidental there is a deep meaning in everything."

I started to prepare for the journey home, and curiously enough, as we were leaving India at the end of 1981, I used my last page in my sketch book. It happened exactly as Baba had said. When we arrived back home, I just went and bought a new sketch book. Baba says, "Your real home will always be here at Prasanthi Nilayam. You will come back when Baba calls and recharge and refresh yourself in order to go back home again to spread my message."

I had a very vivid dream during one of the last months I was at Prasanthi Nilayam. I dreamt that I had got an inheritance. I remember it very clearly. It was before Boye and Poul Erik had left, so I related it to them in the morning. We were a little amused about it and agreed that it would not be bad if it came true. After that I forgot the dream completely until I set foot on Danish soil. The first thing I was told was that there was an inheritance for me, just as I had dreamt.

That was really fantastic. I came home to a lot of unemployment and to get a job was almost impossible, but the inheritance made it possible for me to start my own business. I bought a shop and later I got a flat again. Baba had indeed told me that I could face the future without worries. I would work again as well as get my own home again, and it all came to pass.

As for my son, it happened just as Baba had said. Of course, Kenneth thought that it was exciting to go to India to Sai Baba and stay at Prasanthi Nilayam, and he enjoyed taking part in the Bhajans, but when he realised that we were going back to Denmark, he looked forward to it. And he took for granted that he would attend the same boarding school as before we went to India. He really expected that there was room for him. I was not quite sure, as I know that there are waiting lists for everything in Denmark. But here things again turned out as Baba had said. He got his room again at the same boarding school where he had many friends. He adapted so well, as if he had never been in India. When we arrived home, I called the head of the boarding school and the first thing he said was, "Welcome back to our wealthy country. We have just one place, and Kenneth will get that. You are lucky. Had it been one month earlier or one month later, there would not have been a vacancy."

Yes, I thought, if only he knew! Kenneth was happy.

My drawings were still developing. They were now more beautiful than ever; as if from another world. And Baba said, "You are growing through your tasks, and the tasks are growing through you."

I am now telling my story to people who are interested in Baba's teachings, and at the same time I am exhibiting my drawings so one can see the fantastic development which has taken place. Up to now I have drawn over 200 drawings, of which no two are alike, because I do not know beforehand how they are going to be. I do not decide that myself, as I am only Baba's tool. And I am happy to be allowed to be that. Maybe the drawings will be quite different in a year or two; I do not know. By the way, Baba says that anybody who has a drawing in their home, is helping to spread His message.

On my table, I have a photo of Baba. It is a quite ordinary one, which I bought in Puttaparthi and which is sold by the thousands. I noticed that a little vibhuti had started to appear on it. So I looked at the photo every day through a magnifying glass to see if more vibhuti appeared. In the morning on the day after my fiftieth birthday in November 1981, I was looking at the photo as usual and nearly got a shock. On the right side of Baba, a small, delicate face appeared. Never have I been more surprised. I looked at it again and again and did not understand what it meant. Then Baba said to me, "This is Baba's birthday present for you. You will always be on my right side. In this incarnation, you have the photo to enjoy. In your next incarnation, you will not need a photo, then you will be born in India and from a physical point of view, be very close to me. But remember, we are only at the beginning of the work which Baba is preparing you for, and all beginnings are difficult.

Also remember that nothing is accidental, everything is planned and destined. You tread the path Baba shows you. I am developing and forming you, everything happens in a certain way. The most important things Baba will take care of, the small things you have to manage yourself. And never forget for a second where you belong. Your heart and your thoughts must always be with Baba."

I hope that one day I shall be able to devote myself completely to my drawings and through these, tell a lot of people about my beloved Master,

Sai Baba.

A final lesson concerning my cigarettes

I have never been a heavy smoker, but I liked to smoke after my morning coffee. It was at the beginning of my relationship with Baba in 1979 when I had just had my morning coffee and was about to smoke a cigarette; my lighter and cigarettes were on the table in front of me. I took the lighter and was about to light my cigarette, but I put the lighter on the table again. I thought to myself, "What is going on?" And picked up the lighter again, but the same thing happened. I still did not manage to light my cigarette. I thought it was kind of strange; what in the world was happening?

"Is it you, Baba, who is interfering? This is just too much. I'll decide if I am going to smoke or not. Now, I am certainly going to light this cigarette."

I grabbed the lighter firmly and finally managed to light the cigarette; lovely! I leant back and enjoyed it.

"Here, it is I who am in charge," I said to myself, but I was mistaken. I had hardly finished the thought, before I suddenly felt ill. I became so dizzy that I almost fainted. I could hardly get up, and my legs nearly failed me. I almost crawled into my bed, and I had to stay there all day. Every time I tried to get up, I felt dizzy and the whole bed seemed to rotate. It was not until the evening that I could stand on my feet again, but I was still a little dizzy.

Then Baba said to me, "It is not healthy for you to smoke, so it is best that you stop smoking."

A lesson that I certainly learned. I suppose I do not have to add that was my last cigarette.

"Thank you, Baba."

Drawing no. 134 from 1981

A dream some time in 1979

I dreamt that I was a nanny on an English estate where I had been employed for years, and it appeared to be that I was quite indispensable. I was very popular with the children, who knew me better than their parents, as I had looked after them since they were little. The master and mistress also liked me very much. It seemed that they could not do without me. I had decided to leave and their lives were completely changed as they could not do without me. The children wept, and the master and mistress beseeched me to stay. However, I was unyielding. They were not able to persuade me. I was going to write to a friend about my departure, but stopped abruptly, the pen in my hand and thought, "By the way, where are you going?

"That is, indeed, strange that you do not know where you are going." Just then the telephone rang. The mistress came and said that the master wished to say goodbye to me. When I took the telephone, it was not the master's voice I heard, but a wonderful choir, which was singing OM, OM, OM. In the end, we were all singing.

At that moment, I awoke with OM on my lips. I felt that I was probably saying goodbye to a worldly life, and that I was now going to follow a spiritual path With Sai Baba by my Side. And I am still doing that.

Another dream some time in 1979

I was at a big party with many smartly dressed people. I was sitting by myself, a little in the background and watching at a distance, wondering about the way people behaved. People were drinking and smoking heavily and everybody talked nonstop, all speaking at once. I sat thinking to myself, "What in the world am I doing here? I think I will leave."

At that moment, a woman joined the party, smartly dressed and surrounded by a lot of men. All had a glass in one hand and a cigarette in the other. They were chatting, drinking and smoking, and to say the least, were very loud. They were not drunk, but I thought they were quite ill-mannered and noisy. I certainly did not feel like staying any longer and wanted to leave the party. But then I took a closer look at the woman.

It seemed to me that I knew her. I looked at her once again. Then I was shocked. No, it could not be true, it was impossible. I looked intensely at her; yes, it was true. This woman was me. Ugh, I looked at her with great contempt. This was terrible, I thought. I had never behaved like this. I was embarrassed on her behalf, and the thought again struck me, "I must leave now."

That was too embarrassing and unpleasant. However, at the same time I looked up and right in front of me, I saw a film which slowly unfolded with different pictures of me.

The first picture looked like the woman at the party, stupid, I thought. The woman in the next picture was a little more sympathetic. She had neither a cigarette nor a glass in her hand. In the third picture, she was quiet. I liked her better. In the fourth picture, she was totally transformed. There she was sitting with her head bent in prayer and her palms put together in the Indian greeting.

Suddenly, I understood and I was deeply touched. At the same time, I looked down and there on the floor a ring came rolling towards me. I bent to pick it up, but at that very moment, I awoke. I lay there thinking that it was a pity that I did not see what the ring looked like. However, it was of no importance.

I have no doubt that I am on the right path thanks to Baba's boundless patience. I just wonder when I shall become like her, the fourth woman? Only Baba knows.

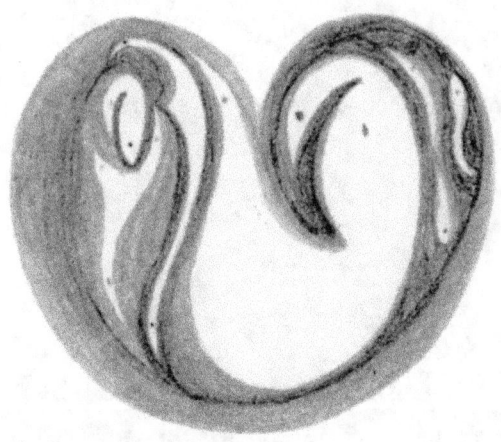

Drawing no. 215 from 1982

An out-of-the-body experience

This incident happened in 1980, at the beginning of my relationship with Sai Baba. It was past midnight, I had just gone to bed; had turned off the light and closed my eyes. I was not asleep yet. I suddenly found myself looking into a dark tunnel and just as suddenly, I was floating in space. Everything was quiet; I saw the stars clearly and in the next moment I was floating next to an aeroplane.

In a blink of an eye I found myself in an unbelievably beautiful temple. I was floating very slowly and there was a heavenly feeling around me. Then I noticed that an old saint was lying to the left of me. First, I thought that it was a statue, but then he slowly got up and when I passed him he nodded and smiled at me. He then said to me, "You are on your way, you are on your way," and then he slowly lay down again. He radiated wonderful vibrations, which cannot be described.

I had now passed him, but continued to turn my head towards him wanting to stay a bit longer, but I was automatically floating on.

Then I exclaimed, "Baba, Baba, thanks for the vision, thanks for the vision!" Immediately I was back in my bed, but I shall never forget his face.

The journey to Pondicherry

March, 1980

My son and I were still staying at Prasanthi Nilayam at Baba's ashram. The Indian summer had just started, and it was extremely hot in Puttaparthi. Baba had gone to Whitefield and travelled around South India. So I decided to go to Pondicherry for some weeks to visit Sri Aurobindo's ashram. Pondicherry is situated next to the sea, so I thought it would perhaps be a little cooler. A strange thing happened there.

We went on a bus trip from Bangalore to Madras. It was unbearable. To travel by bus in India is something we could do without. However, you cannot do without a bus if you travel in India. We drove the whole day. Every now and then, we stopped at small Indian villages and ate some strange Indian dishes.

We brought two suitcases along, which were placed in the luggage compartment of the bus. At that time, I had just got glasses for reading, and I had only brought along one pair, as glasses were something relatively new to me. But now I needed them. I had my glasses, a book and a few bananas in my string bag. In my handbag, I had what any woman has in her handbag. My son had brought some Baba books and also some fruit in his bag. That was all we took with us onto the bus.

At that time, I did a lot of drawing. My drawings had improved quite incredibly. I drew every day, my glasses were of course indispensable, and I needed them to read as well.

Finally, we arrived in Pondicherry late in the evening. We booked into a hotel just for this night, and our only thought was to go to bed. We were dead tired after the long and exhausting journey. We had got our luggage. I was at the reception where I was going to fill in the usual forms. I put my hand into my string bag to get my glasses and could not find them. I was confused and emptied the string bag. My glasses had disappeared. This was really awful, I thought. What am I going to do? Without them, I can neither read nor draw and this happened in India!

"Are you missing something, madam?" the receptionist asked.

"Yes, my glasses. I must have lost them because I cannot find them, so I am sorry I cannot fill in the forms. I cannot read nor write without my glasses."

"Have you looked in your handbag, madam?" he asked.

"They cannot be in my handbag. I always keep them in my string bag. I must have lost them, either on the bus or in one of the villages where we stopped. My string bag was placed in the luggage rack. I had taken it down and put it back several times, so they could be anywhere. I cannot find them, so I must have lost them."

"I am really sorry," he said, "but I will fill it in for you. Maybe you will be able to get another pair of glasses here in India."

Yes, I thought, but I am sure, it is going to be rather complicated.

But then something happened, which really took me by surprise. The next morning I asked the receptionist, "Is there a nice hotel here in Pondicherry by the sea?"

"Yes," he said. "I suggest you stay at the Aurobindo Guestparkhouse. It is a lovely hotel and it is situated next to the sea."

"Well, that sounds like the place we would like to go to," I said and paid my bill. He called a taxi and on my way out, the receptionist said, "I do hope you be able to get a new pair of glasses here in Pondicherry."

"Yes, so do I." And I really hoped it would not be too difficult. We drove to the hotel which turned out to be just wonderful. We went to the reception to book a room. However, unfortunately as I had lost my glasses, I could not fill in the form in a satisfactory way.

"That is okay, madam," said the receptionist, "I only need your passport, then I will fill the form in for you," and he did so. We were taken to our room. It was really lovely with a balcony facing the sea.

I had opened the door to the balcony, and the fresh sea air flowed in. The view was wonderful. Somebody knocked at the door, and I opened it. The receptionist was standing there and said softly, "Madam, your glasses," and then he was gone.

I was standing with my glasses in my hands. The glasses I had lost two days ago. I was dumbfounded. How could that be? It was really quite crazy. I was totally confused and could not understand it at all. I sat for a couple of minutes trying to pull myself together, with my glasses in my hands. I took a closer look at them; yes, they were mine.

Then Baba said to me, "Take good care of your glasses, you cannot do without them." I was deeply touched; tears rolled down my cheeks, and at the same time I felt very happy, but I was still confused. "Thank you, Baba, my beloved." I could draw again, which was of great importance to me at that time.

We had a wonderful time there, and we also managed to see Aurobindo's ashram. He was a philosopher and a mystic and he lived from 1872 to 1950. But it was Baba who was, and still is, in my heart.

A dream in 1981

When my short book about my meeting with Sai Baba, which I wrote in 1981, was printed, and which, by the way, is the beginning of this book, I, of course wanted Sai Baba to bless and sign my first copy. So I went to Puttaparthi in 1982 and took it with me. Then Baba came to me in a dream the last night before I left for India.

The dream

I was in a book shop when an unusual customer entered. It was, in fact, Baba. He said to me, "I would like the little orange book which is at the bottom of those books."

This was my short story. "Certainly," I said, and had to move a lot of heavy books which were placed on top of it. But I got hold of my little book and handed it to Baba. Baba now placed it on a table by itself. He raised His hand and blessed it saying one single word, namely "respect". In that moment, I awoke and felt incredibly happy. Baba not only blessed and signed my book when I arrived at Prasanthi Nilayam, but I also had an interview and further, a photograph was taken of Baba and me. This picture gives me joy every day. At the same time, I bought a large picture of Him, which He also signed when I got my second interview. That was a very lovely stay, which meant a lot to me.

Drawing no. 217 from 1982

Selling my shop

At the end of 1981 when I returned from India, I had, as mentioned before, bought a shop, therefore, I had an income. But it was tough to be in the retail business in Denmark. I often worked ten hours a day, and it was not very profitable due to state tax, but those were the conditions at that time.

My son came home every weekend so naturally I spent my weekends with him. During the week, he was at boarding school. I still drew but not so often, I did not have much time, nor energy, for that. The time came when being in business became too tiresome, and I thought of selling.

Baba then said to me, "You must be patient. The time is not right to sell yet."

Yes, I thought, it always has to do with patience. A month passed, and the thought came back to me. At that time, it was the height of summer in Denmark and very hot. Nevertheless, I phoned the estate agent and said that I wanted to sell my shop. "Oh no," he said. "It is impossible at this time of the year. Everybody is on vacation, and in this weather, nobody thinks of buying a shop."

However, I was stubborn. "I want my shop sold now. I do not feel like being in the shop any longer."

So, he accepted to put the shop for sale. Some people came at the beginning to have a look, but nobody wanted to buy and it was still a very hot summer.

I had almost forgotten that the shop was for sale. Then suddenly one day a man came into the shop. I thought he was a customer and said, "Can I help you?"

"Yes," he said. "I would like to buy your shop."

I was quite surprised because at that time, I had forgotten everything about it. "Did the estate agent send you?" I asked.

"Yes, and it is a beautiful shop you have," he said.

I could see that he was a foreigner, so I asked, "Where do you come from?"

"From India," he said.

"I have been in India myself," I said, but I did not mention Sai Baba.

"Can I have a look at the back of the shop?" he said.

"Certainly," I answered and showed him in.

"Sai Baba," he exclaimed, very moved, and bent over the table where I had a small picture of Sai Baba. He was standing in front of the picture with both palms together in the Indian greeting and, said, "I know Sai Baba has sent me. This is the right thing for me. I will buy your shop right away. Can I call my wife?"

Everything happened so fast that it took me by surprise. I was touched and quite overwhelmed. I could hardly believe it; even the atmosphere was completely transformed.

His wife arrived with an elderly Indian man where all three of them stood with their palms together in front of Baba's picture and sang the Arathi softly. Arathi is a song in Sanskrit at the end of Bhajans, hymns to God. It was very solemn. There was an Indian atmosphere in my shop; quite incredible! "Baba, Baba!" I thought once again. The shop was sold, and I could go to Baba again.

A stay in Puttaparthi in 1983

I had been with Baba at Prasanthi Nilayam some weeks when I met an old devotee of Baba. We talked about my son, who is a diabetic. She suggested that I should go to Baba's hospital and get some medicine, which comes from a holy tree in India. It is supposed to have healing properties for many illnesses as well as diabetes. "Baba has a natural healer at the hospital that you can consult," she said.

I knew this hospital no longer exists. It has been replaced by a much bigger, modern and very beautiful one. I am always aware of what Baba says to me and in fact, He says it again and again. He says, "Only listen to Baba. I am doing what has to be done. Everything is in My hands."

I thought about that, but of course, she did not know it. She was only trying to be kind to me. At the same time, I thought that the whole thing could have been arranged by Baba, and my son really needed that medicine which was available at Baba's hospital.

"What should I do?" I thought. Nevertheless, I said that I would visit the hospital. At the same time, I thought that I would take the medicine to darshan the following morning. I hoped that Baba would bless it. Then I would be sure that it was the right thing for my son. Perhaps that was the answer.

We went to the hospital and talked to the healer who was very kind. She gave me a bag with the medicine and advised me that I should give my son a little, three times a day. This would have a healing effect on his diabetes. Next morning at darshan I was really "lucky" to be placed in the first row and was sitting with the medicine in a big bag. Baba came closer and stopped in front of me. He looked very sternly at me and asked in an angry voice, "What have you got in your bag?"

"It is holy powder, Baba," I answered.

Baba looked again sternly at me and said loudly, "Madness!"

I was embarrassed because everybody was amused, but I was not. Baba had given me an answer. It could not be mistaken, and that was what was most important for me.

I would like to add that many people use the medicine for many illnesses, so nothing is wrong with the medicine, but I was not supposed to use it.

Baba guides me directly. He tells me what to do and say. It does not matter whether He says it in His physical form or in me, or whether He comes to me in a dream. I have to obey Him, regardless of what other people say or do. Deep inside I really knew, but obviously, I had to test it.

If we only listen to what Baba says and try to live accordingly or do our best, we cannot fail.

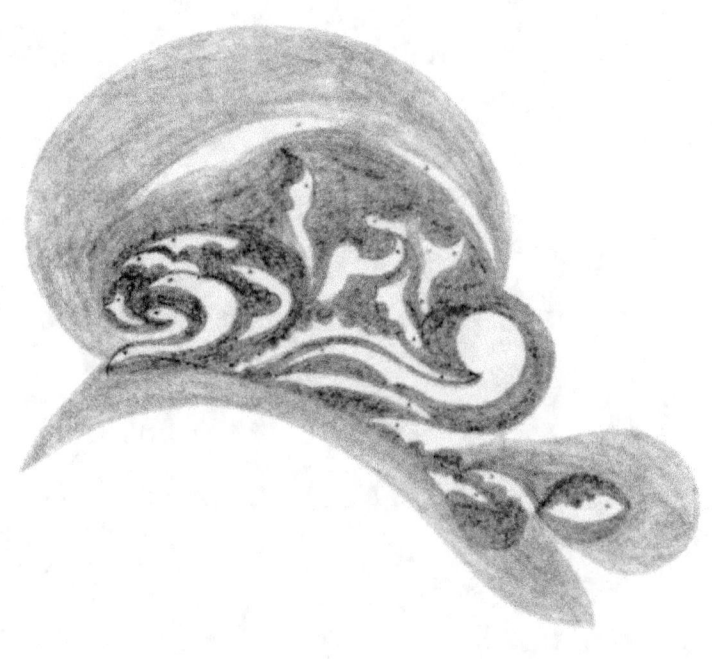

Drawing no. 203 from 1982

Mine and Baba's drawings

My drawings, or perhaps more correctly expressed, Baba's drawings, had really become beautiful, almost divine, as though they were from another world. Many people have seen them, and everybody was fascinated by them, but it was and will be Baba's power and strength which were in them, not mine. I cannot draw and do not have any talent in this regard.

Many of my friends and acquaintances asked me to visit them with my drawings, so they could see them, and of course, I did. Several also came to my home to see them and everybody was enthusiastic about them. People often said to me, "Don't you think they would be lovely in colour?"

"I wouldn't have a clue," I said, and that was really a fact. One day, I thought I would give it a try. I took some of my son's crayons and started to colour one of them carefully, but it looked completely wrong, so I put it aside. I sat for a moment and thought, "No, this is impossible."

Then Baba said to me, "Look at your first drawing and compare it with the last one." These were Baba's words.

Then I understood that I was supposed to begin to work with colours. I am not an artist, and I did not know how to proceed until one night I had an inspiring dream.

The dream

I was standing in a large square looking around. There were a lot of columns where I noticed that the paint had peeled off many of them, and it looked ugly. At the same time, I noticed that there were big holes in the wall nearby. Suddenly, I heard a loud voice coming from outer space. It said, "Yes, you are going to paint, really paint with a brush."

I asked, "But what about the holes in the wall?"

"Don't bother; they have nothing to do with Baba," the voice said.

I awoke and realised that now I was going to paint with colours. But I had no idea how to paint. I had never held a brush in my hand. I felt this when I made the first brush stroke, which later turned into many. Some days after the dream, I went to buy some watercolours. I thought that they would be the right ones, but when I started to paint one of the drawings, everything blurred with water and the drawing was ruined. I realised that it was not water colours I was going to use. At that moment, I was pretty annoyed.

Some weeks passed when I thought about it occasionally. Maybe ink would be the right thing, so I bought some hoping it would do the trick.

Once again, I took another drawing, but the same thing happened; everything blurred. Another drawing ruined. Now I was really annoyed and put the whole thing out of my mind. I did not at all feel like experimenting with colours any more.

"To start something I do not know anything about is quite foolish. I will leave that to those who know more about it. Despite the dream, I will not have anything to do with these experiments with colours anymore."

I did not give it a thought, until one day I happened to be in an art shop to buy something not of any importance, when I saw some tubes of paint in different colours, which were just in front of me. At that moment, the salesperson came, and I asked him, "What kind of colours have you got there?"

"They are artists' colours, so-called acrylic colours," he answered.

"Oh, I didn't know that," I said.

"Yes, you only need to mix them with water. Many artists use them," he answered.

"I think I will give it a try. I will take the red one," I said, paid and left. When I came home, I realised that I had forgotten to buy what I went there for.

I did not start with the red paint immediately. I was still reluctant after the first attempts. But then one day I started, mixed the paint with water and slowly began to work on the third drawing. I had hardly started before I knew that these acrylic paints were just what I should use. I was so inspired that the next day I went back to buy all the different colours. Now the whole thing began to take shape. With Baba's guidance, everything is possible.

I was now in a period during which I painted a lot, and it really got better and better. Baba said to me, "Remember, you grow with the task, and the task grows with you."

One day, a couple of friends came to see me and when they saw the coloured drawings they exclaimed, "My goodness, they are beautiful. Why don't you hold an exhibition?"

"Oh no," I said, "I am not an artist and I don't have a clue about exhibitions." I was not very interested and was thinking along other lines. Then a strange thing happened. A week later I got a letter from a stranger who invited me to an exhibition.

I accepted the invitation and went to see the exhibition. It turned out that she had once seen my drawings. The exhibition was very beautiful and it was of her own creations. We talked, and she suggested that I should hold my exhibition there as the facilities were good, it was right in the centre of Copenhagen, and it was free of charge. "Why don't you talk to the board of the art society in the bank, opposite this place?" she said.

"They own the place and they decide who should hold exhibitions here."

I did not once mention the word exhibition, nor did I have any ideas in this direction, but apparently somebody else had. I had the feeling that everything was falling into place for me, even though I had not dreamt of having an exhibition. "Well, maybe it is possible for me to hold an exhibition," I thought. "Time will tell."

My exhibition in 1984

Some weeks passed and I did not think much about an exhibition, but while I was painting the thought surfaced now and then.

Then suddenly one day I made a quick decision. I put ten to twelve paintings in a case and set out to the bank to talk to the manager of the art society. I was taken to his office. The first thing he asked when I entered was, "Where did you graduate, where have you had an exhibition before and what kind of publicity did you have?"

The questions were like a slap in my face even though they were asked in a polite way.

I waited for a moment and then said very quietly, "I haven't studied anywhere; I haven't held an exhibition before, nor have I had any publicity."

He looked at me for a while, and then he said, "But surely, you must have learnt to draw somewhere."

"Now I would like to tell you something," I said. "I have an Indian master, and it is He who inspires me and He who guides me. It is His power and strength, which are in the paintings, not mine. The paintings symbolise the universe."

Once again, he looked at me and this time was much more interested. "Really, I have never heard anything more interesting. I am eager to see these paintings," he said. "Would you please put them on the table here, it sounds very exciting."

"Yes, certainly," I answered and spread them on a large table.

When he saw the drawings he immediately became very enthusiastic and said, "I have never seen anything so special before. They are very beautiful and harmonious. Your Master must be someone very special."

"He certainly is. Without Him the paintings would never have come into existence," I said.

He continued, "Of course you simply must hold an exhibition. I will book a time for you. You will receive a letter from us when you can hold the exhibition. I will photograph the exhibition."

I was very happy, thanked him and left. I thought about how I had to get started as I had no clue in organising the exhibition. It later turned out that these thoughts were quite unnecessary.

Baba not only shows the way. He arranges everything down to the tiniest detail. A couple of weeks passed and then I got a letter from the organiser concerning the exhibition. He wrote, "We are very pleased to offer you our hall for your exhibition. The hall will be at your disposal in the first eight days of February, 1984." He finished with the words, "I wish you all success in the future with your very beautiful work." I have kept the letter.

I called and thanked him and was now getting busy. There were only three months left. I had finished twenty to thirty paintings, but they had to be framed for the exhibition, so there was a lot of work to do. The only thing which concerned me was the time of the year. It is winter in Denmark at this time and as a rule very cold and grey, so people prefer to stay indoors. However, as I had never held an exhibition before and was not a recognized artist, it was not proper for me to complain.

I suppose three weeks had passed when I received a new letter from the art society. I was asked if I would mind waiting to exhibit until the beginning of May, as a well-known artist had arrived, who could only exhibit in Copenhagen the very eight days, which had been reserved for me, but I could have two weeks in May instead. I was surprised, but happy, because that was just what I wanted. I told them that it was okay, and everybody was happy. Now I had got not only eight days, but two weeks exhibition in May when spring is here. It could not be better. As I had more time I made an effort to have more paintings for my exhibition.

As I improved I began to paint in strong colours. I did not use pastel colours in my pictures. Then one night Baba came to me in a dream.

The dream

Baba was sitting in His chair and called me up to Him. I sat down at Baba's feet. He smiled at me as He raised His forefinger and said, "Please don't paint in such dark colours. You should also use the lighter shades."

From that day on, I included pastel colours. Thus, I had paintings in pastel colours for the exhibition, thanks to Baba.

We were now getting closer to the month of May, the time for me to hold my exhibition. As to my paintings, I was well prepared. I had a lot of paintings, but no experience in how to display them and was there anyone who could help me? I did not need to worry. One of Baba's devotees called me and said that he had heard about my exhibition. "I feel," he said, "it is my duty to help you, so if you wish, I can hang the paintings for you and help you in any way that may be necessary."

I was very happy and of course, I accepted the offer. Everything seemed to fall into place, in spite of my ignorance in these areas. He really did a great job and hung all the pictures. It looked very good with the right lighting. I decorated the window with a big picture of Baba, and a big bunch of orange roses arranged on an orange silk sari with a few of my paintings.

The exhibition was a success, and many came to see it, some even several times. A visitor came three times, "I have never seen such beautiful paintings, a symphony of colours. Where have you got such inspiration?" she asked.

"From my Master in India," I answered.

She looked at one of the paintings for a long time and started to cry. Very moved, she said, "I have never heard anything so amazing. I'll buy your little book and buy any available books about Sai Baba in Danish. It has been a great inspiration to see your paintings and to talk to you. I will look forward to reading about your Master."

Yes, it was truly an inspiration for me too.

Many who came to see the exhibition heard for the first time about Baba, and it was really nice to take part in spreading Baba's message. In this way, I had many beautiful experiences. It happened exactly as Baba had told me a few years earlier in 1980 when I started to draw and did not have any idea how it was going to be. So now and then when I could not see any purpose in it, He often said to me, "Your drawings are beautiful. One day, you will become Baba's great artist, and your drawings will be hanging in many countries. Through these, you will take part in spreading My Message."

In fact, my drawings hang in many countries today. Yes, in not less than three continents. One in Malaysia, one in San José in California, one in Seattle in the state of Washington, and one in New York. Besides that, one in London, two in Vienna, four in Sweden, three in Norway, and of course many more in Denmark. All who bought the pictures felt, that they had to own a picture, a divine picture. I am only a tool for Baba, and I am very happy to be allowed to be so.

"Baba, Baba, what am I to say?"
Words are inadequate.

Written by a friend from my exhibition in 1984:

Through the beautiful harmony
of these forms and colours
We feel a symbol of cosmic power,
of subtle melodious rhythms
and the graceful play of sounds.
We are all a part of this Wholeness,
a spark in the Mirror of Eternity

- Nenne

A Letter from California

A woman from California bought a drawing. Two years later she sent me a nice letter which arrived the day before I was leaving for Baba. She wrote:

"This letter I would have liked to send you long ago, but as I have been very ill, I haven't been able to write until now. As you can see, I enclose a photo of our living room. On the mantel shelf is a picture of Sai Baba. Above that hangs your drawing, but it isn't hanging there anymore. It's now hanging in my bedroom above my bed."

"One night I had terrible pains. I prayed fervently to Sai Baba while I looked intensely at your drawing. Suddenly, it was as if a flash of lightning went through my body, and I was healed. I cried and cried and then thanked Sai Baba again and again. Your drawing is still hanging over my bed. I am still healthy, so healthy that I can now write to you. I hope sincerely that we shall meet again."

I have kept the letter, and her photo is displayed in my living room. I wrote to her from India. I hope she will continue to be healthy. Unfortunately, I have not heard from her again. However, it was a beautiful experience.

Drawing no. 210 from 1982

A journey to India with obstacles

This journey happened in 1985. I always prepare my journeys to India in good time. There is a lot to be prepared as I usually stay in India for some months at a time. At the same time, I have to think of many things: tickets, passport, visa, vaccinations, etc. and not least important, traveller's cheques. Something mystical happened with regard to the traveller's cheques on this journey.

I always go to the bank one week before the journey and order my traveller's cheques, and did so this time too. The day before departure I visited the bank to get the cheques. I had signed all the cheques, and they had just been given to me, when I went to the desk as I wanted to withdraw some cash at the same time. I had placed the envelope with the cheques next to me for a moment while I put the money in my bag. When I was going to take the envelope with my cheques, they had gone. They seemed to have disappeared into thin air. I became quite nervous, looked once again, but they were gone and I was the only one at the desk at that time.

The female bank assistant asked, "Is something wrong?"

"Yes," I answered, "my traveller's cheques have gone. I placed them here for a moment while I cashed the money."

She called the lady, who had given me the cheques. She looked everywhere. They turned the waste paper baskets upside down, but without any results, they were gone. American Express was called immediately, and the cheques stopped, so no one could cash them.

The bank then ordered some new ones for me, which I could manage to get the next morning. What luck as my plane would leave at 4pm. So I left with new traveller's cheques.

But more obstacles appeared. When we arrived at Bombay, my suitcase had disappeared. My son, a friend called Christian, and I travelled together. But their suitcases came rolling along the conveyor belt, although we had checked all of them in at Copenhagen. When we arrived in Bangalore, I was surprised to see that all three suitcases were there - and was I happy!

The next day we went to Puttaparthi. I opened my bag to get something. And what was lying at the top of the bag? The traveller's cheques! They had disappeared before I had even left the bank. I was totally confused. How could that be? Now I had two cheque books.

The one I thought stolen, I had saved as a souvenir. "I think Baba is teasing you," Christian said.

"Yes, so do I," I answered.

Later I went for an interview with a small group of Danes. My son and I went to the inner room with Baba. I sat at Baba's feet. The first thing He said was, "Are your finances okay now?" and smiled.

"Yes, finally, Baba," I answered. However, inside I was quite confused.

Then He said in a teasing tone, "Yes, you will have your ring when the time is right, and your son will have a new medallion."

However, I did not get the ring, so the time was obviously not right.

Maybe I should add that Baba, back in about 1982, had said during an interview, "One day Baba will give you a ring with the whole universe contained in your little ring, but not until the time is right."

Only Baba knows when the time is ripe for this or that. The ring as such is not important to me. What is important to me is that Baba is with me every day. That is of paramount importance and takes place on the inner plane. Then Baba came to me in a dream during the night.

The dream

Baba gave me a small parcel and said, "Unwrap it; it's not important."

I unwrapped it and saw it was an incredibly beautiful ring with diamonds, rubies and other precious stones. I admired the pretty ring.

Then Baba gave me another small parcel and said, "Unwrap it; it's important." It turned out to be yet another ring, but totally different. This ring portrayed a cobra snake, quite thin, pale blue and iridescent; the eyes were two diamonds.

"Gee, it's beautiful, Baba. Is this the ring that you want to give me? "I asked.

"Yes, but not now, but when the time is right," he replied.

Then I woke up. Baba wanted me to understand that it was not the rings that were important or momentous, but the divine. In Hinduism, the Cobra snake symbolises the divine. Baba often mentions the ring in dreams, when he comes to me, and where the ring still has a significance in one way or another.

A dream sometime in 1985

I attended a lavish dinner party where the table with the culinary dishes was so long, that I could not see from one end to the other.

There was a lot to choose from and something for everyone. There were lamb and chicken cooked in various ways, roast beef, fried pigeons, hens and pheasants. They had all had to give their lives for this party. Everything was beautifully presented. There was a lobster, salmon and caviar as well. There was everything. I looked at this orgy food and they served poultry of some kind. I began to eat, but something was wrong. There was a small bone or something that would not get into my mouth. I struggled with it, but without success. At the same time, I had trouble digesting the food, and I chewed and chewed. "What is it?" I thought. I thought I heard a sound; then I heard it again. To my horror, I now quite clearly heard a small "pip, pip". I was terrified and immediately spat out the food on my plate and looked at it with disgust.

What was it? On my plate was a small bird, bitten into half. I felt uncomfortable and shouted, "Waiter, waiter, take it away, I won't look at it." All my food was now carried away; I had totally lost my appetite.

To my amazement, I saw the loveliest little bird in all the colours of the rainbow flying toward me and landing right in front of me. Then I woke up. For a long time, I had been thinking of becoming a vegetarian, but had come no further. However, after the dream, I ate no meat for a long time. Today I am as good as a vegetarian.

Drawing no. 164 from 1981

Another lesson in Puttaparthi

This stay took place in 1986. At the time, I was in Puttaparthi, I talked with a man who had been given a linga by Baba. A linga, or lingam, is a phallic symbol. His wife was sick, Baba had said he was going to put it in a glass of water every day, so his wife could drink it; the water would have a healing effect. Furthermore, he could also help others with it, Baba had said.

He asked if I wanted a small bottle of the water; maybe it was something for my son, he thought. "Yes" I thought, "but what about Baba?" However, I thanked him and took the bottle; one could never know.

The next morning I took the bottle of water to darshan, where I would have liked Baba to bless it. However, that was not to be, because I ended up in the back row, so that was out of the question. When darshan was over, I stayed. Baba gave the interview, and I was sitting in my own thoughts.

Suddenly, I saw Baba come out. He came slowly towards me, stopped right in front of me and looked lovingly at me. Then he said in a tone as if he was talking to a little girl, "What have you got there?"

"It is holy water, Baba," I said.

Baba took the bottle, held it up so everyone could see it, was tremendously amused, smiled lovingly at me and said in a funny tone, "Only water, only water." Then he threw the little bottle back to me, and said in the same tone, "What will do you with it? Only water, only water." He smiled, turned and went inside.

The water from the lounge was meant for the diseased woman to drink, as Baba had said, and others who sufferers were offered the water as well, but I would not use it for my son. Baba again showed me that I only have to listen to him. He gives me what I need when the time comes, and he does what is needed to be done, just like with the powder. Sometimes I forget it and listen to others instead. Therefore, I got this lesson. It is through our mistakes we come a little step further.

Some days later, we would leave for Demark, and it was the most beautiful parting Baba has ever given me. The day came when we would leave, just after the darshan. I had packed, the taxi waited at the doorsteps, and the baggage was placed on the roof. We were ready to travel from Puttaparthi to Denmark. I had just a couple of late purchases to make before departure, but finally, we were ready to go.

We drove slowly out of the ashram, but when we got to the gate, we sighted Baba's red car; we waited a bit to let him get out first, and then we followed directly after Baba. He sat alone in the back of the car. Baba's car drove slowly down the road, and I thought to myself that he would possibly drive to the hospital but Baba drove past the hospital.

"He is going to the university," I said to the driver, but Baba drove past the university as well. It was about to be exciting, because now we were completely out of Puttaparthi, only Baba's car and our taxi were on the road and there no houses; only fields on both sides. Baba's car drove quite slowly.

Now I could see Baba say something to the driver, and then the car swung all the way to the left, drove onto the field, turned and stopped. Baba looked towards us. I became aware that He wanted something, so we stopped at the side and got out. We stopped in front of Baba with palms against each other and waited for what was going to happen. Only then Baba gave the driver the order to start the car. The car came quite, quite slowly towards us. When he was right next to us, He rolled down the window, smiled and waved goodbye to us very affectionately.

Baba knew exactly what time we left the ashram. Yes, of course, because he knows everything. Baba waved all the time, while the car slowly drove back to Puttaparthi. I waved back at Baba; I could see his arm moving, right up to where the car made a turn.

A last farewell, while tears ran down my cheeks. We got back in the car and continued the trip to Bangalore. Baba, Baba, I will never forget it. There was something much deeper in it than just Baba waving goodbye, which I was not aware of at the time but only a few years later.

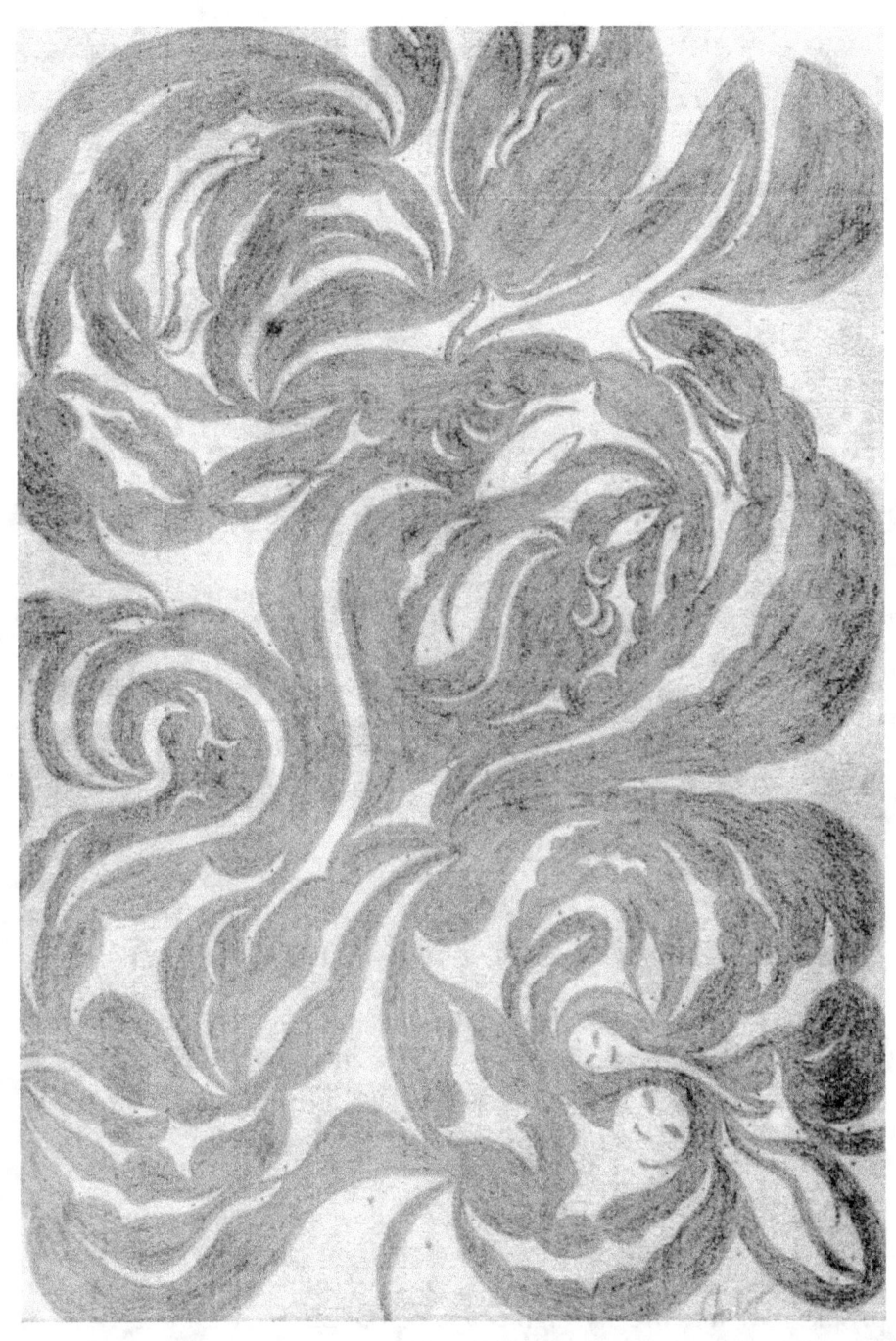

Drawing no. 128 from 1981

Two dreams in Puttaparthi in 1987

It was not a very pleasant stay, since it was filled with problems from the first to the last day. One can do without such problems, or maybe not. The first night in Prasanthi Nilayam, Baba came to me in a somewhat unusual dream. It was something to do with a lesson that I had not learned.

The first dream

I came into the classroom on the first day of the new school year. I had to sit right at the front. I looked around, surprised, since I saw none of my classmates from the previous year. I became increasingly disorientated and thought, "Where are the others?" They were all strangers. Baba was, as my teacher, standing at his desk looking very serious. He then looked sternly at me, pointed at me with his ruler, and said very angrily, "You have not learnt the lesson yet, so you need to attend a second time in the same class." I was totally embarrassed and at the same time sad. Everyone looked at me and I thought, "What lesson is it that I haven't learned?" Then I woke up.

However, today I have learnt the lesson. Later came other homework. All of life is a lesson. We will never be finished with going to school. Actual life here on Earth is a high school.

That dream set the scene for the entire stay, because everything went completely wrong, and I thought a lot about what lesson I had not learned. Baba avoided me entirely and I think we moved to new places four times in one month. I had never experienced that before. It was incredibly cumbersome. At the same time, my son was ill with diabetes, which did not make it easier, but we must take it as it comes which was, of course, what I did.

On this trip to India, I was going to combine the stay in Puttaparthi with a trip to Sri Lanka. I was going to be with Baba one month and then travel to Sri Lanka before Shivaratri. Shivaratri is a sacred Indian feast for the God Shiva. It was to avoid being there at the time when people flow in. Already eight days before Shivaratri, there were so many people that I thought, "Now it's time to leave." I was pleased to enjoy life on the beach. Then I had a dream that changed my plans.

The second dream

I was in the ashram with thousands of people, and I could neither move forwards nor backwards. It was dreadful. I was squashed and pushed from all sides and thought, "I must get out of here!" I started to jostle my way through the crowd towards one of two gates. Finally, I could see the gate and was happy soon to be out of the crowd. Now the gate was just a few metres away from me, but just as I was about to go through the gate, two huge cobra snakes appeared in front of me blocking my path. I was so frightened that I immediately retreated. I could not get out. "Well," I thought. "Then I will use the other gate," and began to jostle myself back to the other gate which I finally reached. "Here I can get out," I thought, but no, the same thing happened. Two huge cobra snakes blocked my way, so it was impossible to get out. Then I understood that I had to stay and I woke up. I did not go to Sri Lanka, since I understood the meaning of the dream.

At first, I was angry with Baba. I really had no desire to be in the throng of people and had been looking forward to my stay in Sri Lanka. At the same time, I understood what Baba wanted to teach me that the divine is more important than to enjoy life, no matter how many people there were. It should be obvious. Yet another thank you, Baba.

The next morning for darshan, I sat in the first row. Baba stopped in front of me, smiled teasingly while He looked lovingly at me and was tremendously amused; which I was not. I had not quite mastered the lesson yet, which should be proven later. Only through our trials and tribulations we grow spiritually.

When we had been in Puttaparthi for a month, and I had had more than enough, Baba went to Whitefield and then to Ooty about 300 kilometres south west of Whitefield. We went to Bangalore and had some relaxing days there. I decided to go to Ooty as well. It is a long trip; we left early in the morning in a taxi and were in Ooty in the evening, only to be told that Baba had just gone to Bangalore. We drove back to Bangalore the next day, because I was quite angry with Baba.

After some days in Bangalore, my son was again ill from diabetes and went to the hospital, where he stayed for a week or so. When he was well again, we went back to Denmark. "Now I've got enough of being in India and my son being sick, and can wait several years before I travel to India again," I said to myself. But after just one year, I left to see Baba again.

Some quite wonderful experiences

Baba gave me some wonderful experiences in the period from January to April 1988.

A vision on 20 January 1988

It was early in the morning, and I was awake. I saw Baba in a blinding white light. He called to me and suddenly I was standing in front of Baba in the light.

He replied to me on a very personal question that I had asked Him countless times over the years I had been His supporter, and where he had led me so directly and still does. It was an incredibly beautiful and affirming experience

A vision on 1 February 1988

Baba came to me as Mother Sai.

I was with Baba in a totally otherworldly, wonderful place, which I lack words to describe.

It was dazzlingly bright and had an atmosphere more beautiful than anything that exists on Earth. There were a lot of people, and they were all filled with love which radiated from them.

My son was with me, and we almost floated around in the wonderful light. Baba called my son and I in for an interview. He sat down at a beautiful table; my son and I sat opposite Baba. Suddenly, my son exclaimed, "You have a nice mouth, Baba."

I now looked directly at Baba's mouth. I saw that Baba had red lips, just like a woman. He was also buxom to look at.

Now I understood that Baba was Mother Sai, the female aspect of the divine.

We were outside again. I looked up and saw an indescribable sea of light. Quite slowly a winged creature, I would almost describe it as an Angel, came quietly hovering down toward us. A beautiful crystal bowl with water was held up to her. She drank a little and floated on. I was deeply captivated by this sight.

Baba came out and called me to Him. He smiled fondly, and said to me, "He should not have the water from the linga."

Baba was referring to what he had said earlier in his physical form in Prasanthi Nilayam. I had been sitting with a small bottle with water from a linga that Baba had materialised and I thought my son was supposed to have. Someone had given it to me; therefore, I sat with the bottle of water.

At that time, Baba stated the same exact words and held the small bottle with water from the linga in his hand, teasingly. "What do you want to do with the water? It's only water, only water."

He had enjoyed himself a lot and given me the bottle back. Now he confirmed it here at this beautiful place, as Mother Sai with the red lips.

I awoke and contemplated on the indescribably beautiful dream that I thought it was.

"Where do I get the imagination from?" I thought, because I was quite sure it was a fantasy dream.

"Now be careful that my imagination, isn't completely taking control of me," I thought and then fell asleep again. Then Baba came to me in a dream.

The dream

Baba sat in his chair in Prasanthi Nilayam. I sat in the lotus position right behind Him. He turned to me and still had the red lips. He raised his index finger and said, admonishing, "No, it was not a fantasy dream; it was real."

Still in the dream, a bit later, I entered the temple square in Prasanthi Nilayam. Baba came toward me. He stopped, smiled and clapped me on the shoulder. He no longer had the red lips.

I woke up for the second time that night and could not sleep again. It was an incredible experience. It is deeply etched into my mind, and I will never forget it.

Whatever experiences at the internal level Baba gives me, I never doubt the accuracy of what I am experiencing, and I never doubt what he says to me. Every day, I have to try to live up to it.

A vision on 15 February 1988

Baba came to me as my friend.

Baba walked with me at the water's edge along a beautiful beach; small waves swept over our feet. That was so incredibly beautiful and so quiet, so quiet. No people, only Baba and me alone in this wonderful place. The atmosphere cannot be described. There was a small fishing boat, bottom up, as if there had once been a fishing village close by.

Baba was my good friend, and He had his arm on my shoulder and talked to me about spiritual things. I felt very happy. I said to Him, "Baba, the only thing I want is to be in your presence." Baba smiled fondly at me.

I awoke and could almost feel the scent of the sea. It was incredibly beautiful.

A dream on 22 February 1988

Baba came to me as my servant.

I was on a trip and one morning I went into a restaurant to get my breakfast.

Baba came to my table as my servant. He put a plate with two cakes in front of me and said, "Thank you, it will be five rupees."

"Unfortunately, I overslept, and came out the door so fast that I forgot my wallet," I said to Baba.

Baba smiled sweetly to me and said, "Yes, it is because you lay and dreamt about Baba."

Thank you for all the sweet dreams, Baba.

A wonderful dream on 1 March 1988

I arrived at the clinic, close to giving birth, and I wondered how this had happened, since I live alone.

"It can't possibly be," I say to the doctor.

"It is real enough. You are pregnant."

I was thinking that this was crazy and said in a facetious tone, "Well then, it must be the Holy Spirit." That made us both laugh.

The dream continues on 6 March 1988

I had given birth to a divine child. The small baby who I held in my arms, was nothing less than Baba. He was the most wonderful baby I had ever seen. He wore a little orange jacket and had the most beautiful curls and big brown eyes.

He fell asleep in my arms and I laid him gently on a blanket next to me. He was sleeping soundly now. Finally, I sat with Baba's cloak in my hands and said to a young woman next to me, "I want to sew something for myself from Baba's cloak, but I dare not begin to clip it, if He would have it back."

The symbolism may be: A spark of the divine was born in me.

It was an incredibly beautiful dream.

A dream on 10 March 1988

I came to a small house which was almost hidden by weeds. I felt connected to the house. I locked myself in and explored the house. It was filled with beautiful things, and I recognised it all.

Finally, I came to a small wardrobe and opened it. There were some very beautiful clothes in wonderful colours and fine silk. I felt it once belonged to me.

There was a wonderful calm and tranquil atmosphere in the house.

I then left the house and came out onto a dusty country road. I become immediately aware that it was in India. A bus came, crowded with Indians and I just got on the bus before it drove on.

A dream on 13 March 1988

Baba was giving a speech. When it was over, He came out. As he walked past me, he said, "Come to my office, you must run an errand for me."

Baba wrote down what I needed to buy. All the time Baba wrote, I walked outside and looked around.

A person came up to me and said, "You must follow me in here."

I went into a room where I became entangled in a lot of silk and something was placed on the top of my head. I looked in a mirror and saw I was turned into a woman from Tibet.

I felt so happy in the clothes that I completely forgot what I had to do for Baba. Then it came to my mind and I rushed back to Him. He lifted his head, looked up and down at me and said, "You look nice."

Then he gave me the note which he had written with the things I was going to buy.

"Get on with it," he said.

I rushed out to shop, but was so intrigued by the beautiful clothes I was wearing, that I completely forgot the errand.

Then He came out of his office and saw me utterly preoccupied with myself, in which he autoritative, yet gently said, "What? Have you not got any further? Gain some speed."

Which I immediately did.

An experience on 8 April 1988

A wonderful experience at midnight.

I lay in my bed and couldn't sleep. I thought of everything, what Baba meant to me, but I have not yet learnt the most important thing, namely to control my thoughts, nor have I learnt to control my temper. "It's just too bad," I thought. "Baba, you may really help me with this."

Suddenly, like lightning from a clear sky, my crystal chandelier turned on by itself. I really got a shock, and did not understand how it could happen.

When I had come to, I got up, turned it off and went to bed again. A little later Baba said some sweet words to me, that I will never forget. It was a message from Baba.

Unbelievable - thank you for the beautiful greeting, Baba.

The trip to Sri Lanka

Finally, I went to Sri Lanka in 1988, but I should probably never have done that. The year before, in 1987, I should have done it, but did not. I had had a dream the night before telling me clearly that I should stay in Prasanthi Nilayam, and of course, I stayed for the Shivaratri, despite the crowd, which I wanted to avoid. I understood perfectly what Baba meant in the dream, so I stayed.

The next morning at darshan, Baba stopped in front of me, smiled and then teased me. He seemed to have fun, but I was not amused. It had not been my wish to stay longer, but it was apparently Baba's.

But now it was time for it. I did want to see Sri Lanka during a stay with Baba, which seemed to be a fine arrangement. With spiritual books in the trunk that I could immerse myself in, I could enjoy the beach life and nature at the same time.

My son and I arrived in Sri Lanka and were picked up by Shiva, an old devotee of Baba, who lives there. He had promised to help with a hotel and so on. Shiva was very friendly and helpful and had reserved a room for us at an exceptionally beautiful hotel, situated right next to the beach. I had planned that we would stay here for some weeks, before going to India and Baba.

Shiva drove with us to the hotel, which was an hour's drive from Columbo. When we arrived, I thanked Shiva and said that I could do the rest myself, but he would not hear such talk.

"No, Swami has sent you, so I'll see you installed first before I go back."

It was incredibly attentive of him. We arrived at the hotel which, as I have said, was very beautiful. It was in white marble and surrounded by an exotic vegetation all mirrored in the sea. It was so appealing. A restaurant, also in white marble, was surrounded by tropical plants as well and had a swimming pool in the background. Should I have chosen, I would definitely not have moved into such an expensive hotel. It was actually not luxury that I sought, but Shiva had arranged everything so well for us and he had done it as best he could, so we followed him, and I enjoyed it for the moment.

I thanked Shiva for his help and thought that he would drive back, but he said, "No, I won't drive back before I know that everything is in order. Swami has sent you, and it's my duty to help. Now we go into the restaurant, where I'll speak with the manager. Later, I'll follow you to your room, so I know everything is in order. I'll not go back before that is done."

We walked into the restaurant. Shiva called on the manager and explained that we would stay at the hotel for some weeks, and that we were followers of Sai Baba. He asked if we could get vegetarian meals at the hotel.

"No, but we would like to make it specifically for the lady and her son," the manager said.

Then he called a chef, and they made a small menu card with four different vegetarian dishes for us. Shiva was very happy on our behalf.

At this point, I felt it was becoming too much. The whole thing was arranged over my heads. It bothered me, that although I was not a great eater of meat, I was certainly not a vegetarian, and I had absolutely no objection to enjoying what this hotel had to offer. Shiva may have gotten the impression that I was a vegetarian, and as I said, he had done everything in Baba's spirit and in the best sense. So at this point I would not say anything, but it was not quite as I had intended. I thought that from the next day, I would do as I like. Shiva thanked the manager on my behalf, and we went to our room which, of course, was very beautiful. Shiva asked if everything was okay, and I could only confirm that. I thanked him for the great help he had provided. He wished us a good holiday and then drove back to Columbo.

It really was a beautiful room. It was on the ground floor and right next to the sea. "It was a perfect place to relax and have peace of mind," I thought, as I opened the balcony doors. There was a fresh breeze from the sea, and the nature was wonderful. We went for a walk on the beach where we, among other things, could get the pleasure of riding on an elephant. My son, however, declined that experience. The sea breeze was nice, and we worked up an appetite for dinner.

When we came into the restaurant, everything was incredibly sumptuous. I had anticipated that the guests were Indians and of course tourists. However, the tourists had come for just one thing: to enjoy life their way. They were dressed up, and I immediately felt totally wrongly clothed in my sari and, incidentally, in the completely wrong crowd. An orchestra played table music, and the waiter came and showed us to our table. I studied the menu and thought I might enjoy a glass of wine. Then the waiter with the small menu card that they had created specifically for us with a few vegetarian dishes, showed up and ordered a bottle of mineral water on the table. All this was done in an incredibly friendly way. They had got the impression that I evidently neither drank wine nor beer, which definitely was not the case. But they tried to do everything as well as possible. The manager had given the message. He had even received a message from Shiva, who had arranged everything so well for us in Baba's spirit.

There we sat, and I felt a little out of place and could do nothing but order one of the vegetarian dishes and drink mineral water. It all felt so wrong. I could only express my thanks for the totally personal service we got, but everything is relative.

Deep down, I was furious because, in fact, everything was turned upside down. "This is too much," I thought. "I would and should probably decide what I should eat and drink. I'll find another hotel in the morning."

I paid, and we left. I had absolutely no desire to be seated in the classy restaurant between all the dressed-up people, who enjoyed the exquisite dishes with equally fine wines, while I felt I was put on water and bread.

Tomorrow I would call Shiva, and apologise for all the trouble I'd caused. I would say that the hotel was not for me, and it was probably best that I took care of things. I felt I was better off with that.

I was truly in Sri Lanka, but who was it really that controlled this? I didn't feel it was myself. The next morning, after breakfast, I decided to call Shiva in order to say that we would leave. I felt he ought to know. Nevertheless, I postponed it; I could not bring myself to do it, when I thought of all the time he had spent for us. I postpone it and said to myself that we would be here for eight days, before we left.

It all repeated itself at lunch, where there was a veritable orgy of food. It was so sumptuous that I had never seen anything like it. We could simply not take the food. It became more and more uncomfortable to be there, and I did not like the atmosphere, although the service was impeccable and everyone was very friendly. In the midst of all this, I thought only of Baba, who was the most important thing in my life.

Three days passed, then I could not bear to be there anymore. I called Shiva up and asked where Baba was for the moment.

"He is in Kodaikanal," he replied.

"Then why am I here?" I said.

"What is it you want?" Shiva asked.

"I only want to be there, where Baba is. Don't you understand?" I said.

"Very, very clear, Marguerite," he said.

"This stay is a mistake. We'll go to Columbo tomorrow, and then to India," I said.

Shiva was happy again and said, "I'll send a taxi and help with tickets for India." Poor Shiva, he was back at work. I packed and in my mind, I was already in India with Baba.

I was thinking of how I, and my life, had changed. Just six or seven years ago, it would have been perfectly acceptable to take a holiday in a hotel like this, but now it gave me no satisfaction, although it was the life that most people would like to experience and pay thousands of dollars for. For me, it was empty. That was what Baba wanted to show me and he fully managed to do that. The taxi came, and we drove to Columbo. Shiva helped once again with the tickets, which had to be altered. Then, finally, we were in India. Baba was in Whitefield, and I yearned incredibly to see him again. We took a taxi from Bangalore, where we stayed at the hotel, and from there out to Whitefield, where Baba gave darshan.

However, never have I been more disappointed. There were many people, and we came at the last minute. Baba had not started his darshan yet.

"Oh, how nice," I thought, "we can just attend it," but it had not mattered whether we had got there in time or not, for just then Baba came driving out of the gate and gave no darshan.

"Baba, how can You do it?" I thought. "Could You not have given darshan before you vent?"

Everyone was obviously disappointed. Most people went back to Bangalore and we also started the trip back in our taxi. I was angry with Baba, but then something funny happened, so my mood rose several degrees.

It was already dim when we began the trip back to the Bangalore. It gets dark in India quite quickly and soon it was just car lights that one could see. There was approximately a half-hour drive to Bangalore.

I was sat immersed in my own thoughts, when the light in the cab's ceiling was suddenly turned on. I was ripped out of my thoughts and asked the driver whether he had dropped something.

"No, I didn't," he said.

"Well, I thought you had, since you have turned on the light," I said.

"I haven't turned on the light. I thought it was you who had lit it, and that perhaps you had dropped something," he replied.

"No, I have not turned on the light and I've not dropped anything."

"It was strange," he said and pressed the button to turn off the lights. However, when he had pressed the switch down, the light was still lit. Now he pulled the switch up and down, but nothing helped; the light would not turn off.

"I do not understand this, there must be something wrong with a wire," he said.

"It doesn't matter for my sake," I said. So we drove on with the light switched on. It took a few minutes. Then Baba said a few sweet words to me; it was wonderful. It was Baba's greeting to me. It is quite a wonderful feeling that cannot be described. I was very pleased and touched and was immediately in a good mood again.

After the driver had once again in vain pressed the switch, he said, "I do not understand; the light will not turn off, should I stop and take a closer look?"

"No, not for my sake," I said.

It was the only attention, Baba gave me during the stay. Never has He ignored me so efficiently and so thoroughly, day after day, as he did here. It was just in his physical form. My relationship with Baba at the internal level is always unchanged. It is from all the way back to 1978, when Baba called directly to me and immediately began to lead me directly, without me asking for it; yes, not even searched for it, but today I could not live without this.

Baba had not been in Puttaparthi for three to four months because of the heat and because the water supply was faulty, so He stayed in Whitefield instead. We stayed at the hotel in Bangalore. Finally, rumour had it that He would come to Prasanthi Nilayam. We left in advance partly to be there when He came and partly to get an apartment, before there were too many people. We got a nice apartment and all breathed peace. We all waited for Baba to come.

The whole of Puttaparthi was getting ready for His arrival, and both my son and I were very pleased to be in Puttaparthi the last month we had in India. It has always been in Puttaparthi that I have felt most at home.

We had waited a week or so and already many people had arrived. It was reported that Baba would come the next day and I was delighted to see him again. Perhaps I would return to favour. I thought I had learned much from my stay in Sri Lanka. I felt I completely and fully understood that the spiritual path that Baba showed me was the only one I would follow. This I had to try to live up to, as best I could.

Then, unfortunately, that night before Baba arrived, my son got a high fever and I had to drive to Bangalore at night, where he was admitted to the hospital. It was complicated due to his diabetes. I was, of course, very sad, but there was nothing else to do. So when we were on our way to Bangalore, Baba was on His way to Puttaparthi. I felt it was just like Him making sure that I never got a single darshan in Puttaparthi. And that was what I most wanted, right from the time we left Denmark and throughout our stay in Sri Lanka, while Baba was in Whitefield and we stayed at the hotel in Bangalore. At that time I felt that we did not come back to Puttaparthi for some time, and I was right. When we drove from Puttaparthi late at night to Bangalore, early in the morning Baba drove from Bangalore to Puttaparthi. It seems it had to be that way.

One of the phrases, Baba often says to me, is, "It is through your trials and tribulations that you grow spiritually. Without them, you would not move forward. Too much attention from Baba will only make your ego grow. We do not need that." That was exactly what I got. Baba gives us each of us what we need. "You did this very effectively, Baba."

When my son was discharged from the hospital, we went to Denmark. I had no desire to see Baba or Puttaparthi again. However, that was not what happened. Only Baba knows what is best for us, but it was hard anyway.

A dream on Christmas Night, 1988

I was with some wonderful divine people. One of them was the Master Jesus who I, deep down inside, knew was Baba.

We're supposed to eat and I laid the table. There were several small tables and I knew that Jesus had to sit at a particular table, so I thought to myself, "At the table, where Jesus must be seated, you must not dish up to yourself." I felt I was not worthy to sit at the same table as Jesus.

I, therefore, decided to dish up for myself by one of the other tables. Then Jesus came to me, patted me on the shoulder and said, "Yes, you may." Then I laid myself a place at the same table and ate sitting on Jesus's right side. Then I woke up. It was an unusual and very beautiful dream.

Another stay in Prasanthi

In 1989, we had been in Prasanthi Nilayam for about a month. It had been a very harmonious stay in every way.

I had asked Baba a question and was now sitting, relaxing between darshan and Bhajans when suddenly one of Baba's teachers came over and sat down next to me. She said a few words about the weather, before she took her Hindu brand off her forehead and put it on mine, "For you."

She smiled, got up and went back to her seat. I was a little surprised, but thought, "Well, yes."

It was, in fact, a beautiful Hindu-mark in light blue stone, it looked like a Cobra snake.

Then Baba came out, facing me and looked intensely at me, saying inside my head, "Yes, this is the answer from Baba."

From that day, I put the Hindu mark on the forehead. Baba often says to me, "In the heart and soul you are Hindu." I also feel that.

The day before we were to travel home, I went all alone on a dirt road in the outskirts of the ashram. Everyone else was at University, where Baba lectured, but I had not been to the lecture and was on my way home, when suddenly Baba came driving by. He had ended the lecture and was now on the way back, when he drove exactly where I was walking. I was so flabbergasted but, at the same time, happy and as Baba passed me, He rolled down the window and waved to me, while He, in my view, sprinkled a little vibhuti out towards me and smiled fondly.

As we left for Denmark, I knew exactly what lesson Baba would teach me. I had really a lot to work on, but did not, unfortunately, start right away.

Baba often says to me, "You take one step at a time, and at each step, you have something to learn, but remember, you cannot skip a single step."

I actually had something to learn. I just think I took a very long time to learn this. Ah yes, the road is long, but I do not walk in vain.

A dream sometime in 1989

I sat between a few people waiting for Baba. Finally, he came carrying some packages, all of various sizes, wrapped in fine paper. We all went up and flocked around him. He began to hand out the packages. Everyone walked happily away with a package. The only one who had not received a package was me.

I went to Baba and said, "Baba, I have received no package, should I not have any?"

Baba looked lovingly at me, gave me a kiss on the cheek and then disappeared. Then I woke up.

A vision sometime in 1989

I was, along with some lovely people I felt were my friends, in an otherworldly place and everything was light.

We were standing, admiring the beautiful white silk I held in my hands. All we knew was that it was the fabric for my wedding dress. They were very happy on my behalf. At the same time, we stood with a great calendar in front of us and said in unison, "When should it be, when should it be?" while we had a good time. Suddenly, we all pointed at the same date which I unfortunately cannot remember. Yes, on that date the wedding should be. Then I thought, "Who should I actually marry? Who exactly is my man to come?" I thought much of it.

Krishna blessed me in a vision sometime in 1990

I was standing looking out of a large window. I bowed my head for a moment. I looked up again, and the window pane was now being transformed into the most beautiful mosaic in colours. It was Krishna with his flute. In all his brilliance, he stood there smiling at me. I bent my head again, and a tear ran down my cheek.

I knew I had been blessed by Krishna. When I looked up, the pane was normal and I woke up.

Krishna blessed my home in a dream sometime in 1990

I was sitting in my living room. It was evening. Suddenly, two thieves came into my apartment and were standing in the middle of the room.

They began to take different items of value to them and put them into a bag.

I said in vain, "Get out of my apartment. You have no right to be here, and you must not take anything that doesn't belong to you. It's my stuff."

They simply laughed and totally ignored me. Eventually, they took a large statue of Krishna and were about to put it in the bag. I immediately stood up, went to them and said sternly, "No, you must not take this statue, it is India's great God, Krishna."

They looked startled at me and said, "Is it India's great God, Krishna?"

"Yes, that's it," I said.

They gently put it back into place as well as everything else, they would have stolen and left my home in a hurry. I actually have a beautiful large statue of Krishna on my house altar. He is still there and I do strongly expect him to continue to be. This time I felt that Krishna had blessed my home.

Krishna
(See the painting in colour the back cover)

My son

We came home from India. I knew then that there should be a change in our lives. My son was going to live his own life. He was 27 years old and should move out of my home.

It was not quite as straightforward. Where should I begin? I had to take into account the fact that my son was mentally underdeveloped, so he couldn't just move from his foster home and start to live his own life.

In Denmark, we have a very good social system, so I had to start there and check out what he could be offered.

When, and if, I found the right solution for Kenneth what, of course, I believed and hoped for, the next step was to sell our present apartment. At that time, it was virtually impossible, and there was another major problem: Where should I move to? How would I find a good and affordable apartment? It would be almost impossible; there is a very long waiting list for an apartment in Copenhagen. If I finally were fortunate enough to get one, it should preferably be at the same time as my son got a place to stay. The waiting was there, no matter what.

It certainly would seem that I should be lucky, if it all should work out. I had to take one thing at a time, and deep inside, I knew with no doubt that with Baba's help, things would fall into place. I could not foresee at that moment how, but I started slowly to think along those lines.

I got a birthday invitation from a friend. During dinner, I spoke with one of the guests, who I did not know well. Suddenly, he said, "We know some people who have a son who is very similar to yours and of the same age. Some time ago, he moved to a nice shared housing with eight or nine other young people. He is happy there and is joining in with so many things. He has become so active that his parents hardly know him. They are so excited on his behalf. Do you think it might be something for your son?"

It was really strange. It was actually what I had in mind at the time and I had not spoken about my son. Now I was confirmed that it was the right thing for Kenneth. However, it is one thing to think about it, something entirely different is to make it happen.

Something similar happened about three weeks later. A lady advertised a little table for sale in a newspaper and I had the desire to buy. I called and agreed to visit at four o'clock in the afternoon. It could not be earlier, because my son came home from the day centre at three. "I'll take him with me," I said, and it was okay.

When we arrived, I was very surprised. She was very friendly and welcomed us, as though we were old friends. She had put on a fine spread of coffee and food, which was unusual, considering that we did not know each other.

We sat at the table and I figured that we should talk about the table, since that was what I had come for, but it was not at all the subject.

She turned to Kenneth, and said, "Kenneth, I have a son who is very similar to you and of the same age. He has recently moved from home and lives now together with eight to ten other young people in a nice house. He participates in different activities every day and attends swimming, physical exercise and dance. He is pleased with his new life and I'm so happy on his behalf. He has got many new mates. Would you like to stay at such a place?"

"Sure," said Kenneth and looked happy. He had been very interested in everything she had told.

I had been listening to her without interfering and could not help but think about what Baba has told me so often, "Remember, everything is happening in a very specific order and everything happening in Baba's ways. Everything is as it should be and everything is happening as it should, so don't create problems out of it; everything is in Baba's hands."

Now I actually felt that He had put everything right, as He so often had done. I asked Kenneth, "Would you like to stay with other young people in a shared flat and be involved in a lot of different things each day?

"Yes, Yes," he said and looked excited, thinking of all the new and exciting things he was about to experience. I must say he was, at the time, starting to get bored at home, so I felt it was the right time for a change, for the benefit of both of us.

My decision was made with not a moment of doubt. I bought the table, which we had actually almost forgotten about, but it was of minor importance. Now I had more important things to think about.

After about a week, I called social services and asked what I should do and who I should talk to. A very friendly woman called back and we agreed that she would pay us a visit, so she could say hello to Kenneth.

The first thing she said when she came into the room was, "Sai Baba."

I have a large picture of Baba, and she had heard about Sai Baba. She was now standing, looking at the picture. It goes without saying that it was Baba, who came to dominate the conversation; it all came to be in a very nice atmosphere.

Many things had to fall into place, not to speak of all the papers, which should be completed and signed. Further, more there was a long processing time, and most of all, if Kenneth could come into consideration for the shared home. All this should be investigated.

"It is a really nice place with many good facilities and lovely surroundings. If it can be done and if there is space, I will do everything to ensure that Kenneth can stay there," she said.

Kenneth was very excited and thought of nothing else. We talked for a few hours and it sounded promising. She said she would call back a week later, which she did, and said she thought it was working out. The headmaster from the place we had talked about, would call me.

He called a few days later, "I think you and your son are going to visit us. I would like to show Kenneth around a bit so he can see what lovely surroundings, we have and where he would be staying."

We went there and it was really unusually nice.

Kenneth was given a space in a shared house, 10 in all. Everyone had their own living room and bathroom but shared a common living room. There was a large kitchen where a woman did the daily cooking. Furthermore, there were permanent teachers to take care of them. In addition, there was a swimming pool, a gym and a lot of different activities he could attend to as needed. The most important thing of all was that there was a very warm and kind atmosphere.

Kenneth should move in within two months, but by then I would have had to sell my apartment, which I left to my solicitor. At the same time, would I even have a place to stay? It was a question I asked myself. Then I remembered a good friend who lives in a special building with only one-bedroom apartments; they were cheap and in a nice location. I called her and asked if I could get an apartment there.

"Hurry into the office to talk with them," she said. That I immediately did.

It turned out that there was a waiting list there as well, but I got on it and the lady promised to call as soon as an apartment became available. After about two weeks, I got a letter that stated that I had gotten an apartment exactly at the same time as my son had to move. It had all seemed to work out perfectly. We moved in September 1991, each to our own new place and to the delight of both of us. I knew who had shown me the way, and who I may thank for everything going well. He came to me in a dream and confirmed it.

The dream

Baba was sitting in his chair when he called me to come up. I sat down at his feet. Baba looked lovingly at me as He took my hand and said, "You travel home next month, but it will be two days later than you expect."

He sat for a long time with my hand in his and spoke to me. I woke slowly and had only Baba in my heart. I knew I had made the right choice.

The same day I called the airline company with whom I had booked the ticket to India and asked why they had not sent an acknowledgement.

"It is because you're still on the waiting list, but we have a seat two days later. Will you have that one?" he asked.

Now I remembered Baba's words in the dream and said, "Yes, please." At long last, I had learned the lesson and used it in life.

The lesson was to take a look at my life with my and give him his own life so he could evolve and go his own way. Before I had done this, I could not move forward in my own development. Now I can see how true it was. He goes his way and I go mine for the benefit and pleasure for us both.

Baba, thank you for your limitless patience.

My son came to say goodbye

Shortly after that my son had moved, he came to me in a vision to say goodbye. It was the inner Kenneth. The other person, the physical Kenneth, now goes its own way and develops in the direction he should with Baba's help. His higher self is aware of this.

A vision on 5 January, 1992

I was sleeping when my son came shivering and wet into my bedroom. Apparently, he had been in the water. I made room for him and he snuggled under the covers. At the same time, another Kenneth stood wet beside the bed and showed me his swimming trunks.

I said to the Kenneth in bed, "Did you come to say goodbye to me?"

"Yes," he said, as he closed his eyes. Then he turned kind of luminescent and faded slowly away.

The Kenneth stood beside the bed went out of my bedroom with his swimming trunks in the hand. He waved them a little gleefully, as if he was telling me that he had been swimming. He attends swimming. Then I woke up.

He had just called me the night before and was, moreover, in a brilliant mood. He called in exactly the same second that I would have called him. It often happens.

A dream on 21 January, 1992

I was in a train station waiting for the train to pick up my son, and the train was very delayed; there were many people who were waiting.

A man came up to me and said, "I'm waiting too. I know your son, Kenneth well."

"Well," I said. "The train is very late, so he's probably tired."

"Yes," he said. "Your son is very tired."

Finally the train came into view in a distance, but I woke up before it arrived.

I can say that he is not tired any more. He is busy as never before, and he has developed tremendously. Thanks to Baba.

Experiences in the summer of 1992

A dream in May

I walked down a long hospital hall and passed a kitchen where two persons were doing the dishes. One of them was actually Baba. He was drying the dishes.

I went to Him and said, "Baba, you should not do the dishes; I can do that."

Baba looked lovingly at me, smiled and said, "Yes, I can easily do the dishes."

Then I woke up.

I had recently returned from India, but I was hardly through the door, before there was both this and that for me to take off.

"Yes," I thought to myself, "there are things that we immediately are hurled into; how typical."

It is to reconcile the internal with the external. It is not always easy, but it can be done. It was that Baba wanted to show me with this dream.

A vision in July

I sat to the left of a woman at a table. Suddenly, a ring dropped from her left hand down on to the table and landed right in front of me. It was certainly no ordinary ring. It was exceptionally large and the ring showed two gates, which now slowly opened.

What a sight. The entire universe revealed itself to me. For a moment, I gazed into eternity; then the gates slowly shut again.

I was deeply captivated by this sight and said, when I gave her the ring back, "It is an incredibly beautiful ring. Has Baba materialised it?"

"No," she replied. We looked for a long time at each other.

"Did He materialise the one you have on their right hand?" I asked. It was a beautiful ring with a picture of Baba.

"Yes, he did," she said.

Then, I was back from the vision.

A vision in August

I was standing with a book in my hand. The title was: *Letter to my Darling*. Happy and amazed, I looked at this beautiful book. I opened it and on the first page there was a picture of someone I didn't think I knew because the picture was very dim. Across the picture a letter was written in a language I didn't understand.

Now I was quite slowly drawn towards a shining figure who apparently was waiting for me. As I faced her, I showed her the letter in the book and asked, "Have you written this letter?"

"No," she said and smiled warmly at me.

"But it is you who gave me the book," I said.

"Yes," she said, still smiling and looking lovingly at me. We had a long gaze at each other; she had a wonderful aura.

I turned around, had an unusually beautiful sight. In an other-worldly place with blinding white light, Baba was walking, wearing a white cloak. He came closer and closer towards me and became larger and larger. Finally, I only saw one eye of Baba. Then everything slowly faded away.

Wonderful!

A vision and a dream in 1993

A vision on February 3

I was surrounded by a bright, white light and felt very light and airy, and very happy.

Suddenly, a luminous figure came up to me and said, "Shall we dance?"

"Yes," I said. We danced, but were almost hovering around in the white light to the beautiful music. The music was *Santa Lucia*. Then I woke up with the music roaring in my ears. It was a very beautiful experience.

A dream on February 21

Baba came very slowly towards me, smiling and stopped in front of me.

I kneeled and kissed his feet. He took me by the hand and made me stand. Then Baba put his right hand forward, and I kissed it. I was completely enclosed by His love.

Now Baba sat down at a table, and I sat down next to Him. He was handed a lot of letters from different people. He went through them, one by one, and I looked as well.

Occasionally Baba looked at me. "No," I said, "it's not my handwriting neither."

"This could be my handwriting," I thought a little later. Baba just smiled and put the letters aside.

Suddenly he got up and I did too. He now had three white balls in his hands. He threw them to me and I threw them back.

Now more people came and it had now become a game, a divine play, and everything was fun. Baba played with us and finally I threw three balls to Baba. He grabbed them and smiled at me. The game was over for now.

Does this dream tell us that everything is a game? Yes, perhaps we should take life as if it was a game, even if that may be difficult at times.

People who are suffering all over the world would not easily say,

"We are taking the whole thing as a game." That is a great question each of us must ask ourselves.

"Baba, Baba. I lack words. You not only guide me directly day after day. You come to me in beautiful dreams, where you give me both good and bad comments, and you give me wonderful visions. Last, but not least, the great trials and tribulations. You draw and play ball with me, as if I were a little girl.

"You are everything to me. Not a second could I do without Your guidance.

"Thank you, Baba."

Baba's miracles

To sit in front of Baba seeing him perform a miracle, materialise a ring or anything else, in itself is so great that I lack words to describe it.

He does it so naturally, without drama and big words, so it comes totally as a surprise. One can hardly believe one's own eyes.

I was once in an interview. There were about fifteen people from different nations. I was sitting right in front of Baba's feet, so I had the opportunity to see what Baba was doing.

Baba said to a young man from Germany in the back row, "Come to me."

He then went up to Baba, who said, "Would you like to have a ring with a picture of Jesus or one with a picture of Baba?"

The young man replied, "I would like to have a ring with a picture of you, Baba."

"That you shall get," Baba said and did a small rotational movement in the air with his right hand. Then he held a large ring in the hand with a picture of himself. One simply cannot see what is going on, before the whole thing is over; it's great.

Baba put the ring on the young man's finger and gave a little speech for him. Then Baba asked him to go back to his seat.

Baba now held a lecture for us all. Suddenly, he made a break and said to the young man who had just received the ring, "Give me back the ring." Baba said this in a strict tone.

The young man took off the ring, and it was passed from person to person until I got it and handed it to Baba.

Baba threw the ring up in the air and then it was gone. The young man did not get it back. Then Baba continued his lecture. We were speechless. Baba knows people's thoughts, so why He took back the ring only Baba knows.

Years ago, I was at another interview. There were about twenty people from different places in the world. This time I once again sat at the feet of Baba.

First, He materialised a little vibhuti and gave it to those of us who sat closest. Then he asked us where we came from. After that He spoke a little about spiritual things, before He paused.

He quickly materialised a ring and gave it to the woman who was sitting on my left side. She was so moved that she begin to cry. Now a second ring appeared in His hand. This ring he gave to the woman on my right side and she was equally surprised and was also unable to keep the tears back. We were all surprised.

Baba looked at me for a moment and smiled, but no more rings were materialised. "Yes, Yes," I thought, "but just to witness this is great."

Several years ago, during a stay in Puttaparthi, I bought a large picture of Baba, and He signed it. It hangs in my home. In the beginning, I looked at it a lot. Maybe, I thought, there will be little vibhuti on it, but there was not, of course, so I stopped thinking about it. But on a small picture I have in my wallet, the vibhuti falls like a waterfall from Baba's right hand over the entire picture. This in itself is a miracle.

But Baba himself is the biggest miracle.

Drawing no. 212 from 1982

Yet again in India

I travelled to India on 2 March, 1993. Baba was in Puttaparthi and it was great to see Him again.

I was sitting thinking of a precious stay when He gave me a very special reception. After my first darshan, when bhajans was finished, a woman came to me with an adorable red rose. She gave it me with these words, "From Sai Baba to you." It was beautiful in itself.

I went to my room and put the rose in front of Baba's picture, lit candles and an incense stick and sat down for a little while in front of the picture.

Suddenly, in the upper left corner, a small white cloud appeared. This circulated quite slowly around the picture for about five minutes and finally disappeared in the right corner. It was very fascinating to look at and a very beautiful greeting.

Now back to this stay. After a week or so Baba went to Whitefield, and so did I. More and more people came, and it wasn't long before I felt that there were too many. Today much is required to be in Baba's physical proximity. The peaceful atmosphere that was around him fifteen years earlier, is no more.

I thought about visiting Ramana Maharshi's ashram, which is situated three hours' drive from Madras. He was a great master, and a master for among others Paul Brown, author of *Behind the Closed Doors of India*. Ramana Maharshi was born in 1879 and died in 1950. His ashram still exists. It is run by His disciples and there was going to be a very fine atmosphere. His spirit lives there still.

A week or so passed while I was wondering whether I should go or stay. I was a little unsure. Then Baba came to me in a dream, and my doubts disappeared.

The dream

I arrived in a place with beautiful surroundings and the beauty of nature. In front of me on a raised platform sat a wise old woman. I knew deep inside that it was Baba. She received me with open arms.

She materialised a small piece of paper from the air; then a pen. She wrote something on the paper and gave it to me. I read it, "No other gurus."

"No," I say. Having a large picture of Baba in my hand, I said, "What about Him?"

She smiled and nodded to me. Then she laid in a hammock and swung back and forth. I understood that I could ask no more questions. I could move on. So I did the next day, 23 March, with Baba's blessing. For me, there will always be only one master.

I sat in the transit hall in Bangalore's airport waiting to be called to the plane. I was going to Madras. Suddenly I got up and sat down somewhere else, I don't know why. I had just sat down when I caught sight of a large picture of Baba, right in front of me. It was a large one, in which he stands up and is waving goodbye. Well, my trip was blessed, I felt, and my heart was quite warm.

I arrived at Madras and stayed there overnight. The next day I would go to Ramana Maharshi's ashram in Tiruvannamalai. In the night Baba came to me in a dream.

The dream

I stood somewhere, waiting for something. I know not what. Suddenly, to my dismay, I saw four people coming toward me, carrying Baba. They laid him in front of me.

I looked at Baba in front of my feet and was sad for Baba seemed to be unconscious or maybe even dead.

Terrified, I exclaimed, "Is Baba dead?"

I got no answer. Instead, they said to me, "Come with us."

I was now led upwards, almost carried higher and higher. I saw a stairway slowly disappearing beneath us.

We found ourselves in a stunningly beautiful and very large lecture hall with thousands of people.

Here Baba was sitting in the first row, very much alive.

"It's wonderful," I thought to myself. "You're alive and kicking."

I sensed the doors closing behind me. Baba was now being handed a telephone. He took it and while he looked intently at me, he said, "Yes, yes, she's here now."

Baba now looked lovingly at me, but at the same time very seriously. At that moment, I understood that in the future, it would not be the physical Baba, who would have the biggest impact on me, but the inner Baba.

In Ramana Maharshi's ashram

I arrived at Rahama Maharshi's ashram on March 25. It had been an arduous trip, five hours by bus in approximately 40 degrees Celsius, but it was worth it. His ashram was so beautiful and peaceful. My mind was immediately tuned to it; it simply could not be avoided. One senses his spirit everywhere. The atmosphere is absolutely wonderful, a silence; I felt it in my body and soul. Here you clearly feel you are in a very sacred place.

I often sat awhile in the small hall, where His sofa still is, and where he gave darshan every day more than forty years ago. It was exactly the same hall where Paul Brunton was for many years. It was a very beautiful experience. Paul Brunton (21 October 1898 – 27 July 1981) was a British philosopher, mystic and traveller. He left a journalistic career to live among yogis, mystics, and holy men, and studied Eastern and Western esoteric teachings.

I was there for a week or so. Then I felt I had to travel to Kodaikanal where I knew Baba would be at the beginning of April. I flew from Madras to Madurai. Then a three-hour bus drive to Kodaikanal. I arrived on in Kodaikanal on April 1. Baba was yet to arrive, but they expected Him any moment; it was said. He came the next day. It was wonderful. I was delighted to see him again and be in his physical presence for a few weeks.

With Baba in Kodaikanal

The days passed quickly in Kodaikanal. Baba lectured every afternoon. Although one often only understands half of what is being said, it doesn't matter. Just to see Baba, when He speaks, between the singing, is in itself a fascinating vision that I would never have done without, no matter how tiring it can be to sit and listen for three hours.

Baba speaks in Telugu, which is his mother tongue. It is translated into English by an interpreter. Although it is something of an ordeal to sit cross-legged, shoulder to shoulder, for many hours, you do it anyway. It must necessarily be so today, where thousands of people come to see Him.

At the same time, the climate often changes in Kodaikanal, because it is a mountain world. It is often icy at night. The rain comes crashing down one day, the next day it can be 30 degrees Celsius. I had to get up at five in the morning, so of course, it demanded a good health.

More and more people arrived, adding to the noise from the many buses with followers and a lot of taxis. All this traffic caused traffic jams time and time again. It made me consider buying ear plugs. Not to mention the pollution from all the vehicles. All of this we must be prepared to endure if we want to see Sai Baba. And you can endure it, when you think about the purpose of the journey.

I had been there for three weeks; in spite of everything and I yearned to go home. However, it was reported that Baba would stay there for a month. So I thought, "I must stay there for the last week."

My plan was that when Baba travelled to Bangalore and on to Whitefield, I would stay in Bangalore, relaxing in a hotel for a few days and slowly prepare my journey home. Then Baba came to me in a dream at night.

The dream

I was employed at a large theatre. I was quite tired of being there and said to one of my colleagues, "I'm thinking about leaving. I do not like being here anymore. I do not think it has the right spirit anymore."

She said, "If you want to leave, you must follow me into the office to say that you are leaving."

Then Baba came out of a door and said authoritatively to me, "No, you should not go in there. You will be with me in here."

Baba opened the door for me and I went into Baba's private residence. He sat in a chair and I sat at His feet. Baba smiled at me, and I said, "Well, Baba, I have been employed at the theatre."

"Yes," He says, "but not anymore."

He looked very fondly at me and said, "Now travel home," while he embraced me and kissed me on the cheek, like a father saying goodbye to his little daughter. At that moment, I felt very happy.

Suddenly, he said, "Look!" In front of us was a completely different Baba. He was dressed in blue velvet and had long black curls hanging down on each side. He stood and smiled at me, this time as Krishna. Then I woke up and knew I could travel with Baba's blessing; what I did the next day.

Baba often says in his speeches, "You're all actors on the big stage. Each has been assigned a role. If you play the role well, it creates good karma. Playing it badly creates bad karma."

It is the symbolism of this dream.

I arrived in Bangalore, moved into a hotel and relaxed. I was fortunate enough to get a seat on the plane all the way to Denmark in four days' time, so I had three days to think about the time with Baba and to say goodbye. Last but not least I thought a lot about dreams. However, the time was approaching when I had to think along other lines: all the practicalities concerning my journey home. Then I got a beautiful vision on my last night in India.

The vision

I was in a place where everything was very bright. I was a little busy, because I had to catch a train. I began to run in order to reach the train.

Suddenly, I feel that there were two of us running. I saw to my amazement that a woman was running by my side. It was as though we knew each other. It must be my higher self. All the time we rushed, I felt there was something I had to tell her, but it was impossible for me to remember what it was. I tried to remember it, but failed. The only thing I knew was that it was something about some dreams about Baba.

Then she said, "I have here the latest photos which have been taken of you," and she threw three or four photos in front of me, which for a moment hovered in the air. I fleetingly looked at them, looks again, of course; it is true; it is me, but certainly changed.

I saw I had changed into a light being. I had a serene expression on my face and wore loose-hanging, luminous robes. My hair was quite bright and combed back. I was very happy. I went to say something to the woman by my side, but she is gone.

The train came rushing into the station. It was a splendid sight. It was the most beautiful train I had ever seen. It shone in all the colours of the rainbow. It stopped and the doors slid open. I looked into the cabins which, surprisingly, looked like lovely, flowery rooms. There were wonderful colours and splendid flowers everywhere. I was speechless.

I shouted, "Where is the train heading for?" But it was apparently my train. Unfortunately, the doors closed and the train drove on. I woke up to reality and just wanted to go back to the vision.

I'm lacking the big words when I must describe those lovely experiences, but then I think of what Baba so often says to me:

Just do what you have to do each day,
as well as you can, then Baba will do the rest.

Home again

I was back home. It was at the beginning in May. It's always great to come home to the slightly cooler climate we have in Denmark.

Yesterday, June 15, 1993 I finally sat down at my typewriter, typing the first chapter of this book. At night Baba came to me in a dream.

The dream

I was sitting in a waiting room, apparently waiting to be summoned. Suddenly, the door opened and Baba came out.

He said to me, "Please come inside."

"Is it for an interview?" I asked.

"Yes, please," He said.

I sat at Baba's side. He smiled warmly at me, and gave me an adorable little book. It was bound in brown leather with small gold roses all over it. Baba signalled that I should open the book. I leafed gently through it, but saw not what it said, and had now reached the last page.

In the back of the book there was a small plastic bag containing some small bags of Prasad, which is divine food. I opened one and ate some of it, while Baba smiling looked at me.

Soon after, he stood up and led me to the door. I left, warm-hearted and very happy with this beautiful book in my hands, that I felt Baba had blessed.

It was June, which should have been summer, but as far as the weather was concerned, one almost thought it was autumn. It was cool with rain and wind, but a little sunshine now and again. With temperatures of only fourteen to eighteen degrees Celsius, I was thinking of taking a trip to one of the Greek islands to get some sun and summer. There it was about thirty degrees and the weather was stable.

At the same time, I would like to continue writing, but I did not have a portable typewriter. One of my friends had a business, partly dealing in antiques, but also with everything else. It could well be that he had a typewriter so I called him and asked.

"Yes," he said, "I have a few, including a lovely small, light one. I'll check it for you."

"Okay," I said, "I'll come next week."

The following week I went to him to look at it. He made it as good as new. It sat at a table to try it. Indeed, it was orange. "Baba, Baba," I thought. I was already on the way.

It was now the beginning of July and I had to travel to Greece in a week. I was busy packing a suitcase, not forgetting the orange type-writer. It would be a combination of work and pleasure and I thought it was great. On the last night before I left, Baba came to me in a dream.

The dream

I sat among a crowd of people and was awaiting Baba. Suddenly, a woman came over, sat down next to me and said, "May I touch the ring given to you by Baba?"

I looked at my hand and said, "I do not see any ring, so I haven't got a ring from Baba."

It is the ring playing its tricks again. At that moment, Baba stopped and smiled at me, but moved on.

Suddenly, He resolutely stopped and came back while he material-ised a large handful of vibhuti for me. Then he turned around and left. I woke up and knew I could once again travel with Baba's blessing.

Today it is August 17, 1993. The last chapters I wrote during my holi-day in Greece are here. They now must be transcribed. I thought it was the ending, but last night Baba came to me in a dream.

The dream

I sat among many people, waiting for Baba. No one really knew if he would show up and people were very much in doubt.

As time went on, one by one left. Eventually, there were only a few of us left, but our patience was rewarded.

Suddenly, a door slowly opened and Baba's arm appeared. "Oh," I thought, "He's coming."

Then the door opened wide and Baba came out. He walked slowly toward us, took a few letters and approached the place where I was sitting... but passed by without so much as looking at me.

I said to Him, "Baba, Baba."

He immediately turned to me and said, "Oh."

He smiled and came immediately back, and stood in front of me. He pulled his cloak to one side and I was allowed to kiss his feet. Then He sat down next to me.

He held his left hand in the air, all the while. He looked at me teasingly. With his right forefinger, He counted the fingers of the left hand: One, two, three and four. Then he stopped and smiled at me. I knew he meant that the fourth is for wearing a wedding ring.

Ego & temperament

Dream on 2 September, 1993

I was with a man in very beautiful scenery. We discussed a topic. I did not remember what is was, but we were deeply divided. He stuck rigidly to his viewpoint, and I of course to mine.

The discussion grew gradually to unimagined heights, and became a quarrel. He was eventually completely furious, just because I had a different opinion. On the contrary, I thought that he was completely stupid.

Now he could not master himself, he lost his temper and suddenly he stood with a kind of garden tool in his hands; it had sharp teeth turned directly toward me.

When I saw it, I was scared and ran. He followed me and caught up with me. We stood face to face. Suddenly I had the tool in my hands, and it turned into a soft metal. It grew smaller and smaller before finally completely disappearing.

We were completely overwhelmed and looked at each other. I was deeply moved and said to him, "Yes, Baba's abilities are without limits."

He looked a bit baffled at me and said, "That cannot impress me."

"Don't you understand anything about it?" I asked.

"What is it you want me to understand?" he asked.

Now I was seriously annoyed with him, and before long the discussion went on again.

The same scene repeated itself. We shouted at each other, and suddenly he once again had the dangerous tool in his hands. I was afraid and started running again, this time he caught up with me and again, we faced each other.

Suddenly, I again had the tool in my hands, and this time it turned into the most beautiful small cutlery. A spoon, a knife and a fork.

We were both deeply captivated and looked at this miracle while we admired the beautiful cutlery. I was very moved. There was complete silence; our discussion was over, we had made peace.

I looked at him, and the tears ran him down his face. He was totally changed and he said, "Yes, Baba's abilities are without limits."

We looked at each other and had only Baba in mind. Who had been right was suddenly not important anymore.

I said, "Yes, this event must be included in the book." It is hereby done.

Here is supposedly something that we can all recognise.

Dream on 10 September, 1993

I was standing, looking at a large picture of Baba. As I looked closer, I saw that from Baba's right hand hung a lovely pearl necklace in all colours of the rainbow. It was very long, reaching the floor.

Perhaps the necklace is symbolising that each vision and dream are a gem, and that's exactly what they are.

I sat down and began to draw and said to a friend who was present, "I really cannot draw."

"Of course you can," she said.

As soon as I started to draw, the drawing changed by itself.

"Hurry up and come in and see. The drawing has changed," I said.

She came quickly to me and looked over my shoulder. As we were both looked at the drawing, it changed again. This time to a portrait; head and shoulders. It disappeared quickly, and unfortunately we did not see who was depicted. Then I woke up.

The day before, we had been together and had worked on the manuscript for this book. In the book I had written about a vision and a dream, in which Krishna came to me.

I had asked my friend if she would draw a picture of Krishna, for the page where the vision and the dream was described. She can draw and said, "I would like to try, but I'm not certain that I can do it."

We talked back and forth and the last thing I said was, "perhaps we could wait to see how much space will be left for the drawing. Maybe it will only be a head-and-shoulders image of Krishna."

A Life Changing Journey with a Master
Part Two

by Marguerite Jalving

An unusual story continuous

This book is primarily dedicated to
Bhagavan Sai Sathyra Sai Baba

"Unless you people see miraculous signs and wonders," Jesus told
him, "you will never believe." - *John 4:48*
*

Humanity should praise itself happy,
we have Sai Baba among us
and try to live up to his message:
"There is only one religion,
the religion of love."
*

Aum Sai Ram

Thanks (for Part Two)

First of all, I thank Sai Baba for all the beautiful dreams and visions... I can't find words to describe them. Thank you for the truly personal guidance. Without that this book would never have been.

Big thanks to Erik Istrup who, in some miraculous way, suddenly showed up at the right time and place to undertake the hard work in publishing my book both in Danish and in English, including the translation. No one could have done it better.

Furthermore, thanks to Karin Valentin, who has done a very good job of bringing together the threads to modify the Danish part of the book, and to May Engel for proofreading the English translation.

However, nothing is a coincidence – Baba guides everything.

SAI RAM

Marguerite Jalving

Introduction (for Part Two)

When my first book, *With Sai Baba by my Side* was published in Danish in July 1994, I did not have the slightest idea that I would write another book, but Baba continued to come to me in dreams and visions. I wrote them down, because they are just as amazing and beautiful as those in my first book.

I was convinced that Baba expected me to do so, and because it is what Baba wants me to do I will continue this second part.

*

A deep thank you to Sai Baba, which gives me these divine experiences, and at the same time gives me this lovely work.

*

Marguerite Jalving

Master and pupil

A beautiful dream sometime in 1993

I was a young girl, who had just moved out of the family home. I had a wonderful father who I loved dearly and at the same time was missing very much. He was worried about how things were going for me and one day he came visiting.

I was happy to see him, so I ran to greet him and wanted to fling my arms around his neck, as I used to do. However, when I raised my arms, he stopped me, laid his hands softly on my wrist, looked gently at me and said, "Shall we say master and pupil?" as he simultaneously transformed into Baba. In this vision, I was deeply moved and said, "Yes, Baba." From that moment, I was a student of Baba. Only then I laid my arms around his neck, saying, "I love you, Baba." I felt like a very happy little girl.

For a moment, Baba stretched his arms to put a little distance between us, looked gently, lovingly at me, and said, "Baba loves you even more."

I can't find words to describe how I felt.

Wonderful!

My son disappeared

On Baba's birthday, 23 November 1993, no one knew where my son was from eight o'clock in the morning to around eight o'clock in the evening, except Baba and my son, but he said nothing be-cause his vocabulary is very small. My faith in Baba was certainly put to a tough test.

I was called at six o'clock in the evening to be told that my son had disappeared. He had not returned from the workshop in the afternoon, as he usually did.

"He is called for in all buses and taxis (which can be done in Denmark). Furthermore, we have called all the hospitals, but without result. We must now appeal to television that they make an appeal for him in the news at 7pm," she said. It was the head of the group home, where Kenneth was living. Everyone was deeply shocked, not least myself after I got the message.

That day it was snowing badly; it was bitterly cold and extremely slippery. It was awful to think that we didn't know what had happened to him. I could only do one thing: pray to Baba.

Twenty minutes later the phone rang. He was found unharmed, in the middle of the Town Hall Square, far away from where he lived. He was a little cold, but otherwise okay. It was one of the staff members of the group home, who found him. Since my son has diabetes and had been away all day, he was immediately taken to the hospital, as the staff member was obviously afraid there would be an insulin shock on the way. At the hospital, his blood sugar was examined. It proved to be perfectly normal, even very good, even though he still had his lunch box in his bag, as he had with him every day, untouched. He apparently had not had anything to eat all day. How could it be, when we know that a diabetic must have his food at specific times during the day? It is very important to avoid insulin shock. Kenneth got insulin both morning and evening, so it all seemed very strange.

When they came home, it turned out that he had not been at the workshop at all. It was confirmed the next day. That is to say, that he probably hadn't had anything to eat or drink for ten hours, but strangely enough his blood sugar was okay, as I've said earlier. They understood nothing of the whole thing. I understood even less, but we were all happy that he was home unharmed.

After I had calmed down and spoken with Kenneth on the phone

111

and ascertained that he was all right, I breathed a sigh of relief. However, none of us could make him tell us what had happened, except then he had been on the bus.

I wondered what he had actually been doing. To ride the bus all day without anyone noticing is almost impossible. All the buses had been contacted in vain, so it all seemed very strange indeed. It got even more mysterious, because Baba came to me in a dream two days later.

Dream on 26. November 1993

I was amongst a lot of people standing in a large, beautiful, circular hall. We were standing in a circle waiting for Baba, all looking at the sparkling crystal chandelier that hung from the ceiling. It was very large and shone out in all directions in all its radiance.

Baba came into the hall, stopped for a moment, and spoke with some supporters on the opposite side of where I was standing. Suddenly, he turned around, came directly towards me and stopped right in front of me.

A woman on my right-hand side at once began to ask Baba a whole lot of questions. Baba just looked at her. She asked endlessly about trivial things.

Finally, I said to her, "Be quiet, can't you see that Baba wants to say something important to me?"

She looked surprised at me and kept silent.

Baba looked strictly at me and said sharply as he pointed up at the great crystal chandelier, "Be careful you don't get it down on your head."

Then I woke up thinking, "I wonder what that could mean? Must I have the big chandelier falling down on my head before I see the light and understand the situation in the dream?"

The following weekend Kenneth visited me. I thought I would talk to him about his strange disappearance. I asked him, "Kenneth, on the day when no one knew where you were, and you were gone all day, did you stay on the bus the whole time?"

"No," he said.

112

"Were you walking the streets looking at shop windows?"

"No," he said again.

"You must have done something, and you hadn't touched your lunch either. Tell me, did you get something to eat from someone?"

"Yes," said he, not in the slightest bit worried.

"It sounds very exciting. There was perhaps someone who invited you to a good dinner?" I said, mostly in fun.

To my great surprise, he said loud and clear, "Yes."

I looked at him for a little while, and then I asked him, "Was it a lady who invited you to dinner?"

"No, no."

"It was perhaps a man?"

"Yes."

"Was it an old man?"

"No, no," he said, and became more and more excited.

"It was perhaps a young man?"

"Yes, Yes."

It became more and more mysterious. From this strange conversation, I understood that when he had been on the bus, there was a young man who had spoken to him. They went to the city where they had spent the day together.

They had dined together, looked at the Christmas exhibition, and later they had tea. In my conversation with Kenneth, I came to understand that the young man knew Baba. He had also seen Kenneth's medallion which Baba has materialised to him many years ago.

Together they had had a nice day and Kenneth had felt that he had been with a friend; this friend had then said goodbye to Kenneth at the Town Hall Square, just before he was found.

"And then you're taken into hospital in the ambulance and your blood sugar was checked, and it was perfectly normal," I said.

"Yes," he said and laughed.

"You have a good friend all for yourself."

"Yes, yes," he said thrilled.

However, what should we believe? And how many may learn something from this? At the same time, I had the dream of a crystal chandelier in clear mind. It all seems so incredible that we could hardly believe it. A few weeks later, something peculiar happened.

Mysterious

Sunday at about 2pm, 12 December, 1993

I was sitting reading the review of my manuscript when the doorbell rang. I got up, opened the door and got very surprised, because in front of me stood a young man most politely asking, "Excuse me, is a small boy named Bent Bogèn living here?"

"No, no," I replied. We looked at each other and smiled, both of us somewhat bemused.

"Please forgive me," he said very politely and went again.

I went back to read my manuscript, but kept thinking that it was a really strange question to ask.

I was thinking of the young man and what he had said. Bent Bogèn – BB – no, it was too unbelievable, but it ended up that I wrote down this episode. Later it would turn out to be even more mysterious.

In the afternoon, I spoke with a friend on the phone telling her about the incident. She found it strange too. She called me again in the night quite excited and said, "Now you just hear this. I have been thinking of what you've told me about the young man who came to you asking for a small boy named Bent Bogèn. Bent, Bent, I thought again and again. There is something called Bent. Eventual I looked in an encyclopaedia and found out that Bent is an abbreviation of Benedictus and Benedictus means blessing." I listened deeply intrigued.

"If you think about what he said: "Bent Bogèn", and remove the accent above the "e" in Bogèn, it spells Bogen (which means *book* in Danish)," I said. This experience should tell me that

my book had been blessed.

It took a little while before I could grasp the meaning of this. I could hardly believe it. Was it really Baba, in the guise of a young man who had come to me and blessed my book? And it might be the "same young man" who had been together with Kenneth all day on 23 November, Baba's birthday! Yes, so Kenneth truly was with a good friend.

The only thing I can say is, "It surpasses my imagination; it is fantastic, although I know that Baba can come in all guises. It is described in many places." At night, I got a vision, that made the whole thing even more strange.

Vision on 13 December, 1993

My son and I were together in a place I didn't know. There were many people here, and it was quite warm.

Suddenly, we all looked up and cried, "Behold he comes, behold, he comes!" There was a great sea of light. Slowly, in the centre of this brilliant light, a shining staircase appeared.

On the staircase, a light figure emerged. He slowly glided down towards us. It was a young man; Divine to look at: He was completely surrounded by white light and dressed in a colourful costume.

He had now reached the bottom of the stairs and stood in the midst of us. However, there were so many people around him, that my son and I couldn't see him, so we moved away from the crowd.

When we had moved away from the crowd and had found a more peaceful place, he suddenly moved towards us with his arms filled with colourful flowers. He was now standing directly in front of us. He looked intensely upon us, smiled warmly, and gave each of us an adorable flower, smiled again and walked on. He was wonderfully clear to look upon; not of this world. Then I returned from the vision and could still see him in front of me. It was an incredibly beautiful experience.

Dream on 16 December, 1993

Kenneth and I were on our way home from a trip. We arrived at the railway station with two heavy suitcases. There were many different trains and a great many people. The situation was very confusing. I stopped for a moment and asked myself, "I wonder which train to take?"

Then a sweet woman came up to me and asked, "May I help you with the luggage?"

"Thank you very much," I replied.

She grabbed Kenneth by the hand, and they went with the luggage in advance. Suddenly, a friend showed up and we started to talk. Suddenly, I saw that the woman and Kenneth had gone a long way ahead of me, so I said goodbye and sped up to catch up with them. I fought my way through the crowd, but when I finally arrived where I had last seen them, they were gone.

I looked around, totally confused; it was as if they had disappeared into the thin air. I was left alone with no baggage.

Baba often says, "You are carrying too much baggage." Baba means material baggage. We are too attached to our material things. Once he said this to me in an interview.

Dream on 20 December, 1993

In this dream, I was inspecting my new apartment, and I was extremely satisfied.

I was looking out of one of the windows at a spectacular view: A beautiful water mill, where wonderful, clean water was foaming from the wheel which was turning. The scenery was unusually beautiful with blooming meadows as far as the eye could see.

When I asked, "Who will be living here?"

A voice replied. "It should ..." was all I heard, and I didn't see who had responded.

I don't know why I asked that question, since it was to be my apartment, but strange things happen in dreams.

Then I turned and was looking into a lovely bedroom. A woman who looked like me was lying on the bed. I went into the bedroom, and the woman asked me, "Can I stay a little longer, please?"

"Yes of course, but no more than a few months," I replied.

I then woke up from the dream. It was almost impossible to bear. It was only a dream. I hope it becomes a reality, but unfortunately, such a view never will.

I wonder how long I must wait.

Some fantastic experiences in dreams in late December 1993

I was lying in a lounge chair on the balcony of a house by a wonderful beach looking at the sea. I said to myself, "You should be sitting close to the sea." And suddenly my chair and I hovered away from the balcony and ended up close to the waterline. I was intrigued.

*

I was in an apartment building on a balcony looking down. Far down I saw a family living in a house with a lovely garden. The family came out into the garden carrying a cash box and several account books.

They sat down around a large table. It looked as if they were about to count the day's sales. It seemed very harmonious. When I looked closer, I saw that all the books had a picture of Baba on the cover. It seemed to be a happy family.

*

I was in space watching angels who were floating; some in crowds, others alone. It was an indescribable view in the most wonderful light blue colour, and everything was covered in diamond dust, which gave the whole scene a sparkling glow.

*

I very solemnly worshipped a tiny figure. There was a spiritual figure by my side.

*

I flew around the whole universe navigating by touching a small knob in my right hand and stepping on some kind of pedal.

*

A small, delightful ballerina girl was running along with the ballet group on their way home from the theatre. She had been dancing for hours, was pretty tired, and suddenly she said very pleading to me, "Oh, carry me the rest of the way home," and that was what I did.

*

I was looking up at a beautiful sky filled with clouds when a small opening appeared, and I looked onto a sunny beach. A quiet, wonderful atmosphere poured out towards me.

A woman, who looked like me, was sitting completely relaxed in a lounge chair. Everything was peace and calm. She looked at me. For a moment, we looked at each other. I started to walk away, but then I thought, "I want to wave at her" but when I turned to wave at her, the opening in the clouds was gone.

*

I was swimming for a long time underneath the surface of the most wonderful clear water with open eyes wondering how this could be done.

Yet another strange experience

On the last night of 1993 something quite bizarre happened. Some kind of noise woke me up in the middle of the night. I raised myself half way up to switch on the light, but my hand went straight through the switch, and the light wasn't turned on. At the same time, I felt very drowsy.

I looked into the living room and saw that my sofa was made up entirely of shiny white bed linen. In this splendid white bed linen, a boy was sleeping. The white duvet reached the floor.

As I looked, he also raised halfway up, and I said, "Just lay down again to sleep, Kenneth. It is too early to get up." He did so, and I did the same.

I laid down for a little while and was now a little more awake. Suddenly, my thoughts were really focused, "What is this about? Kenneth is not even here this weekend." When he is with me at the weekend, he actually sleeps on that particular couch.

I was now fully awake and turned on the light, and this time the contact seemed to work. I sat up in bed and looked once again into the living room. The boy in the white linens has disappeared, and the couch looked like it used to.

Who was it that had been on my couch in the white shiny linens? One can only guess, but it was certainly not my son.

A joyful day in January 1994

On 11 January, 1994 I received a very important letter that told me that I had been offered an apartment, larger and significantly better than the one I had.

I had to move by 1 February 1994, which meant that there were only three weeks left, and I suddenly got quite busy.

The manuscript for my book, *With Sai Baba by my Side* was completed. In a few days, it would proceed to printing. My task was completed.

It turned out exactly as in my dream, where I was told that I had been given an apartment. It was about two months after the dream. However, I had to do without the view of a water mill, but that was okay.

So don't tell me that everything happens by chance. When one is led by Baba, then there is no coincidence. Everything is fantastic.

At the same time, I felt a little sad to hand over my manuscript, for after working on it for so many months it had become a part of me, and now, I should give it to people that I didn't know hoping that it was the right thing to do.

A few days later, on 14 January, I went to the publisher with my manuscript. It should be printed since it was Baba's wish. I had to leave it to the editors, publishers and others, but I was calm, because I knew that everything was in Baba's hands.

As soon as I walked onto the street from my apartment, an elderly gentleman walked towards me. I could not avoid noticing that he was dressed very nicely. He stopped and asked, "Excuse me, have you seen a uniformed policeman who patrols this street?"

"No, I have not," I replied.

"I apologise," he said and walked away.

As I walked I pondered about the strange question, because we have not had walking policemen in the streets for many years.

I went into the bookshop that was also a publishing house and met the man I had intended to speak with. I gave him my manuscript, he browsed a bit and said, "Nice, nice, with drawings and everything, but has Sai Baba also materialised some cash for the printing of it?"

"No, but I expect the publisher to pay for the printing," I replied. "They only do this if it's a very good manuscript," he said.

I said to him, "I leave the script in your hands. Please read through it when you have time, and give me a call." He held the manuscript into his chest, bowed slightly and said, "I'll do that." "We will see." I said and left.

In this context, it was funny with the question regarding policeman. I felt something like, "You can be assured. It will be taken care of in the right hands."

As I previously said, I had submitted my manuscript to where it should be printed. I had this strong feeling that they knew me a little. That night Baba came to me in a dream.

Dream on 16 January, 1994

I was in a workplace of some kind standing listening to a young man talking while he was working. I did not see what kind of work he was doing. I was just listening to him.

Suddenly, a door opened and Baba came in calling for me. He looked happy, took me by the hand and said, "Come with me." We went into a dim room and Baba and I started dancing. It was a joyful dance. While we were dancing, Baba smiled warmly and gave me the impression that we were celebrating something. I was very happy. Suddenly, without warning Baba stopped and went out the door as if he had to retrieve something.

For a moment, I stood completely still. To my amazement, the room slowly became clearer and clearer until, finally, it was quite bright.

What I saw was absolutely fantastic. I went slowly up to a table upon which there was a book. I opened the book and started looking into it, but did not, however, see what it contained. Then I looked up and saw shelves of books everywhere, and I became aware that I was in a printing office.

I awoke and thought, "Well, well, we'll see how it turns out, but I'm sure it will be fine. Everything goes as Baba wishes.

Probably a couple of months went by, and I had heard nothing from the publisher, so I decided to pay him a visit. One thing I knew for sure: it should be printed.

The man, who had taken care of it, came towards me smiling with my manuscript saying, "It is splendid, but unfortunately, we cannot print it. With all the paintings and drawings in colour, it will be too expensive. It costs a lot of money to get a book published today, and unfortunately, we are not in a position to do so."

I had been standing completely calm, listening to him, and now I said, "I understand this very well, but one thing I know: It will be printed because it is Baba's wish. Let us go into your office, and I will tell you about a nice dream I've had."

"Yes," he replied, and so we did.

I told him about that dream in which Baba and I danced, and how it eventually turned out that we were dancing in a printing office. When he had heard the dream, he changed his mind. Now, he wanted it to be printed, including the drawings; and that is how it went.

Deep down, I knew it would be that way. I went back home, knowing that my manuscript would be published.

No one can stand up against Baba's divine will.

Dreams and visions in 1994

I have moved

I had been very busy, because I have moved into a wonderful apartment. It went exactly as I had dreamt, so I was very happy. On the first night in my new apartment, I had a beautiful dream.

Dream on 2 February

I went into an apartment where there was a mess due to moving. In the middle of all the mess there was a miniature Krishna temple. I thought, "It must be for me, because no one seems to live here." And I picked it up. Then I saw a Krishna figure lie close by. "I must have Krishna too," I thought so picked up Krishna as well. Then I went out through the door with Krishna under one arm and his temple under the other.

Krishna has moved along.

Dream on 19 February

To my horror, I discovered that I was in a hospital for the mentally ill and I did not understand why. It was horrifying.

I tried to explain to one of the carers, that it had to be a mistake. I had no reason to be there.

He listened for a while; then he said, "If you want to speak with the consultant, you must go through that door."

"No, it is the office of the consultant for this department!" I said.

"Yes, it is," he replied.

"But I don't want to see him. I want to speak to the director of the entire hospital," I said.

"Then it is the other door," he said.

I went through the other door and as soon as the door was closed behind me, I was in Prasanthi Nilayam by Baba. I was very happy to know that it was with Baba, I belonged.

We can only guess what the hospital for the mentally ill was supposed to symbolise. Sometimes we might think that it is the mentally ill who govern this world as it looks these days. Is there anyone on

Earth today, who can live in peace and harmony with each other? We can only hope.

Dream on 8 March

One evening, when I was sitting listening to music, a thought came to me, "I wonder if Baba can hear the music too." It was just an idea that struck me, maybe more in fun. That night Baba came to me in a dream.

I was standing looking out a window, when Baba suddenly walked by. He turned and smiled at me and showed me that he had a hearing aid behind his right ear. It was so large that it reached down to his shoulder. He pointed at it, amused, and smiled.

Yes, Baba sees and hears everything.

Dream on 19 March

I was driving in my car, but slowed down a bit. I saw five major highways ahead. When I reached them, I stopped because I suddenly had a big doubt as to which one was the right for me to take.

A young man in a long robe appeared and said, "May I see your driving licence?"

I looked in my pocket and said, "Oh, I've forgotten it!"

He then called elderly man in a long robe, who came slowly towards me.

He looked seriously at me and wrote something in a big book. Then he gave me a letter with a strict look. I opened the letter and saw that I had received a fine of five hundred kroner.

I certainly hope that in the future, I will be driving properly and not forget my driving licence again, because then something will go wrong.

Vision on 2 April

I was at a very beautiful and completely silent place. Suddenly an unusual book was handed to me. However, I did not see who gave it to me. The book was very beautiful and approximately 50cm long, 25cm wide and 10cm thick. It was a very special book framed in a small, beautiful, brown wooden frame, bound in light brown leather. The lettering on

124

the book was in gold. It was an old, beautiful writing, but in a language I didn't understand.

I carefully opened the book and on the first page was a picture of an ancient saint, completely in gold. I did not know who it was and when I gently closed the book I woke up. It was a very beautiful and solemn experience.

Dream on 21 April

I was aware that Baba was giving darshan. A lot of people, including myself, ran to the spot where it took place. At that moment, I forgot all about good behaviour and as we all ran it was a free-for-all.

To my dismay, I realised that I had forgotten to take off my shoes so had to hold them in my hands during the ceremony.

Baba saw all this as he steered towards me. As he approached, my shoes fell down in front of his feet. I was very embarrassed. Baba ignored it and went onwards.

A little later I sat in a quiet place, all by myself thinking how terribly I had behaved.

Then Baba came towards me smiling warmly. He gave me a beautiful album full of pictures. I looked at the pictures for a short while, but unfortunately, I cannot remember any of them. When I closed the album, I noticed that my name was on the front.

From this, I understood that if my behaviour were correct, then Baba, as time goes by, gives me everything I need. I am looking forward to the day when I will see the pictures. I woke up.

Dream on 23 April

My son once again came to me in a dream: I was at home waiting for Kenneth. I waited and waited, but he didn't come.

A man came with a message for me saying, "Follow me, he is over here." So I followed the man.

We were now standing in front of a big door and he told me to go in. I went in and found myself in a large, bright studio. An older, beautiful Indian woman was painting a portrait of Kenneth, who was sitting in a chair. There was a wonderfully nice and clean atmosphere in the room.

125

As I came in, she tucked away the brush and sat down on top of a couch. They both looked at me. Kenneth seemed to be happy and the woman very relaxed. I felt that I should not interfere and went back home.

Sometime later Kenneth came and showed me a nice little box of glass. Inside there was a piece of soap. He then began to talk to me, which surprised me.

He said, "Mum, try to turn the box and see the other side." So I did. In there I saw a small corner of my living room in miniature. Kenneth said, as he pointed at the different things inside the little glass box, "I just said 'table' and the table appeared, then I said 'chair' and the chair appeared, then I said 'wall' and 'picture', then there was a wall with the picture on it." While he was telling me this, he looked very intensely at me.

"It is very nice; did you get it from the woman?" I asked. "Yes," he said and seemed very pleased. "Well, I must meet her," I said. "No, you can't, because I told her that I was leaving today," Kenneth replied.

The dream ended, leaving the question: where was he leaving from and where was he going?

Dream on 24 April

I was decorating an apartment. Everywhere, there was a shining light coming from all around; it was incredibly beautiful.

When I had finished the decoration, I stood looking at a blank wall. "What should I put up here? I was thinking.

Then a very discreet man, whom I did not know, gave me a gift. I opened it and saw a very large and beautiful bottle of perfume. The bottle depicted a heart surrounded by wonderful flowers in all colours of the rainbow. The bottle was about 50cm in diameter!

I was totally in awe of this beautiful gift and said, "Yes, I'll put this on the wall." I was about to thank the man, but he had already left.

Vision on 28 April

I was in a place where I was sitting talking with some people. Suddenly, the wall in front of me disappeared and instead I looked into a lovely temple.

I enthusiastically exclaimed, "Look, this is Baba's temple. I will go in." I walked up the aisle and suddenly there were a lot of people.

As I entered the temple, I felt that my shoes slide off. I looked down at my bare feet and at the same time I sensed that one piece of clothing after another was disappearing.

When I had reached the altar, I horrifyingly acknowledged that the last item of my clothes was about to disappear. At the last moment, my eyes caught a large piece of silk fabric that was lying on the floor and I wrapped it around myself.

Everyone had left the temple and I walked slowly out again, while I thought of the strange incident when my clothes had disappeared.

A woman came to me with some clothes and a pair of shoes and asked, "Are these yours?" I looked at them and said, "No, they're not mine," and left the temple.

The symbolism must be this: I did not need my secular clothes any more. Now I walk the spiritual path, hopefully in a different dress.

Some strange phone calls in 1994

The first call came a few months after I had moved to my new apartment. I moved in February 1994.

One morning in April my phone rang, and a lady asked, "How may I help you?"

What do you mean?" I asked.

"You have called us. Your phone number is right here on my screen," she said.

"What do you mean? What is the phone number you can see and who do you want to talk to?" I asked.

"Well, is this not your phone number?" she asked and told me my phone number.

"I don't understand anything about this. How can my phone number, which is ex-directory, come up on your screen, and who am I speaking to?" I asked.

She mentioned a name that I can't remember, and that it was for the hard of hearing. "If you are hard of hearing and need help, you can call this particular number. You tell us your name, address and telephone number. In that way, your number is forwarded to our screen and we ask how we can be of assistance. I understand that you haven't called us, and I do not understand how your phone number shows on my screen, especially when you have an ex-directory phone number. It is very strange. I am really sorry," she said.

"It is okay, but I am not hearing impaired, and it is not me you need to talk to," I said.

Later, I thought about the episode and found it was a weird call to get. I could not help thinking a bit about how it would be to be hard of hearing, "There may be something that you can't hear." I gave it a little deeper thought. Perhaps it had some meaning after all. Only Baba knows.

Second phone call in May

I am almost a vegetarian, but at one time I unfortunately got a craving for beef. The urge was so strong that I had to eat meat several times a week. Perhaps I was missing proteins; I do not know, but I had to have beef and I ate it with great pleasure. I was a little surprised by myself. Then I received the second strange phone call.

I had just finished my meal when my phone rang. A gentleman asked, "Is that the Angelus Association?" (I'm not sure I got the name right).

"No, it isn't. You must have got the wrong number," I said. He told me the number and indeed it was my phone number.

"Yes, it is, but it surprises me that you can call my number because it is ex-directory. Where have you actually found my number?" I asked.

"There is a note here on my desk, telling me to call this phone number," he said.

"You have to look it up in the phone book to get the correct number. What is this association that you want to talk to?" I asked.

"It is a cattle association," he said.

"This is most definitely not a cattle association," I said.

We were both amused and eventually he said, while he chuckled, "You must forgive me, but you might have become a member of a cattle association."

After this event, I could not help but thinking about all the meat that I had been eating. Slowly I again lost the taste for beef, and I am certainly not a member of the cattle association any more.

Later, I came to understand that there is something called Angus cattle, and that it would reportedly be the finest beef, we can get. So it was probably Angus Association that had been asked for. Whether there is an association with that name, I don't know.

I am waiting

I am waiting for the book *With Sai Baba by my Side*. It is in the process of being printed in Danish. Otherwise, I am ready to travel to India and hope that I can take a copy of the book with me. So I must have a little patience. Then Baba came to me in a dream at night.

Dream on 24 May, 1994

I looked down at the temple square in Prasanthi Nilayam; it was completely empty. I looked up and high up on a mountain Baba was standing performing a speech. Apparently, it was a place where he currently gave darshan to a few disciples and I saw some kneel at his feet. There were only a few people, but it was apparently a darshan for those few.

There was an entire mountain between Baba and me. I was walking towards the mountain with a book in my hands and finally, I reached the foot of the mountain. I was thinking, "Should I climb up this steep mountain?" Then I saw a few people struggle down the mountain slope. It looked to be a dangerous task.

A woman was standing by my side, and I said to her, "Can you see the few people who had fought their way up the mountain, and are now slowly on the way down again? It is a steep mountain and by looking at them, we can see that it is very dangerous. They have to be careful not to lose their grip. That is why it is a slow process. No, Baba has not given darshan yet, so we have to wait."

Sadly, I did not wait. Yet another lesson was waiting ahead.

My book has been published

On July 4, 1994 my book *With Baba at my Side* was printed and ready for the market. I was just about to go to the publisher to see the book and even to have some copies, when the phone rang. An adorable female voice said, "It is Saba, is this Saba?" Before I managed to reply, we were disconnected. Shortly after that the resemblance between Saba and Baba struck me.

Well, I went to the publisher and got my book. It was exactly as it should be in a beautiful blue Krishna colour. And of course, the book was as it should be, because when Baba intervenes, nothing is left to chance.

Now there were five days until I once again travelled to India. How it would turn out this time, only time could tell.

Back in India

July 13, 1994.

I had gone to India with my book, *With Sai Baba by my Side.* Everything was chaos. I lost one of my suitcases back in Frankfurt. "What a nice start," I thought. When I arrived in Bangalore, I was missing all my toiletries and other stuff. But that was only the start of my problems. There would be many more, but thank God I was unaware of that at the time. Otherwise, I would probably have returned home.

Baba was in Whitefield and holding a major conference, so it was impossible to get a room. After much difficulty, I got a room in Bangalore and later in Whitefield, so now that part was settled.

It was the monsoon, so the rain crashed down, and it was cold. There were thousands of people, and everything drowned in conference and rain. Of course, it was great to see Baba again; it always is. But the stay was difficult, filled with problems. I really could have done without it, since I have been through this so many times. I know by now that all the trials and tribulations are part of it all. That is just the way it is.

Several times I did not go for darshan because of the rain. When I went there the space was usually reserved for the many conference participants and that was quite natural. I thought quite a bit about my book. Should I try to hand it to Baba? But it was just as if the right moment never occurred. Finally, I came to the conclusion that I simply would not give it to him. He has blessed it. What more could I ask for? He knows that I have brought it with me to India, so if he wants to see it, there will surely be an opportunity to give it to him.

Because of the bad weather, I was coughing; my sciatica was hurting as well as my back. I was not worth a penny. Furthermore, we all knew that Baba would not come to Puttaparthi for two months due to a large construction project in Prasanthi Nilayam. "Now I've had it!" I said to myself. "I'll leave for home."

I got hold of a taxi to Bangalore and went to Air India to book a seat on the plane back home. I was lucky to get a seat within three days. "It was luck," I said to the driver. "Now we are driving straight to the hotel, where I want to order a room from tomorrow." We did so, and I got a room. "Here, it will be great to relax for the last two days, before going home. It is just what I need," I said to myself. However, I soon got something else to think about; just not quite what I intended.

One of my suitcases was missing, as I've told, so now when I was at the hotel, I asked if they had heard anything from Air India about it. I had given the hotel's name and phone number to Air India, and asked them to notify the hotel if the suitcase appeared. "We have not heard anything yet, but it is likely to be in a large building where all lost luggage ends up. I can, if you wish, give you the papers concerning your suitcase, they are right here. Then you can ask there yourself; the building is on the road to Whitefield," he said.

"Well, yes, why not? If I can get it before I leave, and it's on the way to Whitefield, is it worth wasting twenty minutes. It's okay," I said and got the papers on my suitcase, and then we drove on.

If I had known what I was in for, I probably would have left the suitcase where it was. However, at that time, I was happily unaware of what was to come. I was going to encounter India's bureaucratic system and unfortunately, it was too much for me.

At last, we came to the building, and luckily, I had a nice driver with me, who directed me into the first office. There was indeed a great many of them. Here new forms had to be filled in, then on to the next office and the same thing occurred. Yet we went for a third office where other documents had to be filled in. At that time, I lost my patience and said, slightly annoyed, to the Indian official, "This cannot be right. Now I have completed several sets of papers, and I must still fill out more. It is Air India, which has thrown my suitcase away, so please find it. I will not fill in more papers!"

A friendly Indian gentleman, who had overheard this conversation, came to my rescue and offered to fill out the papers for me. I breathed a sigh of relief, thinking, "This is not the way to do things, now I have to relax; I have to really master myself. I cannot allow my temper to take me over. It will be too ridiculous."

I did remember the headline in the last chapter of my book called "Ego and temperament". It would be embarrassing if I could not live up to what I had written, so I took a few deep breaths.

The friendly Indian gentleman had finished filling in the papers, and I thanked him kindly and thought that I would now go to a room where they kept the baggage.

My friendly chauffeur was still by my side and I was glad of that.

Otherwise, I would never have figured out which doors I had to use.

We had walked around and around, up and down, in and out of the various offices and indeed, I was in yet another office. I couldn't believe it, but it was true. When I came in, my papers were examined, first by one, then another other, and finally by a third person. It was almost as if it was I who had done something wrong and not those who had lost my suitcase. There also was a police officer present to see that everything was done in an orderly fashion.

Finally, it seemed as if they were in agreement, and one of the officials came up to me and said, "Madame, your passport!"

"My passport!" I said not very gently. "Don't tell me that you must have my passport, you have all the information and the passport number in the report from Bombay. Furthermore, you have all the papers which I have filled in here telling you everything, now it has to stop!" I felt that my patience was coming to an end.

Everyone started to shout; everyone interfered. Nobody could seem to agree on anything. Suddenly, it was too much for me. My patience had run out, and my temper entirely took over; there was nothing I could do. I quickly went to the man who had the papers and tore them out of his hands, tore them to shreds and threw them up in the air, absolutely furious, while I cried, "Forget it!" And then I immediately left the office. Their discussion was over, as was my patience.

Unfortunately, it would not be the last time I was brought out of my composure on this trip. I was really put to the test, and more of the same awaited me.

We drove to Whitefield. I went up to my room and relaxed. The next morning, I travelled to Bangalore, while the rain crashed down. I had had enough. "Now, it would be nice to rest at the hotel before the trip home. A warm bath and a good dinner would do wonders, and then I will go to bed nursing my back." I needed to rest, but it was soon apparent that there would be no rest.

I had a nice room, and after a warm bath I had just laid down on the bed, when a horrible noise started. There was a banging and knocked in the room above me, and I could neither read nor sleep. "What on Earth is that?" I thought. "I have to investigate this."

I went, somewhat irritated, up to the next floor to see what caused the noise, and what I saw chocked me. Some workers were in fact tearing down all the rooms. They were about to modernise the hotel. All I could do was try to get another room. I went down to the hall porter and complained about the noise. "Yes, we're sorry, but we are in the process of modernising the hotel. The workers will stop in about half an hour," he said.

Satisfied with the answer, I went up to my room and waited for the noise to stop. It took half an hour and then an hour. This continued endlessly, and it felt as if I was on a construction site. Suddenly, it was just too much, and so I ran out of patience once more.

Again, I went down to the hall porter, and said not really politely, "I have used this hotel for 17 years and have never heard noise like this. You said that it would end in about half an hour. It was more than an hour ago and if they do not stop the noise instantly I will have to move." The noise stopped immediately but my inner peace was gone.

I felt as if I was constantly provoked, and thus brought out of balance. "It's strange," I wondered, "what will happen next?" I should find out soon enough.

The next day I left the hotel to spend the night in Bombay. I had arrived at a hotel and was given a room. I could hardly believe it, but as soon as I placed my head on the pillow to get some sleep, five hours before I had to continue my travels, hammering was coming from the floor above me. When I heard it, I was enraged. I phoned the hall porter and asked what the racket was about.

"Madame, we're sorry, but we are about to modernise the hotel. We are about to tear the rooms down on the floor above you, but I hope you still get a bit of sleep."

"Indeed, I hope too," I said. But obliviously I got very little sleep. In fact, I was so tired that I was eventually indifferent to it all. "It will be probably my last trip to India. I have my limits, Baba," I said.

If I had just listened to what Baba was trying to tell me in the dream on 24 May, 1994, I could have avoided all the hardships. But sadly enough I did not. It was very unfortunate.

Back home

I got home completely exhausted. There was nothing other than problems throughout the journey. The only thing I wanted was to be in peace and quiet in my apartment and think about what had happened. I did that for several days and eventually got better. I came to the conclusion that the only thing that I had not lived up to according to was what I had written in my book, specifically the last chapter, entitled *Ego and Temperament*. Both the ego and the temper controlled me throughout the journey. It was embarrassing, therefore, another lesson. And my suitcase never showed up.

It is actually embarrassing that my ego and temperament had uninterruptedly controlled me throughout my trip and that I hadn't given it much thought at that time.

On the contrary, I thought seriously about whether I should forget, at least for a time, everything about India and my relationship with Baba. Time would tell. I had no desire to think any more about it for the moment. My focus was about whether I should begin to live a more outward life. Maybe it was better for me. As ludicrous as it may sound, I had no desire to think of Baba, and was almost ready to turn my back on him. He gave me nothing but trials and tribulations. "Admittedly, I get all the beautiful dreams and visions, but can they really be useful?" I once again said to myself.

When I had put the trip to India with all its trails and hardships behind me, I decided to make another trip, but to anywhere except India. I'd had it with India. I got some different travel brochures and looked through them, but only to come to the conclusion that I had no desire to go there. "Perhaps I should engage myself in something, but what?" I thought of many things to participate in, but they stayed as thoughts.

"No, I'm tired. It will have to wait a little while. Just take it slow." It was as if I had no appetite for anything. Somehow I was still tired. My son, of course, and sometimes a few friends came visiting me, but otherwise, I just toddled around. We had, in fact, high summer in Denmark and I had just come back from the monsoon in India, so I got in trouble with my stomach and was forced to be calm.

Shortly before my trip to India, the very same day my book was published, I got a nice Indian picture from a friend. At that time, I thought that this was the picture that is on the cover of the book Bhagavad Gita.

It depicts Krishna and Arjuna in the war chariot in the battle of Ku-ruksetra. The chariot is pulled by five white horses. I had not thought more of it, since I got it just before I went to India and therefore, only had the journey in the mind.

The strange thing was that although newly arrived back home and totally exhausted, I had to buy a frame for the picture. It did not help that I told myself that it was nonsense and it could wait. It wouldn't matter when it was put on the wall, but for some reason it did matter so the frame was purchased and the picture was placed on the wall, although I was sick and tired and could see how ridiculous it was. Somehow it could not be otherwise.

I stayed in bed for the next couple of days because of my stomach. I read a little, but no matter which of my books I started reading, I quick-ly got tired of it. It is not indifferent books I have. They are all about spiritual topics and books that I like to read. I think I managed three to four paragraphs, but all books ended up on the bookshelf again.

At last, Bhagavad Gita was the only book left on my night stand. It is always there, and it was a long time since I had read anything from it. I was looking at it for a while without particular interest, "Well, I can always take a peek in the Bhagavad Gita." Bhagavad Gita is considered to be the Hindus' bible.

Slowly, I began to read the Bhagavad Gita from the beginning, and as strange as it may sound, I did not become tired, but continued to read.

All I seemed to read was that Krishna explained to Arjuna that the most important thing of all is to learn to control one's senses. Before you have achieved that, you'll not gain higher spiritual development. The next thing was that the fruits of one's work belong to Krishna, be-cause it is He we work for. Never had I understood the Bhagavad Gita better than this time.

I started to gain more understanding of what Baba is teaching me and, at the same time, I had clearly in mind all the trials from the trip to India. I understood that what Krishna was explaining to Arjuna was exactly what Baba had tried to get me to understand.

While I was reading, the female friend who had given me the pic-ture with the chariot called me on the phone to ask how I was.

"I'm a little better now," I said. "I'm lying reading the Bhagavad

Gita. And by the way, I have put a frame on the picture I got from you. It hangs beautifully on the blue wall. It depicts the front cover from the Bhagavad Gita by Krishna and Arjuna."

"No, it does not. It is the five horses, symbolising the five senses. The driver symbolises the mind and the little timid person who sits behind the carriage, symbolises man. The image symbolises the senses which have completely taken over. You saw it once in my book and thought it was so beautiful. Therefore, I thought that it was precisely what I should give you," she said.

I was silent for a moment, and then I said, "Well, then the five horses on my picture symbolise the five senses. I'd better take a closer look at the picture." She did not know about my situation and what she, in fact, had touched.

I went to the picture and looked at it. The symbolism was not to be mistaken. Now I understood why the picture had to be framed and placed on the wall. I could now see how it all fitted together. From where I was lying I could look at it and not for a moment forget what it was, I had to learn. No, nothing happens by chance.

I read my own book once again, but with a deeper understanding of the meaning of the many dreams in which Baba came to me.

I realised how much I still had to learn, although Baba had led me so strictly for many years and still does. It was certainly food for thought.

I now clearly saw how much the senses had controlled me on my journey and how embarrassing it was to have to admit that I had apparently forgotten all about what I had written in my own book. It was not good. Also, I saw clearly, "It is only by Baba's limitless love and patience that I again and again can take a small step forward. He led me, quietly, and without me knowing it, directly to the Bhagavad Gita, so I could read about the senses that we must learn to manage. That's why the picture had to be placed on the wall symbolising the five senses, so all came to fit together."

"Baba, Baba, how could I, for even a moment believe, that I could do without your guidance?

It all ended up in that I did not do anything. I probably better take it slow and stay calm.

Baba showed me the way. He came to me in a vision that is too personal to be told here. Baba showed me what I had to learn from all my experiences and how I should live my life. It was certainly not a secular life I should live. It is described elsewhere in the book.

There are no limits to the wise one, who has control over his mind,
his senses, his nerves, and his temperament,
and which has his focus on God.
When a man has become one with God, it radiates all the skills,
all the knowledge and all the wisdom,
and the entire perfection, that is known as divine.

Yet another phone call

6 August, 1994.

When I came back from India at the beginning of August 1994, I was pretty tired of it all and wondered whether I should engage myself in some activities. At the same time, I almost turned my back on Baba in my mind. Then I received another phone call.

I picked up the phone, and a gentleman said, "Is that the moped repair shop?"

"What did you say?" I asked. I thought I had not got it right.

He posed the same question again, "Is that the moped repair shop?"

"No, this is most definitely not a moped repair shop. You must have the wrong number, and in addition, my number is ex-directory, so where have you got it?" I asked. Before he had a chance to explain, I broke the connection, quite angry about all these silly calls. "It is ridiculous," I thought. "I have an ex-directory phone number, and everyone is calling me."

Later I was thinking, "Moped repair - a symbol,; maybe I am like a moped driving much too fast down the road so damage happens which means the moped has to be repaired all the time?" I could not help thinking this way. But to compare myself with a moped that was driving too fast... what should I say about it?

When my book was released in July 1994, I did not think that I was supposed to write more, but Baba continued to come to me in dreams, so I know that it was Baba's wish for me to continue my writing. And so I did.

I had bought a nice little desktop, but lacked an office lamp. I called a friend who had the shop where I had bought the orange portable typewriter and asked whether he had an office lamp for me.

"Yes, I have a few," he said.

"Then I'll visit you tomorrow and take a look at them," I said.

Now that I had got a desktop and hopefully also an office lamp, I had the idea of an office chair with wheels as well, but I quickly gave up the thought. I would not spend that much. The next day when I visited the shop, the first thing I saw when I entered was a nice office chair with wheels in the middle of all the antiques. "That is strange," I thought, sat down and turned around in the chair.

He had a few other customers to attend to, but finally came up to me and saw that I seemed to be very enthusiastic about it, and asked me, "Say, are you looking for an office chair as well?"

"Yes, you bet," I said and purchased both items for a reasonable price. Now, I had a desktop, an office lamp and an office chair, so I could work in the right surroundings.

I must add that the shop owner did not know about my relationship with Baba; just as he did not know that I have written a book. He only knew that I had been to India many times. Because I know he was not interested in the spiritual, I would never tell him about my relationship with Baba.

By now it was October 1994 with the cold, the wind and the rain of autumn, so in about a week, I would, once again, travel to Greece with my orange typewriter, visiting the sun and summer, with Sai Baba by my side.

I got the wrong phone number

From the day (part one of) my book was published, Baba continued to come to me in dreams and visions. I knew that I should make a fair copy of them because they are just as significant as those made in the book, but I just did nothing about it.

Instead, I visited a friend in Sweden; a follower of Baba. He has four of my Baba pictures on the wall. I was there nearly a week. When I was leaving, he asked me if I would visit one of his friends in Denmark and give this friend my book from him as a gift. He thought it would be funny if it was me who delivered the book. I promised to deliver the book, and he gave me the address and telephone number for his friend.

When I was back home, I called the phone number up, as he had written it down, to tell his friend that I would pay him a visit to bring him a book from our friend in Sweden.

It was not his friend I got hold of, but a rather cheerful office girl saying, "Everything for the office!"

"Excuse me, I have been given the wrong number," I said and tried again, because I thought that I had dialled wrongly.

The same thing happened and again, the cheerful voice said, "Everything for the office!" This time I just hung up. I had to look up the correct number. My friend in Sweden had apparently given me the wrong number.

The name started with Ax… and when I got to the names starting with Ax…, the first I saw at the top of the page can you believe it, was BABA? Here the names starting with B…. "Baba, Baba," I said, "this is very peculiar."

At last I found the phone number. The number 1 was written incorrectly. I spoke to the friend and later paid him a visit.

What about "Everything for the office", what was that supposed to mean? I thought of all the beautiful dreams and visions that I had just written down quickly with a pencil. You should look to the typewriter. There is probably something about it: You are a little bit hard of hearing.

I had made myself a small office, so I just had to go on with the work because I had got:

Everything for the office.

Today it is Sunday, 18 December 1994, and there is a full moon. It may be why the spirit comes to me and I have typed these incidents about the mysterious phone calls.

Two dreams in November 1994

Dream on 9 November

A lot of people, including myself were sitting waiting for Baba to give darshan. Beside me sat a very loud group, continuously talking, showing no respect.

Now Baba started his darshan and came slowly towards us. Despite the fact that He had almost reached us, the group just kept on talking. Eventually, I said to them, "Please stop talking. You might not have noticed that Baba gives darshan." Only then, they were silent. Finally, there was calm.

Now Baba stood right in front of us. He approached a woman in the group, and said, "I know that you produce something that you think is vibhuti. May I be allowed to taste a little of it?"

"Yes, I have brought some with me," she said and gave Baba a little of it. He tasted it, smiled indulgently, and moved on.

Baba showed how crazy people are these days. They think they can do anything; soon they think that they are God themselves. They forget that there is a higher power that controls everything.

Dream on 12 November

I was working in a very large and beautiful house. There was a wonderful atmosphere and I was very happy to be there.

I was sweeping the floor, which had a very large, beautiful and bright terrace. Suddenly, my son came visiting with an elderly couple. "Welcome," I said delightedly.

Then Baba appeared in the doorway, and I said to them, "It is the lord of the house; I think it is Sai Baba."

Baba asked my son to join him, and they talked for a long time. Kenneth looked happy, so he must have been pleased with what Baba was telling him. Then I woke up.

Yes, it really was blessed work to sweep Baba's terrace. No wonder that I was happy.

Vanity

Vain; yes, who is not vain? Are there any of us who can tell me that they are not?

Unfortunately, I cannot. In general, I am terribly vain, especially concerning my hair, so Baba came to me in a dream.

Dream on 28 December, 1994

Baba was sitting in a chair, looking with great interest and intently at his mirror image. He looked at his hair and smiled because of the lovely hair he had.

He slowly became younger and younger and at the same time, he became more and more beautiful. Now he had got the finest black curly hair and the look of when he was young. He was continually busy with his lovely hair; even though it was perfect. Yes, the mirror showed him that he had a lovely hair.

While he was looking at himself in the mirror with a funny and content smile on his face, he occasionally looked at me. I was standing just beside Baba, watching.

He was still growing younger and younger and finally, he turned into a baby. The baby was not Baba, but a completely different child of light skin colour. The dream ended, and the intention was quite clear; namely, reincarnation. We are born again and again. We have lessons to learn, as long as we are born into the flesh, and the most important lesson is not only to think about the body, but to think about the soul for the soul is immortal.

Baba says, "Deep inside is the human Atma, spirit. It is not the body and must never be identified with the body that is simply a temporary garment."

The higher self, soul, spirit, or whatever you want to call it, is the one that needs to grow; it is that we must strive for and not the external.

"Give your body what it needs and no more," Baba says.

"This applies to all the body's functions; which mean to learn to control the five senses. Before you have learnt that, you get no higher

144

up the spiritual ladder and that is the very purpose of life."

After the dream, I cannot look at myself in a mirror without seeing Baba sitting in front of the mirror and making a fool of me and my vanity.

Another lesson about vanity

For quite some years I have had to wear glasses, because we all know that vision declines with age. It is only natural and something that happens to most people. First, I got reading glasses; later, I got glasses I had to wear daily.

It has always annoyed me that I was about to wear glasses in my everyday life. They do not suit me, and I would not use contact lenses. One day, I choose not to wear glasses anymore, "Reading glasses may be adequate and moreover, my sight is very good." So I put them away.

It was January with sales, and I had only one pair of reading glasses. I thought that I had probably better use the sales to get an extra pair, in case the others should break.

I was on my way to the optician when a blind man came up next to me and asked if I would help him find the correct number on the street door, so he did not miss it. "Yes, of course," I said and led him to his destination.

"Thank you very much," he said, and I left him.

A little later, another blind man came up to me asking if I would help him to find his way. "Yes, of course," I said again, and helped him as well.

I began to think a bit deeper about being blind. "Imagine if you were completely blind as the two people you just had to help. Imagine how awful it must be to be totally blind."

Then I thought, "It is odd; you are just going to the optician to buy new reading glasses, but for vain reasons you will not acquire glasses for everyday use. What should the blind really do? Not even a pair of glasses would help them; they have no choice. Even if they bought the most expensive glasses, they would not be able to see."

I was outside the shop thinking just before I went in, "I should be ashamed of myself; it is nothing more than my vanity!" I bought two pairs of glasses and was happy that I needed them; as I would not if I had been completely blind.

On my way home on the bus there was a lady sitting opposite me sending me a beautiful warm smile. Yes, not only to me, but also to the man sitting beside me. He also began to smile, and I couldn't help but smile too. It felt quite natural. The woman sent out a wonderful vibration, without even realising it. It came from inside and she smiled warmly at everyone, as if she had an inner happiness. It got to all of us. It was really unusual, for unfortunately it is something we rarely see, quite the contrary.

Finally, I could not help thinking, "Imagine if we all smiled at each other. What wonderful vibrations we would send out. We would feel good with ourselves and with others. Think positive." I was given some lessons on my little trip, which we can all learn from.

A funny experience

On a Saturday morning some time ago I was in my kitchen when I suddenly heard a crash, as if something fell down from the wall.

I walked around looking and saw to my surprise that a very beautiful Indian image, depicting Master and disciple, painted in beautiful colours on black lacquered wood, had fallen from the wall. Strangely enough, it had not fallen straight down, as a picture normally would do, but had fallen half a metre to one side, behind a cupboard, and I could just see the corner of it.

I tried to move the cupboard a little to get the picture out, but it was completely impossible, so I gave up. "It is a pity that it must stay the cupboard all weekend," I said to myself.

Then I got a bright idea. In the building where I was living, there was an office, an assembly room and a retirement centre on the ground floor. I went down to the vestibule with tables and chairs, which residents often used to relax and socialise. As I was about to go out I thought, "Maybe one of the residents is sitting there, preferably a strong man who can help me move the cup-board, so I can get the picture out."

When I stepped into the vestibule, indeed a man was sitting reading a book, and it turned out that he was from India. I said hello, and quickly told him my problem. "Yes, I would like to help you," he said.

We used the lift up to my floor, and as he entered the apartment, he exclaimed, "Well, your home is entirely Indian, and the old man in this picture was the master of my grandmother." He pointed at a picture showing Sai Baba of Shirdi. "I remember it was in her room," he said.

"Yes, it is Sai Baba in his previous incarnation, and here is Sai Baba in this incarnation," I said and showed him a large picture of Baba on the wall.

"Sai Baba is here on Earth today. He lives in Southern India, in His hometown, Puttaparthi, where he has a large ashram. People from all over the world are visiting Him, and you can do that as well. I am a follower of Sathya Sai Baba and have been guided by Him for 17 years. He is the absolute reference point in my life," I told him.

He was absolutely speechless and surprised. He looked at the various Indian figures in my apartment: Krishna, Rama, Sita, and many others. Likewise, he looked at all the Indian pictures on the walls and was very stunned to meet his own culture in Denmark, so far away from his homeland, India.

Then he moved the cupboard, just so I could get out the picture from behind it. It was not damaged. He said, "You say that Sai Baba is an incarnation of my grandmother's master, that is to say, he who is in the picture up there! It is very interesting, and I have to think about this."

"Yes, it is true," I said. We went down to the vestibule again. The whole thing had taken about ten minutes, and my picture was back in its place. Now he had something to think about, and it will certainly come to mean a lot to him. All this happened because my picture had fallen from the wall and ended up behind the cupboard which I could not move without his help.

Later, as I had been thinking more about it, it amazed me that I had shown a complete stranger into my home, which I normally would never do, but in this case, it was quite natural for me. I did not think that it was actually wrong, but in this case it had to be. It turned out, of course, that there was a sense to it.

Baba shows us the way in many ways.

In Baba's divine home

An experience in a dream on 6 February, 1995

I was on my way to visit Baba. I felt that I had to see him; I could not wait any longer. I arrived in a place where there were many people and began to walk around. I went to a superior and asked whether I may visit Baba. "Where do you come from, and what is your name?" he asked.

I told him my name and where I came from. "I will go and ask Sai Baba," he said. He returned from a staircase which apparently led up to Baba's private residence. "I'm sorry, Sai Baba is resting, but I can offer you a meal." I was a little sad, but sat down on the floor waiting for the food.

Suddenly, Baba came down the stairs. He came up to me, smiled and said, "Come with me," as he took my hand.

I was so surprised and pleased and said to Baba, "May I visit your private residence?"

"Yes, you may," he said. I followed Baba up the stairs.

Baba showed me inside. I solemnly entered into Baba's home. It was unbelievably beautiful and simple and I sensed the silence very intensely. Baba asked me to look out of the window. I went to a very large window.

What I saw was indescribably beautiful. It was a divine park of supernatural beauty. I will try to describe what I saw, although no matter what words I use, they will never be comprehensive.

Right in front of me a waterfall was foaming down from high up babbling over large, unusually beautiful stones in all the colours of the rainbow. The stones were reflected in the water and a wonderful symphony of colours could be seen everywhere. To the right of the waterfall the most amazing fountain was surrounded by a sea of flowers of which I have never seen the like. In addition to this, the water shone like a sea of light and everything had a pink glow and was delightful to look upon. By this amazing fountain, a small baby elephant, decorated in colours and gold, was slaking his thirst.

A little further away some flamingos were walking around in a group in the absolutely wonderful surroundings with small fountains and splashing streams everywhere, in an incredible, beautiful and colourful scenery. All of this appeared in a brilliant flood of light. It was Baba's garden in one of his Divine dwellings.

I woke up and once again, I was in the secular world. Yes, undeniably a world of difference.

> *Thank you, beloved Baba.*
> *It was the sweetest of the sweet,*
> *and the fairest of the fair,*
> *you had ever showed me.*

My heavenly and earthly guide

Dream on 27 February, 1995

In this dream, I went to see a supervisor of some kind, to ask if I had got everything that belonged to my apartment. "No, you have not. My paperwork says that something is waiting for you. This is very strange. It has been here for a long time and I have been wondering when you would come and get it," he said.

I followed him down a long hallway. Suddenly, we found ourselves in a large, bright room, and in the middle of the room, there was a beautiful pram. He went to the pram and stood smiling for a while, then called me over. When I looked in the pram, I was surprised to see the prettiest small blonde girl smiling at me. She was around one year old.

I was very surprised, took her up and asked her, "Have you been sitting here and waited for me for a long time?"

"Yes, I have," she replied and sent me an adorable smile.

I held her a little while and then asked her, "Are you staying here with me?"

"Yes, I am," she said and smiled sweetly.

"Do you eat plain food?" I asked.

"Yes, I do," she replied.

"Well, you have been here a long time waiting for me, without food," I said. "No, but food is not so important," she said and smiled again. She was certainly not an ordinary child.

Suddenly, I was alone and a voice from above spoke gently to me, "I am your Heavenly guide and Sathya Sai Baba is your guide on Earth. It is also Sai Baba, who guides you on the inner level. You are to follow Him. He loves you very much."

It was very beautiful and solemn. It was like the voice of God speaking to me. I assume that the small child was the symbol of my higher self.

Message from Cosmos

A few days afterwards, I had a peculiar experience. I was waiting at a bus stop when I noticed a small white van passing by. On the windscreen, I could see there was writing, in capital letters, covering the whole pane. When the car came closer, I saw it said "COSMOS". It stopped for the red light just next to me. On the side of the car, it said, "EVERYTHING FOR THE OFFICE" in big, red letters.

I looked at it and thought about my phone call from "EVERYTHING FOR THE OFFICE". Baba, Baba, I have long since got "EVERYTHING FOR THE OFFICE" and am working at full speed." This was a message from the Cosmos. The small, white van drew off, and I got on the bus smiling at this fun event.

I don't bother

One evening I was watching a film on television. It was a Chinese film called *The Big Parade*. However, it started to bore me, since the Chinese soldiers did not do anything but march or perform drills morning, noon and night over and over.

"When will they move on to doing something else? The film can't continue this way," I thought, but they continued to march or perform their drills, so I ended up falling asleep through sheer boredom. When I woke up, they were still marching, so I turned off the television saying to myself, "Now I've had enough!"

I always do some small exercises in the evening before I go to bed, but I was so tired of looking at the Chinese soldiers and their discipline, that I said to myself, "Surely you're lucky not to be in the Chinese army being forced to do this sort of exercise, day in and day out. Here I decide whether I want to do my exercises, and I don't feel like it tonight," and then I went to bed. That night Baba came to me in a dream.

Dream on 4 April, 1995

Somewhere I was waiting for darshan with Baba, together with many other people. Suddenly, a door opened and we looked into a beautiful dining room. Baba was sitting at a large dining table with some disciples around him. They were apparently waiting for dinner to be served.

Unexpectedly Baba stood up and came out to give darshan. He took a letter which a follower handed to Him. Then he walked up to me and stood in front of me. I bent down and kissed Baba's feet. Then he took me by the hand and showed me that I should come in and dine with him.

I followed Baba into the beautiful dining room. When we had entered, Baba took me to one side and began, right in front of me, to perform the exercises that I do every evening and he said to me in a firm voice, "Now you go out and do your exercises, and afterwards, you can come back and dine with us." I awoke.

It was indeed the last time I had said to myself, "I won't do my exercises this evening."

I am not, admittedly, in the Chinese army, but I am a student of Baba and when you are in Baba's classroom, there is no saying, "I won't bother."

Once again some strange phone calls

2. May, 1995

I had been very busy at my typewriter throughout the day. The same was the case the day before. What I write about is very important. It is about a legacy.

I try to write the facts. The day before I had been writing all day, so when I woke up, I had no desire to get out of bed too early. I rolled over and slept on, but woke up when the phone rang.

A woman asked, "Is this the moped workshop?" She sounded like an old woman.

"No, it is not. What phone number did you call?" I asked.

She replied, "It is on a piece of paper, but my eyesight is very poor. Now I can see the number clearly," and she said my number.

"You see, I have a moped with supporting wheels and it is at the workshop, but I have probably dialled the wrong number. I apologise," she said.

"It is okay, but this is not a moped workshop," I said.

I went back to bed trying to fall asleep, but less than a minute later the phone rang again. Once again, I got up. It was the same woman, starting all over again, but I stopped her. She said, "I am sorry, but I do not understand."

Now I had lost the desire to sleep and got up. I thought about these calls while I was making coffee. At the same time I could not help thinking about how much I had to retype. "Perhaps it is best to have speed, just like a moped driving out the road." At once, I went to my typewriter. I thought it was really odd that an elderly lady with bad eyesight was driving a moped!

I was well under way with the typing, when the phone rang again. A lady asked, "Is this Tava?" or something like that.

"No, it is not. It must be the wrong number, you dialled. What number did you call?" I asked. Then she said my number.

"It's strange, my number is unlisted," I said.

"I do not understand; it is the number on my note," she said.

"What is it about?" I asked.

"You see, I'm using a corset, and have a question about it, but I do not understand how I got your number when it is unlisted. Please excuse me," she said.

"Don't worry," I said, but could not help being amused, thinking, "A corset supports the body... supporting wheels." I continued my work.

When I, a few days before, had begun this work, I thought that it would be funny if I got one of the mysterious calls here and now, because I knew that what I was doing was right. But of course, no one called. About ten minutes later something came through the letter box. It turned out to be a flat package. I opened it and saw that it was my book *With Sai Baba by my Side*. I felt it was an answer from Baba. It was from a lady who had borrowed it, now returning it accompanied by a beautiful card.

6. May, 1995

I had been in the city that day. When I got home, there was a letter from the probate court, in which the judge told me that the counterpart in this case had employed a solicitor to pursue the matter. The fact is that there would be a trial and I must attend. Do I actually want to attend?

That night I had a very symbolic dream that made me think deeper about it:

I was looking down into a deep and very broad valley, not filled with flowers, but with mud: disgusting, thick mud. In this great valley of mud people were working in long rows. They made large mud piles with approximately three metre intervals. That is to say, they were dragged up and down in the mud all the time and were covered in mud. At the same time, there was a terrible noise from their bodies when they were dragged up and down. It was dreadful to look at.

I was standing along with some people looking down on this mess and was disgusted by it. I said to someone who stood beside me. "Look, there is a woman. She is thumped constantly. How can she endure it? See how exhausted she is, and completely covered in mud." However, she had to continue, up and down in the mud bath in rows with other humans who all fought in the same way.

Then I looked down myself and saw that I was spattered with mud. I wore a beautiful loose white mantle, now completely destroyed. I looked at the mess and took off the mantle and threw it in a soiled-linen basket. Then I woke up.

It was food for thought. When I thought more about the court case, I decided that I would not participate in a lawsuit about money. Of course, I would not involve myself in a secular game about money. It is, after all, nothing more than mud throwing. I only need to walk the spiritual path, Baba shows me. I know now that is what He wants me to do, rather than win a lawsuit.

Baba will tell me that it must be my higher self who guides me. No matter what I meet, I will be on the spiritual path and not letting myself be carried away by secular matters. Nothing but my relationship with Baba has importance.

Yet another lesson about not allowing oneself to be controlled by the senses and one's ego.

Yet another dream with a message from Baba

I was sitting in a coffee shop enjoying a cup of coffee before going to an event of some sort, and had plenty of time.

I was looking at a large picture depicting a boxing match. It was very nicely framed, so it has probably been some well-known names and a match of significance.

Suddenly, the figures in the picture came alive, and the fight had been going on for some time. I was absolutely amazed and deeply captivated viewing the match.

Suddenly, the two participants stopped and forgot all about the fight because something peculiar took place. They looked up with terror painted on their faces. From above something came floating down towards them in the ring, something that they had never seen before.

I witnessed something quite unbelievable. Baba came floating down into the centre of the ring and participated in the fight. Baba gave them some decent punches. They had been given a worthy opponent and they could not beat Baba. They were knocked out and the match was over.

"The bill please!" I said to the waiter.

"Yes, madam," he said, and returned a large bill.

"What on Earth are you thinking? I have not had that much," I said. He approached me so I gave him a slap in the face. "Please come with a bill for the correct amount I owe," I said. He was embarrassed and returned with a bill for the correct account and helped me with my coat. I left.

The symbolism of this is that the boxing match was the battle for money on the inheritance. Baba came floating down into the ring mingling and won, and the fight was over. My higher self has been watching the event. Finally, I understood. Of course, I never took part in the trial concerning the heritage. For the money meant nothing to me. Only what Baba showed me in the dreams had meaning.

Amazing.

A couple of strange incidents

I went into a supermarket to do some shopping. I had taken a shopping basket and got all the way down to the other end of the supermarket where I was looking at the goods.

An elderly lady with a cane was standing beside me. Suddenly, she said to me, "I forgot a basket."

I nodded and pointed in the direction of the baskets and was about to move on, when she repeated, "I forgot a basket."

Then I got her point: She wanted me to go all the way back to get a basket to her, although I was actually in a hurry. But then it struck me, "Baba, this is one of the usual tests you're setting for me."

Immediately, I told her, "I'll fetch a basket for you, madam."

I went all the way back to the entrance, without being annoyed. The odd thing was that she followed me, which was completely unnecessary, since I was getting the basket for her and she was walking-impaired. It was indeed odd. I had now reached the entrance where the baskets were situated. I picked a basket for her. She was standing just behind me. "Here you are," I said and gave her the basket.

"Thank you very much; how kind of you," she said, put back the basket into the pile and left.

I looked somewhat surprised and thought, "It's really strange how people behave." But when I came home, I thought a little deeper about the meaning of it, "Are we really so busy with our own doings, that we do not have time to pause for a moment to help an elderly lady with bad legs? If so, it most definitely does not look good for us."

A lesson from Baba.

I was sitting on a bench in wonderful sunshine waiting for a bus. A blind woman came and sat down beside me, "Will a number 10 be here?"

"Yes, but it has just left; but with this lovely weather, it doesn't matter if we have to wait for five minutes. It would be worse if the rain was pouring down," I said.

"It is easy for you to say; you can tolerate the sun. I cannot, I have psoriasis. You see that I have to wear gloves in the heat. It is unbearable," she said.

"Yes, I can see it is not suitable for you to sit in the sun. Perhaps there is a bench in the shade," I said.

"No, don't worry, I am so used to it," she said.

"By the way, I have just enjoyed an art exhibition at the National Museum and it was very beautiful," she said.

"That is nice to hear, but here comes my bus and I must leave. Your bus will probably arrive soon, so goodbye," I said and got onto the bus.

It must be terrible not being able to tolerate the sun. The week before, we had the peak of summer and I had been at the beach every day enjoying the sun. Then it came to my mind how strange it was, that a blind person would visit the National Museum to see an art exhibition!

This is the kind of situation Baba constantly puts me in, so I automatically come to think deeper about things. It is certainly necessary for all of us, so we in thought, word and action are trying to comply with the message of Baba.

A new phone call on 30 May, 1995

My phone rang, and a lady said, "Is this the solicitors?"

"No, it is not. You must have used a wrong number," I said.

Two minutes later the phone rang again, and the same lady said, "It was me who called you before. I just want to say that your phone number is in the phone directory."

"Well, I'll have to investigate further. It is strange because my number is unlisted. What category is it in?" I asked.

"Solicitors," she replied.

I then called the phone directory and explained the case to them. A friendly lady investigated while I waited. When she returned, she said, "There are no solicitors who have this phone number. Let me just get your address and I will look it up and see if there is anything wrong there."

A few minutes went by and then she said, "It says ..." and she read my name and address, and that I have an unlisted phone number. "So unfortunately, we cannot get any further; I'm sorry," she said and we disconnected.

"Hmm," I thought, "phone directory. Yes, there is probably someone who shows me the direction, and I have to follow that direction."

The phone call later turned out to have a significance in respect to solicitors. A few days later, I received a letter from a solicitor who asked me to talk to my solicitor about the trial, which I did not want to participate in. He wrote, "There must be a private administration of the deceased person's estate, so you have to talk to your solicitors. It will then be myself who will represent my client and your solicitor as a negotiator on your behalf. This must be done before we can conclude the case."

I called my solicitors, and she said, "Yes, it is true that you cannot prevent the private administration of a deceased person's estate. It is the law in this country. Succession, probate law and so on are very complicated, but do not worry, I'll take care of it. I'll send you a form which you must sign giving me full permission to act on your behalf, and we will close this case in no time." And so it happened.

That is to say, that "The solicitors concluded the case." We can only guess who got me listed in the phone directory under solicitors, especially as I have an unlisted phone number. What should one believe?

Yet another phone call

Once again, my phone rang. A woman said in a funny way, "Is this the diners' club?"

"No, it is not. You must have used a wrong phone number," I said and thought, "Diners' club, what on Earth was that supposed to mean?"

Later, it came to my mind that in all the many years I have been travelling to Baba in India, I have stayed in the same hotel in Bangalore and every single time I had been standing in front of the reception desk, my eyes fell on a board which says, "You can pay with Diners Club and so on." Then I remembered that every time I drove from Bangalore to Whitefield, I had noticed a large advertisement for Diners Club which we pass on the road. Strange that I suddenly had to remember the two incidents with Diners Club, but perhaps it soon will be time to go to India once again. Time will show.

A few days later, I went to the bank. There was a long queue, but finally it was my turn. The man behind the counter said unsolicited, "You should get yourself a card."

"No, I have had my passbook for many years, so I'll keep it," I said.

"That's no problem; please join the queue," he said.

I asked him, "By the way, do you know anything about Diners Club?"

"Yes, but I use Masters (Mastercard, the author). It is just as good," he said. When I walked out of the bank, I thought, "Master, it is almost too funny, Baba." It is probably a sign from my master that he wants to see me soon.

The pencils

Dream on 6 July, 1995

I found myself in a wonderful place with light coming from everywhere and with many people in a very nice and relaxed atmosphere.

Baba showed up unexpectedly and walked among us. He now
stood in front of me, smiling lovingly. Then He went inside, but returned quickly with a handful of pencils. They were in a mess in his
hand, and Baba gave them to me. I was surrounded by many people,
and everyone wanted a pencil. Before I knew it, they were all gone.
Baba came out again, this time with a bunch of neatly arranged pencils
and gave them to me. Those I kept for myself.

I was sitting looking around, and not far from me, a woman was
sitting, totally unpretentious and very lively. Baba approached her and
as he stood before her, He magically invoked a great beautiful rose
pink stone. As he put it in her hand, it turned into beautiful rose petals
in rose pink mother-of-pearl. They were ravishing. She was completely surprised and looked for a long time at the beautiful rose petals of
mother-of-pearl, which lay in her hand. I could tell that she was very
moved.

Baba had left and the people dispersed a little. Some stayed seated
as I did and some were standing talking in small groups. Everyone felt
wonderful, but the woman to whom Baba had materialised the stone
did something very special. I once again looked her way and to my
surprise, she actually danced the Charleston. She danced at a blazing
pace and the dust whirled around her. All the time she danced; the sun
was shining on her, and I could see that she amused herself and had a
delightful time. I said to myself, "She is incredible; she actually dances
the Charleston!"

A little later I was standing talking with some friends. Suddenly,
Baba came out again and rushed towards us. He approached me and
asked in a very loving way, "You should be dancing in front, but can
you do that?"

Totally overwhelmed of this honour and at the same time somewhat nervous I replied, "No, I do not think so, Baba."

At that moment, a loving person came to me, laid a gentle hand on
my shoulder and said, "I will teach her." Baba looked happy. He went

on and stopped in front of the woman who had now ended her awesome dance.

He gave her a lot of attention and said something funny, which was amused her very much. Baba then went inside and the darshan was over.

The woman was now standing all alone and looked very thoughtful. I said to myself, "I'm happy on her behalf, that Baba gave her so much attention." For some reason I felt at one with her, as she was standing in deep thoughts. Then I awoke.

The meaning of this dream: Baba came out with a handful of pencils, all in a mess in his hand. When he came out the second time, the pencils were laid in neat order in a bundle. Although I wrote the book *With Sai Baba by my Side*, in fact, Baba himself was the author, since most of the book is dreams and visions, in which Baba came to me and in each of them there is a moral, which we can all learn from.

In the morning when I wake up after Baba had come to me in a dream at night, I immediately write down the dream. I always use a pencil for later editing and typing. In the beginning, I just wrote down dreams quickly and did not do anything more about the text. All the beautiful dreams were simply written down on loose sheets of paper with a pencil, and so they remain.

In this context, the meaning of the dream could be as this: The pencils that Baba gave me first, were all in a mess, which shows that there was no order. Only when it came to me that Baba wanted me to write a book, I got a system to my writing. Today loose sheets, written in pencil are edited and typed right away. The symbol of this is the pencils that Baba gave me the second time, which were in a neat order in a bundle, shows that now there is order of things, and I still write down dreams and visions with a pencil.

When Baba came out saying to me, "You should be dancing in front, but can you do that?" He referred to the book I have written, *With Sai Baba by my Side* and to the moral of all dreams: Have I even learnt to live up to them myself? If I cannot live up to what I have written, am I then worthy to be allowed to write another book in Baba's name? When it comes to dancing in front you must know the steps, otherwise you are not right for dancing in front. In other words, will I be allowed to write the second book?

The woman who danced the Charleston of course should symbolise my lower self. While the one to whom Baba gave the pencils, and which was to dance the lead, symbolises my higher self. I am happy that I got help learning the dance. Otherwise, it would not look good.

Whether you have to dance in the front or do other things that are necessary to move forward in your spiritual development, you must fully walk the path that Baba shows you, even if it can be difficult at times.

Incidentally, I had planned to travel to India on 2 August, because I felt that Baba wanted to see me. I was looking forward to seeing Him again. I wondered how this journey would proceed.

Back to India in 1995

How did this trip go? It is difficult to say because I do not know where I should begin and where I should end, but let it be said right away; It was the most beautiful stay I had ever experienced by Baba; so intense and full of love.

I did not know at the time, but Baba wanted me to be in India for Krishna's birthday on 18 August. This I found out later.

When I wrote my book, *With Sai Baba by my Side* , which was published in 1994, it was odd that the colour of the cover must be light blue, the colour of Krishna. It was not something I had planned. The last word in the book was "Krishna" as well. Nor did I plan this; it just seems funny that it had to turn out this way. Lastly, a small picture of Krishna was painted, and was added at the exact page where I described a dream and a vision, in which Krishna came to me, I had certainly not planned that this picture of Krishna was painted to end up in the book.

From time to time, I have been amused, both before and after it was published, "Why must Krishna be so present in this book? Baba, is it because you want to show me that You are an incarnation of Krishna? What else could it mean?"

With regard to whether Baba is an incarnation of Krishna, I have never fully understood. How could I know? That had been my position, even until the morning of Krishna's birthday when I, with thousands of other people, entered the temple square, which was beautifully decorated for the occasion. When Baba came in to the square wearing a light lemon-yellow gown, general rejoicing broke out, and from that moment on, the tears ran down my face. I couldn't help it. It was like a stream that would not stop. And it even got worse when Baba's elephant Geetha came in to the square in full regalia, followed by some of Baba's cows, which were also beautifully decorated. It was a marvellous sight. When Baba went down to feed Geetha with bananas, it seemed the rejoicing would never end, and I was simply dissolved in tears. It was as if it was to continue in perpetuity. I did not understand this behaviour because I do not normally cry easily, but apparently in this case I had, and at this time my love for Baba was paramount. Baba walked among us and there was a joyful mood. Finally, he gave the sign that we all ought to have prasad (divine food), and while I sat eating my Prasad, it was mixed with my tears. It was a very intense experience that I will never forget.

Finally, Baba lit the holy flame and went to his residence, while thousands of people sang Arathi. In the afternoon, Baba gave a speech; and indeed, among thousands of people I was lucky enough to get to sit in the front row, so I could clearly see Baba on His platform, while He gave a wonderful speech in honour of Krishna.

My doubts were gone. At this moment, I knew, "Baba is an incarnation of Krishna".

The week when I enjoyed Baba's presence and all the attention He gave me were lovely. On one of the first days He nodded to me during darshan, without saying anything, but He smiled warmly at me. I felt very welcome. Also, he allowed me to go close, where I was allowed to touch his feet, many times. A couple of times when I sat in the front row, He stopped and bowed down to me and looked lovingly at me, while he received letters from people around me. And often, I saw Him embody vibhuti, which is holy ash, not far from where I was sitting. When one has resided for a time in the Western world, far away from this kind of phenomenon, it is wonderful to see it again.

Prasanthi Nilayam has been rebuilt. It has been made incredibly beautiful. The entire square in front of the temple, where people sit for darshan, has been covered with a beautiful pink ceiling and with large, beautiful crystal chandeliers, hanging everywhere. Large marble pillars are placed on the square, and the floor has been covered with a kind of marble, which is comfortable to sit on, and people are thus protected from both sun and rain. In the centre of the ceiling, there is a construction that can be pulled back and forth, depending on the weather.

This construction was not quite finished, and a team of craftsmen was working up there. One day when Baba walked among us, He regularly looked up, and suddenly he called out to the workers. When they were down on the square, they kneeled one after another and touched Baba's feet. At one point, Baba materialised a ring to the head of the group and put it on his finger. It happened unexpectedly and went so quickly that it took us all by surprise, as it is extremely rare that Baba materialises something while walking among the people. The leader of the group wore a huge smile. He was probably the most surprised. They fell to their knees thanking Baba and then Baba calmly moved on. It is small beer for Baba, as he does not make something special out of it, but it is most definitely not small for us to experience this kind of miracle.

After about three weeks, the attention from Baba had ended, and I was okay with that. He had given me so much. Then he came to me in a dream.

I was in a darshan in the first row, when Baba suddenly stood before me. He looked intensely at me, gently took both of my hands and pulled me up, and then we merged into one. I awoke. In addition to the merge, the point of it all, the deeper meaning of the dream came to me in the afternoon.

I always sleep after dinner between one and two o'clock. It is necessary, when one is up at five in the morning. On this particular day I had slept as well. I always set my alarm clock for two o'clock and go to darshan at 2:30pm. When I had prepared myself and was ready to go, I looked casually at my wristwatch and to my surprise, it showed three o'clock. I was surprised, because my alarm clock showed that it was only 2:30, and the two always matched. "It's strange. I do not understand this, and the battery is brand new!" I said to myself. I had to hurry, if I were to arrive to join the ceremony, before they closed the entrance at three o'clock. But alas, when I arrived, it was already too late, and I was not let in. Then I remembered the dream and understood that it was a sign from Baba, that it was time for me to return home.

While I was taking my afternoon nap, Baba had put my alarm clock half an hour back, then I should not be in any doubt about the meaning of the dream. It is great to get the clear message, so I know what to conform to. Many years ago, Baba did incidentally the same, so I've experienced it before.

From that day, I was not close to Him anymore, which I felt was okay. I left three days later completely filled up and at the same time quite run down, partly because of the high temperatures and partly as a result of the harsh life in the ashram, but perhaps most of all, because the stay had been so intense. I left very happy and without knowing when Baba wanted to see me again. I know it is something which He determines. He gives me what I need and not necessarily what I want. What he does is right; no question about that.

On one of the last days before I left, something very interesting happened. During my stay, I occasionally complained about the lack of respect shown by some of the people who come here today. Furthermore, the self-importance and fanaticism, which I also experienced, seems wrong. The atmosphere has in recent years been different.

It was just before the Bhajan in the morning. I was sitting absorbed in my own thoughts, but felt that I was sitting a bit squashed and asked the woman beside me if she could move a little, which she did. At that very moment, we began singing Bhajan, and all concentrated on singing OM, I was looking down and was surprised to see a small Hindu magazine with one of the Hindu goddesses on the cover laying in my lap. The writing was probably Sanskrit or Telugu which is Baba's mother tongue. I did not know it but guessed it could be Telugu. I immediately asked the Indian woman who was sitting beside me, whether it was her magazine, but she denied it. I also asked an Indian woman who sat behind me if it was her magazine, but she said no too.

When the Bhajan had finished, I asked the others who were sitting around me, but no one knew anything about the magazine. "Well," I thought, "it must then be for me. But it surely cannot have dropped down from Heaven or can it?" When I got outside, I asked an Indian woman if the text was in Sanskrit or Telugu and also about the goddess on the front page.

She said, "Madame, it is the goddess Kali and the text is in Telugu."

"Thank you," I said.

The goddess Kali represents the Kali Yuga, the age we are living in now. It can clearly be felt everywhere and, of course, also here in Baba's place. It was perhaps what he wanted to show me.

The small Hindu magazine that entirely was laid by an invisible hand in my lap, unnoticed, is now on my home altar.

Remarkable.

I arrived in Bangalore and went to Air India to book a seat on the plane home. Here my patience was certainly put to the test. It turned out that there were no seats on the plane for a week. I was absolutely appalled by the idea that I should stay in India another week; run down physically, as I was.

I was sent to a superior, who would take care of it. For two whole days, I was sitting in front of his desk, only interrupted by eating lunch somewhere else and driving back to Air India. There was still no prospect that I could get a seat on the plane, because every message from Bombay said "fully booked". In the afternoon on the second day, Mr. Govinda asked me whether I was a follower of Sathya Sai Baba, I could only respond with a "yes". He asked me whether Baba had ever come to me in a dream. It told me what he thought was very interesting. He was not even a follower of Baba, but had great respect for Him.

It was three o'clock in the afternoon, but there was still no place. I was about to leave for the day. "No, wait a little. I'll try again," Mr. Govinda said. The time passed four o'clock, and my moral hit rock bottom. The time was eventually five o'clock, the Air India office's closing time and I felt that all hope was gone regard to the next day. "I am sorry, but we are closed now," he said.

"I know that you have done all you could," I said. The time eventually became 5:30 p.m., and he was about to close saying he felt tired. It had been a hectic day for him, because sometimes he had indeed handled many other customers who were heading to all parts of the world. It was no wonder that he felt tired.

Then he suddenly said out loud, almost resigned, "Why is Sathya Sai Baba giving me this problem?" In less than a minute, the phone rang with a message from Bombay: There was a seat for me on the plane for the next day's flight. And both I and Mr. Govinda were happy.

When I left, I said to him, "Thank you for all your patience. Without it, I would never have gotten my seat. It was why Baba gave you this problem. Patience is important too. I must learn that. I hope that you will sleep well tonight and have a sweet dream, in which Baba comes and thanks you for all your patience."

He was amused. If you are patient, you usually get results. Here was the evidence. I was on the plane to Bombay. It had been incredibly hot while I had been there, with only a few days of rain. The monsoon season was coming to an end, but it can suddenly begin to rain so heavily that, in no time, the streets can turn into streams, and it was that kind of weather when we took off from Bangalore.

When we arrived in Bombay, we had a storm that has seen no match. The rain poured down, and when it rains in India, it really rains. I had my suitcase and had to go out to get a taxi because I was going to the international airport. Finally, I got hold of one. It was a very old car: The doors were almost about to fall off, and the windows could not shut. I couldn't believe it worked, but we went. The driver himself was as old as his car. I think he must have been around 70 years old and he had hassle in getting the car through water. You would not believe that he had driven customers to the international airport before. I had been on this route many times and I knew it very well, but he apparently knew a very different way. He turned off from the main road and into the worst slum I have ever seen; far from everything, which at the same time was a big detour. Indeed, an experience I could do without, especially in this hazardous weather with an old car, whose engine felt like it was about to stop several times. The rain came through the window that could not be closed, making me wet. One would think he enjoyed making the largest diversion as possible. But this is just a part of the experience when you travel in India. You have to learn to be patient.

However, the worst thing was to look at all the poor people who lived in tin shacks, seeing them sat in the middle of the rain surrounded by waste heaps, where the children were running around together with pigs to see if they could find something edible. It was so terrible to look at. One cannot fail to be concerned by this. It seems completely grotesque that some people on this Earth have to live that way.

Suddenly, I became rather annoyed at the driver because of the situation. I wondered why he had to go out here in the slums, in this old car and in this awful weather. If the car broke down, I would be pretty much in a mess. I said, "Tell me, do you not know the road to the airport? What on Earth are we doing out here? Please take the direct route. I am not interested in staying in this car with windows that cannot be shut, and in this weather, more than absolutely necessary."

"Only Hindi Madame, not English," he said. Well, then, I just hoped that we ended up at the airport, which at last we did.

It was late in the afternoon and my flight to Frankfurt was scheduled for 11pm, so I had time to go get something to eat in a restaurant. Finally, at 8pm, we were supposed to check in, and I was waiting for Frankfurt to show on the board, but it continued to show Hong Kong, and now it was 8:30. Finally, I went to a policeman asking whether he knew anything about the Air India plane to Frankfurt at 11pm. "Yes, the flight has just been changed to tomorrow at 5pm.," he said. It was all I needed. My patience was once again put to the test. "Where can I ask for help?" I asked.

"I will take you to an office where they will take care of it," he said. I followed him and came into a small office.

A woman was sitting at a computer surrounded by a bunch of confused people all shouting at the same time. After a while, it was my turn, and the woman arranged that I could spend the night in a hotel at Air India's expense. She gave me a card that gave access to the hotel. I should just go outside and somewhere, the hotel's bus would take me to the hotel and then, the next morning, bring me back to the airport.

It is most certainly hard to find what you are looking for at Bombay Airport, since it is huge. When I got outside, the rain crashed down. It was almost like stepping out in a large lake, and I was only wearing a thin dress and sandals. At the same time, I had to carry the baggage. "Sai Ram," I thought. It was close to be the worst thing I had experienced.

I asked high and low, if anyone knew where I would find the bus to the hotel, but no one knew. One said, "You need to go this way. I know it's up there somewhere."

I went to the designated place, but there was no bus so I left. I asked again and this time I got a different answer, "No, it is the other way. You'll find it at the furthest end of the road."

Back again. It was impossible to get a taxi, and I was now completely soaked. "Baba, Baba, what in the world should I do?" I thought.

I went a little further, and suddenly I saw dimly in the rain a small car in front of me. In the middle of the windscreen, it had a lit sign with large letters, "SAI SERVICE". I looked again. I had to take my glasses off and polish them since they were fully misted up by the rain, to see if it was true or whether I was dreaming. But it was true enough, "SAI SERVICE". I went to the car. There sat a native of India behind the wheel. I asked him if he knew where to find the bus to the hotel and at the same time, I showed him the card now completely soaked. Immediately, he said kindly, "Please get in and I'll help you," He took my luggage, and we drew off.

At that moment, I knew that Baba had helped me, like so many times before, and I sent Baba thanks once again. The man was now driving in the pouring rain and after going quite a long way; he stopped the car and got out with an umbrella over himself. I assumed that he thought that it was the place, but it was apparently not, for he talked to some people, and as far as I could see, they explained that we should take a different road. He came back, turned the car around and we drove off in a completely different direction. He went out again, inquired and it looked as though we were about to succeed.

Happily, he came back saying, "Now we just drive a little further, and we'll be there." We drove the last bit, and once again, he got out with the umbrella over his head and spoke to some people. He quickly came back and said, "Yes, we are here. The bus to your hotel will arrive in five minutes." He helped me out of the car, all the while holding the umbrella over me as he got me into shelter and then retrieved my luggage.

I cannot say with words, how deeply grateful I was for the friendly way in which he had helped me. Without him, I would never have found the bus. I said, "It was very kind of you to help me. I am very thankful; how much do I owe you?" Smiling, he said, "You owe me nothing. I was happy to help you." And just as quietly as he had shown up, he drew away in the rain. I stood marvelling. Five minutes later the bus arrived, and we drove to the hotel.

For the first time in almost 18 years that I have been travelling in India, someone has done something for me for free and certainly not in the Bombay airport.

Imagine that one had to experience this, but indeed, it was:

Sai Service.

There was a large group of us from the aeroplane, at the hotel. The hotel was so lavish that it could have been from the *One Thousand and One Nights*. Actually, I thought that it was from the time of the princes, at the time when India was a country of great wealth.

A lackey in a white silk dress with a colourful turban and white gloves was situated outside. He did the honours for us, as if we were someone special. We came into some rooms that resembled large salons. Each salon was in various wonderful colours with thick Indian blankets everywhere and deep armchairs and sofas, which matched the colour of the carpet. A large fountain was surrounded by marble pillars and the beauty of India's art was on the walls. I have never seen anything similar to the luxury in this world.

We were shown to one of the salons, because it would take some time before we all got a designated room. I eventually got tired of all the fuss and just the idea that I was to get up at four in the middle of the night got me even more tired. I was about to fall asleep in the soft armchair. The others did the same more or less.

As I looked around at all the splendour of the hotel, I thought about the taxi driver who had to drive me around in the worst slums I have ever seen in India. When one encounters such large contrasts within so few hours, one become pretty shaken, even though one knows that is so in this world. But it is horrifying to think about, and I cannot understand why it should be this way. Poverty is a problem in the East. But we have quite different problems in the West which are just as appalling. They are just of a different kind. One can only say, "It's a sick world we live in. That is precisely why Baba is among us today."

Finally, I was on the plane to Frankfurt, thinking about my previous trip to Baba, when he gave me such great hardships. This time it was patience, Baba would teach me. One must hope that I have learnt a bit of it.

A divine experience

2. September, 1995.

I was in a wonderful place, together with some other people. There was a divine atmosphere pouring out over everything and everyone. It seemed to be a place for resting and relaxing. Everything was in such wonderful colours and exquisite taste, that it would make everything earthly pale into insignificance.

Scattered around there was a kind of deep armchair in beautiful colours. They were lowered so you could lie and rest. Also, there were beautiful, thick rugs on the floor and, not least, rich, divine art on the walls.

I was in one of the deep armchairs, which was lowered, relaxing while I was looking up at the divine art on the walls. Everything was at peace, and I was in a deep state of exalted calmness. The art showed gods and goddesses; wonderful to look at and surrounded by the beauty of nature with a colourful bed of flowers that mirrored themselves in moving springs and small waterfalls. The atmosphere and the emanation from the pictures cannot be described.

Suddenly, I saw a small part of an image come to life. "Oh, now some of the gods and goddesses are moving," I said. We all looked up at the picture and were deeply impressed by what we saw. Now more and more of the gods and these deities came alive, and finally, all the pictures were full of life. A divine vision unfolded before our very eyes.

At some point, a divine creature of the female sex came to me. She was very quiet, almost gliding, and then she stood right in front of me. She was so beautiful and gentle to look at, with a face that reminded me of a madonna surrounded by beautiful black hair.

She wore a long yellow silk jacket, and over that she had a beautiful black shawl, also made of silk, which matched her black hair.

She said nothing, but was just looking at me. Actually, I felt that she was looking right through me. Her aura was so strong, and her gaze so full of love that it went straight to my heart and I was about to burst into tears. She went away as silently as she had come.

I felt it was Baba, who came to me in the form of this divine creature.

Home for Christmas

I had originally intended to go to India for Baba's birthday on 23 November, 1995, when Baba turned 70. Please be aware that in India you are one year, when you are born.

"I have to celebrate Him," I thought. I ordered the ticket to India for 6 November, but it was obviously not be. My son was taken ill and was in hospital. It dragged on and my trip neared. I was very unsure if I should postpone my forthcoming trip to India.

Suddenly, I was no longer in doubt. I felt that my place was with my son in his current situation. I took an unexpected decision, called the travel agent and said, "I will go to India for Christmas instead of November; can I postpone the trip a month?"

"Yes, no problem; what about 6 December?" The lady who always takes care of my travel asked.

"I'll leave exactly one month later than originally planned." I said.

Kenneth fared well in the hospital. He had no fever and was not seriously ill. It was just an infection that dragged on and one can never know what it may become. He had visits every day by the staff from the group home and me, who went daily. My son had brought my book *With Sai Baba by my Side* to the hospital, so a few people read it who might not have done if all this had not happened. Naturally, they were occasionally talking about Baba, and I felt that something good came out of it all. At the same time, I received a letter from a good friend who did not know that my son was hospitalised and the letter had a nice picture of Krishna. It seems that Krishna is by me. At this time, Baba came to me in a dream.

Dream on 17 November, 1995

Baba was sitting talking with me. He was in a good mood and was teasing me a little. We were sitting at a table in a small hut, and all around more people were sitting by other small tables. Baba said lovingly to me, "Yes, you will be home for Christmas. I will make sure that you come home. Are you ready?"

"Yes, I am, Baba," I said. Then I looked out the window and saw that it was snowing heavily. It was real winter weather and very cold. Then Baba said, "Now make yourself ready for the journey, and I shall provide a means of transport for you. It will be waiting outside in a few minutes." Then he left.

I packed my last few things and was ready to go. A little later I went outside the hut. It was almost a blizzard. I looked around for the means of transport that Baba had said would be there for me, and which was supposed to bring me home to India.

Suddenly, my eye caught a small sleigh, and Santa Claus stood up and said, "Yes, it is me you must travel with." I was surprised and pleased to see that it was Santa Claus who should transport me the long way to India. I did not give a thought that it was, in fact, a sleigh and not an aeroplane, I entered. However, it would properly be an Air India flight I'd board a few weeks later.

When I sat down in the sleigh, there were a few other women who wanted to get on board. I said to them, "No, you have to go out again. I know I must travel alone."

One got out immediately, but the second would definitely not get out. "I too want to visit Baba," she said.

"No, I know that you are not going now. You must pray to Baba and try to get an answer as to when to go to see Him," I said. Finally, she accepted and got out.

Santa Claus gave me a sign that he was about to take off. We both looked back at a small house behind us, and in the window saw Baba waving goodbye. He looked intensely at Santa Claus, and said, "Get her safely home." I looked up at Baba and had to take off my mittens and laid my palm of my hands against each other for the Indian greeting Namaste; a last goodbye and a 'see you soon'. Baba smiled to me. We took off, and the tears run down my cheeks in love for Baba.

A true Christmas tale. Yet it is not a fairy tale, but real. I hoped that I would not freeze too much. In any case, I suddenly landed, not in India, but in my bed.

While I am writing these lines, we have got serious winter here in Denmark. It is almost a blizzard, and a part of the traffic is completely stuck. It looks like a scene from a postcard when I look out the window, but it is certainly not pleasant be in, and I am glad that I am not to travel today, but if that were the case, it could only be with a sleigh.

From that perspective, one can very well do without the snow.

However, to go by sleigh with Santa Claus, is quite a different matter. Then the snow would indeed be indispensable. Yes, everything is relative. It is not until Christmas that I would be home in India.

Baba determines everything.

Of course, it turned out that as soon as I had changed my travel plans from November, for Baba's 70th birthday, to Christmas, my son was well and out of the hospital.

Dream on 2 December, 1995

I was amongst a lot of people gathered in a large hall. We sat at small tables with six people at each and I was sitting at the head of a table.

Baba walked towards our table. He stopped in front of us and welcomed me warmly. He put forth his hand towards me and gave my hand a hug in the same way as one welcomes an old friend, very informal. Then he went on.

By invisible hands and to my great surprise, suddenly a fantastic, brilliant crystal was placed right in front of me. It was probably 30cm in height and 20cm in width. It was not round like a crystal ball, but more like a large diamond that was cut into various facets and therefore looked different from different angles, exactly as when the sun hits a crystal, and a colour symphony emerged in all the colours of a rainbow. At the same time, it sparkled and gleamed, and was filled with shining stars everywhere.

I turned it around a bit and asked whether they all could see it. The two people on one side of the table, said, "Unfortunately, we can only see it from one side."

"Well, we will leave it this way for five minutes, and then we turn it so everyone can see it from all sides," I said. I was thinking that the crystal was to symbolise the universe.

Marvellous!

Now there were only four days until my departure to India.

Back to my writing

April, 1996: I have been taking a break for three to four months with my writing. It has been necessary, because I hàve done other things that were important to me. While I was doing other things, I always felt deep down, "Now you need to get started." That is why I have sharpened the pencils and pulled out the writing pad. I know that this is what Baba expects of me.

As I said, I went home for Christmas to Puttaparthi as Baba had told me in the dream that I would. However, it was not with Santa Claus in the sleigh, but with Air India. There was a blessed peace and quiet when I arrived. The activities after Baba's 70th birthday had subsided, and the influx of people we expected would come to Puttaparthi for Christmas had not yet begun. I welcomed different disciples and met some old supporters, who had been there for His birthday and they all said, "You're lucky that you arrive now and not earlier."

I understand that everything had been a bit chaotic, when the police had lost control and some people had been trampled to death. Others got their passport, ticket and money stolen. People told me that there had been more than a million people, but of course, no one knows the exact number. Everywhere in the ashram and also in Puttaparthi town and many kilometres outside the city, there had been a compact mass of humans that could move neither forward nor backward. As seen in this light, it had not been easy to be there. There are, of course, all kinds of people who go to visit Sai Baba today; not just supporters. When I heard this, I was really happy that Baba had spared me, because I had intended to come here for His birthday, but was prevented because my son was sick. Then it was that Baba came to me in a dream and said, "Yes, you will be home for Christmas." And here I am.

The peace and quiet did not last for long, as people began to arrive due to Christmas. With so many people, I soon felt it was unbearable to stay and had the desire to leave. Of course, I would never do so because Baba had called me "home for Christmas" in a dream, but in certain moments, I just wanted to get away from the noisy human masses, even though I stayed. Before long, I had no choice, because suddenly, as lightning from a clear sky, I got an infection and had to stay in bed for four days. I just recuperated in time for Christmas and participated in the Christmas celebrations on 24 and 25 December. There were beautiful moments, and all the hassle was immediately forgotten. I was really happy that I had got the infection that had prevented me from leaving. And since I had been ill, I was lucky to get a chair during the celebrations on both days, so I sat comfortably and relaxed. It was very nice. Nevertheless, I now believe that sitting on the floor, like sardines in a tin for five hours would have been impossible for me, since I had just got out of my sickbed. Everything fell into place in a good way.

I left at New Year and stayed in a hotel in Bangalore a few days before the trip back to Denmark. I was ready to leave and was sitting at the front desk organising my bill and so on. It was the first day of the New Year, 1996, and there were both Christmas and New Year's decorations: balloons and garlands everywhere and a large beautiful heart with "Happy New Year". But the most beautiful of it all was a great colourful decoration, which showed Santa Claus in his sleigh, surrounded by snow and pulled by six little mice. I then remembered my dream, and felt a warmth in my heart.

I came home to winter, coldness, snow and a dense fog that swathed the city day after day. A friend of mine became 50 years old, so I was going to attend their birthday and was busy with writing a song. In between I looked out the window, where everything was in grey shades and thought, "I really want to go to Bali with permanent summer, blue sea and swaying palms and experience their culture." I indeed would give it a closer thought.

However, I arrived for the birthday; a nice party with many people. At one point, I was sitting talking to a good friend.

She suddenly said, "Svend is making a trip to Bali; is it not wonderful?"

"Well, that was funny, because I would also like to travel Bali," I said. Of course, it ended up with that our common acquaintance, Svend and I met in Bali in early February and were there for three weeks. It is a wonderful island with a subtropical climate. It was a nice stay.

The most interesting thing is that I was not aware that they are Hindus in Bali. It is the only island in Indochina, where the populations are Hindus. On all the other islands they are Muslims. It was a very pleasant experience, and I felt completely at home. I stayed in a hotel named Shanti, which means peace in Sanskrit. Village Beach was peaceful, harmonious and beautiful, with small lotus lakes everywhere and with Hindu gods in the midst of a unique vegetation. One evening we were out at a large outdoor theatre watching the great Indian play, Ramayana. It was absolutely beautiful. I really felt that everything was organised for me. Baba was with me in Bali too. Nothing is by chance.

180

I was back home at the end of February, back to the winter, but I was energised, refreshed and with a tan, and the contrast in life is always beautiful. In March, Baba came to me in a dream.

Dream on 16 March, 1996

I was sitting in a hospital, apparently waiting for a message. Then a nurse came up to me with my journal in her hand and said, "It will be 9 January." Then she went along the corridor where a superior was waiting for her. To my great surprise, I saw that this person was Baba. She showed Him my journal and explained something and Baba said loudly, "It will be 9 January."

All the while, I was sitting wondering about what Baba was doing in a hospital, not to mention what I was doing there. To my knowledge, I was well.

A little later I was called for the consultant doctor, who turned out to be a nice, warm person of about sixty years old. I was fully aware that it was Baba, who was sitting there, although He now had the white coat on. He sat in his office chair by his desk and was now slowly turning the chair towards me sitting at the end of His desk. He smiled warmly and looked tenderly and lovingly at me. Straight away I took his hand that rested on the desktop and kissed it, saying, "It has been a long time since I have seen you."

Smiling, he replied, "But then it has been a long time since I have seen myself."

I returned His smile, and then he said, "It will be 9 January."

Then the dream ended. What was it with 9 January? I did not know, but it would become apparent when the time came. One thing I knew for certain was that:

Baba is by my side.

At the dental school in April, 1996

For my whole life I have had good teeth so dental visits have never been a big deal. However, over the last year or so I had noticed that something was wrong with a filling and I went to my dentist.

"It has been indeed more than three years ago since your last visit. I can see that you've lost a bit of a filling. I'll fix this right away and at the same time you'll have a dental cleaning. After that everything should be fine. You're lucky to have good teeth," he said.

He treated me and after half an hour, everything was in order, or so I thought. Some time passed and there was still something wrong with the filling. At the same time I began to become a bit sore on the other side of the mouth, where I have two fillings that have been there for many years. I thought that I possibly had become allergic to the mercury that was used previously.

I had to once again visit my dentist. He looked in my mouth and said, "Well, you've lost a bit of the tooth. I'll take care of it right away."

"What about the other side? Why am I sore?" I asked.

He looked a little at my teeth in general and said, "There's nothing wrong with your teeth; you can forget all about paradentosis. You've very fine teeth."

Satisfied with the message, I left quite sure that all was well. But I was wrong. It continued. I was now more or less constantly sore on both sides and was eventually fed up by the dentist. Anyway, a few months passed before I did something about it, because I thought that it would disappear with time.

One day, I got a bright idea. "I simply go to the dental school, to the experts. Something must be wrong," I said to myself. So the next day I checked the phone book and called the dental school. There I was informed that new patients should show up in person on weekdays between 8 and 11am. Again, I took a few days to decide. My dentist had indeed said that there was nothing wrong. In addition, I was not sure if everyone could use the dental school.

One morning I woke up early and was determined to visit the dental school. It was a cold morning with rain and storms. I had hardly set foot on the street before I felt like turning around to go back to my warm apartment. When I arrived at the *University Park*, a postman told me that the dental school had moved to the *Panum Institute*. This led to an extra tramp through the park and added additional fuel to my irritation. I thought about how ridiculous it was to be tramping around so early in the morning in such weather, perhaps to find out that it had no purpose. "What an idea to come up with," I thought, but continued nonetheless.

All the while, I went through the *University Park* with the various buildings, I passed a building where I, to my surprise, saw a sign saying in large blue letters, "About the house". In Danish it is spelled "Om huset". I turned around, looked once again and was amused. OM, the sound of the Universe. However, I am almost sure that at the educational establishment the letters "OM" is reserved for something quite different. But for me it means "OM", the sound of the Universe. I continued into the cold wind lost in thoughts.

Finally, I reached the dental school, showing my health insurance card at the "information and register" counter. I was given a journal with my name, date of birth and so on, and was asked to go to section 3 and hand over the register, and everything would be taken care of. I found section 3, delivered the journal and was told to take a seat and wait.

While I was sitting waiting, I noticed that it actually looked exactly like a hospital. Everyone wore white coats. They were not, however, doctors and nurses, but dentists and dental students. I waited a while and picked up a magazine from a small table beside me. The first thing that caught my eye was the title of a lecture by a physician about an Indian master's philosophy. This master, however, was not Baba, but the master Maharishi Mahesh Yogi, who brought TM (Transcendental Meditation) to the West. The lecture was called *Renewal Begins from Within*. Wise words. I inevitably came to think of Baba who, of course, is my master.

Finally, it was my turn. A dentist's surgery assistant showed me in.

"Please sit down on the chair," the dentist said and continued with the following sweet words, "Marguerite is a beautiful name. The ox-eye daisy, which is called marguerite in Danish, is a beautiful flower, and I can see that so are you. What brings you here?"

A nice reception. I felt immediately welcome and said, "Yes, it might sound strange. All my life I have had good teeth and have only had treatment on three. The last one I've just got fixed because it had lost some of the filling, and at the same time I got a tooth cleaning."

183

The dentist listened attentively, and I continued, "Something was not right. I continued to have pain and could hardly chew with that side of the mouth. At the same time, It got worse in the other two teeth, so I went to my dentist again and explained the situation, because I thought there must be something wrong."

I explained further about the piece which was broken off and that my dentist's confirmation of my healthy teeth and assurance that I could forget about paradentosis. "So I decided to come here to the dental school. You must of course be experts in the field," I said as the dentist still listened patiently to me.

"We will find out what is going on. Now I'll check it out," he said kindly. He examined my teeth and it took only a few moments to find out what was wrong, "You have an incipient paradentosis and I don't understand that your dentist has not informed you of this. It can be seen very clearly. You are lucky to show up just now so that we can deal with it in time. If you'd waited any longer, it would probably have been too late. You'll get treatment right away."

"It cannot be the case that I have paradentosis. There has never been anything wrong with my teeth and my dentist assured me that there was no paradentosis," I said somewhat surprised about his message.

To this, he replied, "Now you're here and it is good. Now I send you to the x-ray department and the treatment starts. I would ask you to take a seat outside and my assistant will give you further information."

A little shaken by everything I had heard, I was sitting collecting my thoughts and feelings. At the same time, I was happy that I finally had pulled myself together and had visited the dental school. I had most definitely come to the right place and on time.

I looked around and everything was still looking like I was sitting in a hallway of a hospital. Regularly dentists were passing me in their white coats and a little further down the hall some dental students were discussing something. They also wore, obviously, white coats. At the same time I looked at all the beautiful colours, as each section had its own colour. Section 1 was blue and the section in which I was treated was orange of course.

I came to think about the dream when I was waiting in a hospital. I waited to be called into the senior physician. Finally, I was called in. He was sitting in his white coat; as a doctor, although I knew it was Baba. The dream is described at the end of the previous chapter, *Dream on 16 March, 1996.*

As I was sitting at the dental school, currently immersed in my own thoughts, I thought, "Yes, You were probably not only senior physician, You were probably also a dentist. You are everything."

I was deeply moved and touched by the concern that Baba showed me. Baba knew that I had paradentosis. Yes of course, because Baba knows everything. Even I knew nothing about it, and my dentist was evidently not going to make me aware of it, but Baba did and sent me to the dental school, where I would be treated properly and free of charge. Later, I heard about a few cases of paradentosis and realised that it required very expensive treatment.

A little later the clinic assistant came to me and said, "The treatment will start next week." I thanked her and left. At the time of writing, the treatment is in fine progress, but it is very time consuming. I visit there once a week and will continue to for many weeks.

Thank you yet again, Baba.

Today, 29 May, was the last day at the dental school. It has been hard to sit in the dental chair for two whole hours every week. But anyway, when I think of what could have happened if Baba had not sent me there it was worth it. I am always deeply grateful for that. Thankfully, it is now over and my teeth and gums are good. I will be called back for a check-up sometime in September. Yes, I am in good hands, thanks to Baba.

When I was completely done with the treatment and was heading for the exit, happy that it was over, I walked behind a small boy and his mother. The boy wore a wind jacket in many colours and on the back of the wind jacket it said in large blue letters, "Indian Paradise".

Fantastic!

Visions, dreams and miracles

Vision on 14 May, 1996

I hovered around the most beautiful white light. It was like a thousand suns that shone at once. I was feeling wonderful, peaceful with myself while the light expanded slowly, eventually becoming a sea of light.

In the midst of this fantastic light, Baba came walking slowly towards me. He wore a white gown and white figures hovered around Him. They came from everywhere, so he eventually was completely surrounded by them. Maybe they were spiritual beings, maybe they were angels. I do not know, because I was not close enough to see them clearly, but I was allowed in for a short while to get a glimpse of the spiritual world. After that, everything slowly faded away. It was a wonderful experience.

Divinely beautiful.

Dream in August, 1996

Baba knows that I love classical music, which I usually listen to when I am at home. One night he came to me in a wonderful dream.

I was sitting in the front row of a large, very beautiful concert hall, about to enjoy a symphony concert. A large symphony orchestra was about to be ready, waiting for a very important person, namely the first violinist. It was apparently a violin concert we were about to hear, and in a violin concert whoever is playing first violin, of course, is the most important.

We all waited. Then he came in, and everyone applauded. I was so surprised and did not believe my own eyes. For the first violinist was indeed Baba. He was wonderful to look at, as he came in with the violin in his hand and received the applause. When it died down, we all waited for the concert to start, but it did not. Instead, Baba came down to me and welcomed me warmly. He seemed very happy, and I felt it was because of me. Long he held my hand and I was almost intoxicated with happiness.

Everyone was waiting for the concert to begin, both the large symphony orchestra and the audience. They waited and waited, but Baba was standing, holding my hand. He eventually let go of my hand, looked lovingly at me and left. But it was not to play the first violin. He left the concert hall and I did the same. Then I woke up.

I wonder when I'll hear the concert, Baba.

Dream in November, 1996

I was employed as a typist in a corporation, sitting at my desk with my typewriter. My boss came in; it was Baba. He came and gave me a sheet of paper, and said, "This is very important; would you be kind enough to write it?" He said this in a loving tone, but at the same time was very specific.

"Yes, I will," I replied. It really was a nice boss I had.

A little later I went down a long corridor. Baba came after me, stopped me and said, "May I ask you something?"

"Yes, you may," I said. "What is it that you have around your neck?" He asked.

"Oh! It is a medallion with Krishna, India's great God," I said.

"Oh, I always knew it was something special," he said. "May I ask you one more thing?" he asked.

"Yes, you may," I replied again.

"Are you always so happy?" he asked.

"Yes, I am," I replied.

Then I woke up.

I am, after all, a typist and employee of Baba, so he is my boss, and at this very moment, I sit in front of my typewriter typing.

But first and foremost, Baba is my master.

Prasanthi Nilayam, Christmas 1997

I am by Baba again, and will stay for Christmas and New Year, as so many times before. It is always wonderful to see Him again. There are a great many people here. One of the first days I was here, I had a very interesting dream which made a certain impression on me.

Dream on 14 December, 1997

I participated in a party with quite a few people. Suddenly, a little girl of about two years old came and spoke to me, as if she was an adult, "I do not really belong here. I am adopted but my parents do not understand, so you should not say anything to them."

A little later she lay in her bed, speaking Indian to herself. I called her parents who were Westerners and said to them, "Can't you understand that your daughter really is Indian and belongs to the culture. Can't you hear it is Indian she speaks?"

"Yes, but we do not understand," they said.

I took the little girl in my arms and danced *The Farewell Waltz* with her, played by a large orchestra. We danced and danced, and eventually she said to me, "Your old mother is still alive."

When I woke up, I was very absorbed with the dream.

In the last year or so I had had a little trouble with my stomach and thought that I had probably better get a check with my doctor. At the same time, I would have measured my blood pressure; maybe it was a little too high. Finally, I pulled myself together, and got an appointment for 7 February. It's best to know with certainty that one's health is okay. The day before, I had ordered a sight test at the optician because I had the feeling that I probably should have renewed my reading glasses. Here as well, I had been slow to make an appointment, but apparently that now was the right time. The night before Baba came to me in a dream.

Dream on 6 February, 1997

I was resting in a bed. There was a nice atmosphere, and everything was peaceful and calm. I was completely relaxed but I did not sleep.

A woman came and placed something on a table beside me. When she was quite close to me, I saw that she had a medallion around her neck that Baba had materialised. I recognised it because years earlier Baba had materialised a similar one for my son, one that he still has. At the same time, I saw some books written about Baba. His picture was on the cover of them all.

Suddenly, Baba himself came walking slowly towards me and now stood beside me. He looked kindly and lovingly at me and began to examine me while he said something to me. I did not understand, however, what Baba said; I presume He spoke in Telugu, His mother tongue. Then a woman came to translate, "He says that you shall marry him."

"Oh yes, I understand, because I have been travelling so much in India," I said.

Baba was now quite close to me and looked me deep in the eyes. He looked lovingly at me for a long time. His eyes twinkled like stars and slowly He faded away.

There was a wonderful atmosphere at Baba's presence, and I felt very comfortable and warm hearted. And I will continue to be.

The trip to Mahabalipuram in 1998

This time, during my stay with Baba, I intended to end this trip in Madras, in a hotel by the beach to get a little sun and sea air in the marine atmosphere and think about the stay with Baba and let the whole thing sink in. I had brought my swimsuit with me.

Every time I have been with Baba over the last 20 years, it has always been so incredibly intense for me. To be in his physical presence and at the same time have such a great relationship with him at the internal level, means that I almost can't take more than a month at a time; I am filled up, and it is like one long cleansing that I cannot describe. At the same time, I am indeed physically worn down by the pace of the ashram.

As I now had intended to go to Madras, I would visit the small temple in Guindy, managed by Miss Leela Mudalia, formerly a lecturer in botany, but today dedicating all her time to the leadership of the temple. The history of her and her family's relationship with Baba goes back to 1943 where Miss Leela was only 14 years old and at that time, the small temple did not exist.

Howard Murphet has written about the incredible events and miracles that this family was allowed to experience in his book, *Sai Baba, His Message, His Miracles* on page 169. It was, therefore, this temple I would visit and hope to have a little talk with Miss Leela.

As I was walking in Prasanthi Nilayam thinking of travelling to Madras, it was probably more the opportunity to relax at the beach I had most in mind. I felt that I needed that very much. However, one thing is what I want, something completely different is what Baba said. It is not always a match. I realised that many times.

Many times I had wished to visit the temple in Madras, but it had never been fulfilled so now I was a little unsure about whether I had found out where it was situated. I, of course, did not have the address and I had no desire to rush around to find out where it was located.

Suddenly Baba gave me an intense thought that were running around in my head: I should visit the temple in Madras. In the afternoon after darshan when Baba gave the interviews, I was sitting, relaxing with quite a few others in front of Baba's temple. A lady, who was sitting next to me, showed me a book and asked, "Have you read this book?" It was a book Miss Leela had written.

"No, I have not," I said and looked into it.

"You really should read it; it's fantastic," she said. After reading a little, I thanked her and gave her back the book. I went out and purchased it after the Bhajan and was in no doubt that I would visit the temple this time.

The next morning I was sitting in the canteen thinking a little more about it. For one reason or another, Baba would have me visit the temple in Madras. "But too bad," I thought, "I do not know its location and Madras is a big city."

Suddenly, one of Baba's old disciples came asking, "Can I sit here?" First, she had been sitting at another table, so it was quite strange and she was not one I had been talking to. We welcomed one another and then she sat down right in front of me; It was quite okay.

"Yes of course you can," I replied. Then I said to her, "Do you know the address of the temple of Guindy in Madras? I intend to visit it."

"Oh yes I do. Miss Leela is an old friend of mine," and she gave me the address.

"It was wonderful, thank you," I say. Eventually, we stood up and left the table.

If I was tired or not, I had to visit the temple in Madras. It was Baba's opinion, so relaxing at the beach had to wait a little longer. However, it turned out to be totally different.

I was now on the way to Mahabalipuram, with Miss Leela's book in my suitcase, which I wanted to read while I lay on the beach enjoying the sun. At the same time, I was planning to make a stop in Madras and visit the temple. To get to Mahabalipuram, you go through Madras because Mahabalipuram is a little further south. I had heard there was a fine beach for swimming, without too many tourists.

I dedicated one day in Madras to visit the temple and moved into a fine hotel. After finishing lunch I drove out to the temple. Miss Leela was in Puttaparthi, I was informed by her nephew, "But she will return tomorrow at 10am. I will give you her phone number and suggest that you call in advance just to be sure."

"Thank you, I will do so," I said.

"Do you want to see the temple?" he asked.

"Yes, thank you, I would very much like to do so," I said. He showed me into the small temple, and it was really something special. So incredibly peaceful and with a wonderful atmosphere. Everywhere I looked there were pictures of Baba, right from His younger days. I walked around looking at them for a long time.

I was thinking, "They must have been very happy to be so close to Him in His younger years." Baba only called for me in 1979, and has led me since, quite directly, and today I could not live without that. And so it has to be for me.

When I was walking around in my own thoughts in this quiet, fine atmosphere, an Indian man who apparently was the supervisor of the temple, came up to me, asking if I would like to have two packages of vibhuti. "Oh, thank you, I would very much like to," I said.

"You really must come tomorrow, Thursday, where the temple is open and there will be Bhajan singing. It happens every Thursday and Sunday; come again tomorrow," he said kindly.

Thank you very much, I will do so," I said and went back to my hotel.

Finally, the journey continued to Mahabalipuram, which was my main objective, but before I left the hotel, I called Miss Leela. She had come back from Puttaparthi and answered the phone. Immediately, she said, "Please, come."

"I will be at the temple in about half an hour," I said. I checked out from the hotel, got a taxi and drove to the temple.

This time it was a somewhat different experience to visit the temple. It was open and filled with people singing Bhajan. There were so many people sitting close outside, because it was absolutely packed inside the temple. It was an unbelievably beautiful view. I was involuntary moved by the intensity of the song in the Baba's honour, although he was not physically present. The Bhajan sounded different than the Bhajan in Puttaparthi. It was only Indians who were here; many undoubtedly old disciples of Baba.

I was introduced to Miss Leela, who lived in a house right next to the temple. She gave me a warm welcome and showed me many of the pictures on the walls depicting Baba when He was quite young. She showed me a large picture of her father who, many years ago, had built the temple in honour of Baba and it had something to do with Baba's previous incarnation. Here I must refer to the book of Howard Murphet.

It was a lovely meeting. She radiated serenity and an inner peace and yet she was so plain and straightforward. I sensed that here was a woman who was totally in balance with herself. And I felt that Baba's spirit was everywhere. She asked if I wanted to eat a little with her, but I said, "No thank you. I'm on my way to Mahabalipuram, but I felt that I had to see the temple first, indirectly shown the way by Baba, for some reason, or another. I purchased your book, which I will read when I get to Mahabalipuram."

She smiled kindly and said, "When you come back from Mahabalipuram you must participate in Bhajan before travelling home."

"I would very much like to do so," I said, and said farewell. I would indeed travel to Denmark directly from Madras this time. Finally, I was on my way to Mahabalipuram, where I would relax for a couple of weeks while reading her book before heading for Denmark. What I came to experience there was just not what I had intended. It was quite different, but it was what Baba had in mind for me. It came as a complete surprise to me.

I arrived at the hotel in Mahabalipuram but was somewhat surprised when I saw it had two floors and a total of 16 rooms, like a kind of terraced house. It was very nice, and the rooms were lovely. It was right next to the sea with a small pine forest in front. But we could not swim there; it was too dangerous because there was a very strong undercurrent and there were signs on the beach saying "swimming not allowed".

At the same time, it turned out that there was no restaurant, only eight small metal tables, which stood in the small pine forest. It was just not what I had expected. It was very desolate with only a few people living there. I could walk along the seafront for a long time without meeting a single soul.

I got a good room on the first floor and stood for a while on my balcony looking out at the roaring Indian Ocean. There was a silence that seemed almost oppressive to me. I only heard the murmur of the waves and felt, at that moment, completely isolated from the outside world. "What am I actually doing here?" I thought. "Okay, I will stay here for a few days, now that I have finally got all the way out here; after that I'll move into a large hotel, with a nice beach, a good restaurant and so on. I simply cannot stay here."

In the evening, my dinner was brought to my room and I enjoyed it on my balcony. The meal was excellent; there was certainly a good cook at the hotel which was a ray of comfort. In the night, Baba came to me in a somewhat unusual dream.

Dream on 15. January, 1998

I was somewhere in my home. Then suddenly a UFO was in front of me and I couldn't believe my eyes. However, it was true; there was a UFO there in the middle of my home. I opened a hatch and climbed on board. Then, with me inside, it took off, smashing through the ceiling and further out in the universe. Higher and higher it climbed. I was all alone in the UFO and was controlling the craft all by myself. It was a fantastic experience to glide between the planets and stars. The atmosphere could not to be described, but at the same time I felt very happy.

When I had been gliding around there for a while, I saw something strange coming towards me. It came closer and closer and was now quite close to my windscreen. To my great surprise and astonishment, I saw - good God - right into Baba's smiling face. He smiled warmly and lovingly to me. It was a wonderful feeling and I felt warm hearted. He gave me the feeling that there was a sense in hovering around in the universe in my own UFO. He was with me for a while and then he faded slowly away.

I hovered silently down towards to Earth again. As I climbed out of the UFO, a lot of people were running towards me shouting, "They have landed, they have landed!"

"Who have landed?" I asked. "The UFOs, the UFOs," they said. Then I woke up... unfortunately.

What the meaning was here, I am not fully aware of.

An unusual encounter

As I said, I woke up and instantly wrote down the dream. The waiter came up with Indian breakfast, which was quite excellent, and I enjoyed it on my balcony with the magnificent view, only in the company of crows and a small squirrel.

Then I went for a walk by the sea, thinking about the dream with the UFO. The dream had lifted me so high that I decided to stay at the hotel a little longer. I had, of course, Miss Leela's book, which I had intended to read. At the same time, the food was excellent, which was a big plus, especially here in India.

So for now it was no sunbathing for me, even though it was very hot. It was more the spiritual side I, came to deal with. It could simply not be second. I started reading Miss Leela's book, which was absolutely wonderful, with all the really incredible miracles that she and her family have experienced with Baba, dating back to around 1940. At the same time, I wrote down some dreams in which that Baba had come to me in Puttaparthi. Everything was in itself a nice sadhana.

I became very balanced with myself. Each morning and afternoon, I went for a walk along the seafront and was quite comfortable with my solitude. I was completely fulfilled by Baba's love. Morning, noon and night, the waiter served the most enchanting dishes I have ever tasted in India. There really was a good cook at the hotel. At the same time, I read and wrote about Baba, what more could I hope for? This went on for several days.

Then something mysterious happened. I went for my usual walk by the sea, wrapped up in my own thoughts. An Indian man was slowly walking towards me. He had a basket over his arm and stopped right in front of me. Naturally, I did the same thing, since it had been extremely rare to meet anyone. He smiled warmly at me and seemed very friendly, absolutely not intrusive, like someone who would possibly be selling something. I looked a little surprised at him. Suddenly, he told me in a gentle tone, "I am Maha Sai."

"What did you say?" I replied.

He repeated, "I am Maha Sai."

"I do not understand what you mean. What is the meaning of Maha Sai?" I ask.

He pointed to me and then himself, and said again, "I am Maha Sai." It was all said in a loving tone.

I became slightly amused and said, "I still do not understand what you mean."

"Many people come to Maha Sai," he said.

"Yes, but I still don't understand," I said, for one last time, and was ready to go. He looked at me for a little while; we smiled at each other and went on.

I walked at the water's edge, while the waves were foaming at my feet, and I thought, "What could he really mean?" After I had been walking for a while, a light bulb popped above my head. I stopped immediately and looked back. He was just a small dot in the distance. "Maha Sai," I thought. "Yes, but surely it couldn't be true. It was really You, Baba, in the form of this gentle Indian who came to me here at my lonely walk along the sea!" I was absolutely elated, but did not really know what to think."

"You big idiot!" I thought to myself. "He was of course presenting himself; Mara Sai." As usual, I did not understand anything before it was too late. It was almost impossible for me to bear.

When I was back at the hotel, I took a shower and laid down to read Miss Leela's book. And indeed, I could hardly believe it. The very first thing I read was Baba, who said, "We now go to Mahabalipuram..." It appears on page 133 of the book. When I read it, I was really elated. I could only think as often as before, "Oh, Baba, Baba." Later, Baba confirmed in a completely wonderful dream, that

it was Him.

I will talk about the dream later.

I stayed in Mahabalipuram for a week and, of course, wrote down the experience of this quite special meeting. I continued my walks by the sea, but I did not meet him again. A few days later, I was travelling to Madras. At that time, I mostly felt like I wanted to go home. It was a Wednesday; I travelled from Mahabalipuram and arrived in Madras at noon. At the end of the week I would go back to Denmark, so the next day I went to Air India to see if I could get a seat on the plane. And indeed, it succeeded. I got a seat from Madras via Frankfurt to Denmark; everything was stamped okay and I was happy.

It was on Thursday that I should leave, and suddenly I remembered what Miss Leela had said to me that I must go to a Bhajan in the temple before I went home. I had to leave in the afternoon the next day. I felt that everything had been prepared. The next morning I went to the temple to attend Bhajan but there was not a single place for me in the temple, and many people were sitting outside. The Bhajan had already started. Miss Leela was not there at this time.

I was somewhat angry because I could not get inside the temple to attend a Bhajan there. Suddenly an Indian woman came to me. We talked a little, I said that I had to travel in the afternoon and would very much like to get inside the temple, since it was the first time I had been to a Bhajan there. She immediately took me into the temple and asked those who were sitting there to move slightly together so I got a seat. It was a very beautiful experience and at the same time a beautiful farewell to India.

It did not turn out to be a stay at a beach hotel with swimming and so on, although it was what I actually had planned. Instead, Baba sent me on a pilgrimage. It was what Baba intended, and so it happened. I went home with a deep gratitude for Baba in my heart.

Some dreams in 1998

A dream in April

I was sitting, speaking confidentially with a good friend. She said to me, "Oh, I'm quite nervous; I must attend an important exam."

"Well, what is it about?" I asked.

"It's about the ego," she said.

"Well, so it's about the ego. You should not be so nervous. I would be much more worried if it was mathematics, I had to attend." I said in a rather casual voice. Ah yes, how clever one is. We were both amused and then I woke up.

I just hope that I will pass on the day I have to attend an exam about the ego.

A dream in June

I was lingering in quite a wonderful place. I think it must have been in one of the higher realms. There was an absolutely fantastic light around me and, at the same time, there was a wonderfully serene atmosphere. Here Baba allowed me to witness something very special, namely that he hands out diplomas.

I believe there was a group of about twenty people, or souls is perhaps more apt to say, all dressed in long white coats, sitting together in tense expectation. I sat right next to them, but knew that I was not one of them. They were very beautiful and all radiated an inner peace. I waited just as tensely as they did.

Finally, things started to happen. Baba came slowly with the diplomas in one hand. Everyone who was sitting there, has passed a very important exam, everyone that I know.

Baba called their names, one after another. And they all received their diploma; happy and humble. Baba was nearly finished and was now getting to where I am sitting, watching. He said loud and clear, while He looked lovingly at me, "Yes, these are the last two." At that, he gave the last two students their diplomas, which they received with great gratitude for Baba. Then He looked intensely and very lovingly my way after which he left us. At that moment I knew that the next time it would be me who attended the exam. I woke up.

I wonder when it will be?

Dream in September, 1998

A letter from Mahabalipuram

A close friend of mine came to hand me a letter. "There is a letter to you," he said.

"Well, from whom?" I asked, as I took it. To my great surprise, I saw that the letter was from Mahabalipuram.

I thought, "It is strange; I don't know anyone in Mahabalipuram," and then I opened it, and suddenly I remembered sitting by the sea in Mahabalipuram. That extraordinary meeting, which is described in the previous chapter, *"An unusual encounter."*

When I unfolded the letter, my hands grew large and became a wonderful Christmas decoration. I was absolutely amazed when I looked at this very special letter. I think it probably measured about 50 x 60cm. The paper was a pale blue silk. All over it was interspersed with small gold stars and angels in gold that hovered around the pale blue silk. In between, there were spruce cones that hung on a small branch.

In the midst of all this quite enchanting Christmas adventure, there was small fine handwriting in gold letters, a letter written to me. I did, however, only see the title and the signature. The headline read, "Dear Marguerite," and the signature, the reader may well guess, "Baba." Then I recognized Baba's handwriting.

I knew it was a Christmas invitation and confirmation that it had been Baba, who came to me in Mahabalipuram on my trip along the seafront.

"Baba, Baba, what can I say? I lack words."
All I can say is:
"Thank you for a lovely Christmas invitation."

Christmas in 1998 in Prasanthi Nilayam

It was November and I was busy with travel preparations. I would travel to Baba for Christmas and looked forward to being in His physical presence. Shortly before I left, He came to me in a really funny dream.

Dream in December

I was standing with quite a few people waiting, apparently, for something very important. Then finally something happened.

Baba came in with a list in his hand, on which there were some names. He stopped right in front of me and read out the first name. It was the woman standing next to me. Baba gave her a large jar. I had no idea what it contained and what it should mean, but I found out later what it was. Then Baba said yet another name and, more than surprised, I heard Him say, loud and clear, "Marguerite Jalving." I was just going to reply but before I managed to say anything, He turned and walked on.

At that moment, I was angry with Baba, as I had been so many times before, but at that moment He returned and stood in front of me. To my great surprise, I saw that he had transformed into a very independent and self-confident young woman in a fashionable dress and with high heels. I knew instantly that he (she) represented a cosmetics company. And now Baba, who was the female representative, stood right in front of me saying, "I have here a small bag with cleaning powder for you from the company. There is just a little left that still needs to be cleaned, that is why you only get this little bag. The company and I are very happy. You're improving." Then she turned and walked away.

I looked puzzled at the beautiful, small bag. It was of very thin, fine transparent silk in gold filled with a fine red powder, and closed with a small gold pin.

I was of course overjoyed to get the message. I opened the bag and took a little of the powder into my hand. It looked like red kumkuma. At that moment, I woke up.

Baba's imagination is fantastic and without limits.

I arrived in Bangalore in wonderful sunshine. India, India, here my heart and soul belong. Here I feel at home.

It was the beginning of December and at this time of year, Baba usually spends his time in Puttaparthi and that was what I expected him to do this time too. I always stay a night in Bangalore. It is simply necessary for me after the long journey from Denmark to India. The following day I would always travel to Baba, and I expected to do that this time as well.

I was given a room at the hotel in Bangalore, where I always stay and had been taking a refreshing bath after a whole day on Air India. At last, I could look forward to getting some sleep. Just when I laid down on the bed there was a knock on my door. It was my driver who was going to take me to Puttaparthi the next day and he said, "I have just heard that Baba will go to Whitefield tomorrow. He should stay there for three to four days because of building work so we must not go to Puttaparthi yet. I will come back later with more details."

"Well, it was just at the last minute I got to know that," I thought. "How lucky I am." I knew that if I was just arriving at Puttaparthi, only to be told that Baba had just arrived at Whitefield, I would have been terribly disappointed, although I know that it is all part of His plan. No one knows exactly where Baba is at any given moment except Baba himself, but it turned out this time, that the rumour was true and the next day Baba went to Whitefield. I arrived in Whitefield at 11am and participated in receiving Baba, who arrived at 12:30.

There were only a very few of us as Baba's car came through the gate to Brindavan. I felt it was a very beautiful and personal reception that Baba gave me. As the car passed us, Baba looked out of the window and smiled warmly at me. I felt that it was a good beginning for my stay, and thanked Baba in my mind, that I had not gone to Puttaparthi but had received the message in time. And it was also an unusual stay, where he gave me a little of this and that. He came to me in a couple of dreams, where he simply let me understand what he wanted from me, and that he expected I would be up to it. I will come back to that later.

Baba stayed in Whitefield for nearly a week and there were some lovely, peaceful days with Him, with only a few people around, since the vast majority of course were in Puttaparthi. But the days went quickly and suddenly it was time to go to Puttaparthi. The Christmas holidays were ahead and there were now quite a lot of people coming to Puttaparthi from all over the world, and I had become a little tired of the pace of the ashram. Up at 4:30 each morning; it is after all not the pace I have at home and one must take my age into account too; we are not getting any younger. So I decided to miss a few morning darshans, until I was fresh. I did so for two days in a row and felt wonderfully rested. Then Baba came to me in a dream.

Yet another dream from December

Baba walked slowly towards me. He looked very lovingly at me, and said in a gentle voice, "I am sorry you did not come," to which I replied, "But Baba, I was too tired to get up that early. Yesterday I sat for three hours in front of Your temple. So I felt tired, that was why I did not come."

Baba said as he gently embraced me, "I know that, I know that."

Finally, I laid my head on Baba's shoulder and said, "Oh, Baba, Baba." Then I woke up with his name on my lips.

From that day, I attended all His darshans, even if I had to get up at 4:30 in the morning. In the afternoon after darshan, I was also seated in front of His temple, in order to be as close to Him as possible. I did not leave before Arathi was ended.

I knew that was what He wanted of me. Discipline and perseverance. He gave me the strength to do it and, after all, that is why I come; namely to be in His physical presence. He also lets me get physically close to Him. When I went to the first darshan after the dream I got a seat in the first row. Baba walked straight to where I was sitting and took a few letters, while at the same time, he smiled, teasingly me. I felt warm in my heart.

It was, as always, a beautiful experience to be with Baba at Christmas, especially on Christmas morning, when He blesses us all from the balcony. It is so indescribably beautiful and hard to put into words. Also New Year's morning is something special with Baba. We feel His spirit and blessings all around.

Christmas and New Year were over and then it was the year 1999. We approached 9 January, which appears to be a day of special importance for me. In a dream Baba allowed me to understand that, in the chapter *Back to my Writing*, with the title *Dream on 16 March, 1996*. I was curious about whether something special would happen or if it just had a deeper symbolic meaning. I would have to wait to see what would turn out.

It is said that nine is a sacred number, so 9 January 1999, must of course be a special sacred day. Baba pointed that out to me, in a unique way. On 18 January I attended the afternoon darshan, and once again, I got a seat in the first row in front of the temple, sitting with thousands of people, waiting for Baba like so many times before.

Finally, He came but He only gave a very short darshan, and suddenly it was over. He had not called anyone for an interview, which he always did. He went directly to his interview room and a little later He came out again. He ordered His car be brought forth. The red carpet was quickly rolled out so that Baba could drive out of the driveway.

The car drove slowly into the square and stopped in front of the temple, with the licence plate pointed directly toward us women. At the time, I was well aware that this meant something symbolic to me. Many times Baba had in various ways made me aware of His licence plate, the last four digits being 9999. I looked at them now, and they were very close.

9 January 1999 is the four nines and the next day was 9 January 1999. Baba asked a few of his closest disciples to get in the car and they came down and got in. Finally, Baba went slowly towards the car. Just before he got in, he sent me a glance so direct and intense that I was almost moved to tears.

I was taken completely by surprise and thought of the dream in which He came to me a few years back. In the dream, he finished by saying, "Yes, it will be 9 January," although not the year.

It must have been a very small drive, because after about ten minutes, he was back. He got out of the car and turned to us women who sat closest to where he was standing, sending us a brilliant smile that went straight to the heart. Then he went slowly into the interview room. The following night he came to me in a very beautiful dream.

Dream on 9 January, 1999

Baba came slowly walking towards me, stopped, and looked very intensely at me. I was aware that He would say something of importance to me.

Then He said, "We need to talk a lot more about your future. You travel home on the 10th but first we must make another trip." Baba took me by the hand and led me into a very dark tunnel; we could see absolutely nothing. We walked slowly forward. I thought by myself, "Oh, it is good Baba, that I have you to stick to; otherwise I would have been scared." I stayed very close to Baba.

We walked in the darkness for a long time. But slowly, we began to see a light at the end of the tunnel. We got closer and closer to the light and it became brighter and brighter. Now it was like a thousand suns, turning into an enormous sea of light. It was a fantastic sight. I was nearly blinded by the light. Then we reached the brilliant light. In that wonderful light that seemed to continue forever, I saw people who lived there; it was a fantastic experience. Baba said, "We will stop here, for those who live there, live on the other side." Then I woke up.

It was early in the morning, and I was laying in bed thinking about the dream. I understood then that Baba showed me, that He led me from the darkness to the light. 9 January 1999, which was that day, apparently, was the landmark that Baba had set. That day, I would go into a more enlightened phase of my life. What impact that would have, only time would tell. I only knew that Baba was showing me the way.

In the morning, at darshan, right after the dream, I got a good seat where I would be close to Him. The question was if he would look in the direction where I was sitting, or turn His back on us and look the other way. I was curious about what He would do.

Finally he came and turned directly towards me, sending me a warm smile. "Baba, Baba," I thought, "it was a wonderful message You gave me." I travelled home the next day, entirely fulfilled by Baba's love.

What might the future bring?

February, 1999

We had entered the year 1999. I had just returned from India, where I was with Baba for Christmas and New Year. It was a very intense stay; I will come back to that later. First, I would like to talk about what had happened in the meantime.

I had been with Baba in 1997, arriving on 3 June. During that stay, he did something very funny. I was sitting in the front row for darshan.

Beside me, I had a young Indian woman with a letter to Baba. He came toward us and stopped in front of me. Now the young woman handed her letter to Him, which he took, and then he materialised some vibhuti and gave it to her, but she was very unhappy. However, He gave me no vibhuti. While he did this, he was teasing me and come so close up to me, that I could touch his feet. He stood there for a long time, all the while receiving letters from the people behind me. Eventually, He smiled warmly at me, and walked on. It was a nice darshan. I went home on 11 July, and arrived to find an unusual surprise.

I have a small hand-painted, light blue bowl, in which there once contained vibhuti, which Baba had given me during an interview, but it had been empty for a long time. Then one day, 25 July, I wrote this event down on a small slip of paper: I was dusting and I knocked the small bowl so the lid fell off. I was surprised because on, the bottom of it, and just in the middle was a small amount of vibhuti, exactly as much as Baba materialised to please someone, now and again, when He gives darshan. It was sitting on the light blue bottom, as if it had been dropped straight down from Heaven, which in a manner it really had been. At that point I understood why Baba had smiled so teasingly at me. The young woman got vibhuti at darshan, I got it at home in my bowl.

Unbelievable. Thank you for the vibhuti, Baba.

An Indian wedding

It was May, and I once again with Baba. He was in Whitefield and said that he would be there for about two months due to a construction project in Puttaparthi.

During the days I was there, Baba celebrated Buddha's birthday. Many Buddhists came from around the world; around 4,000 people came from Japan alone. I couldn't believe was room for so many people in Whitefield but, of course, there was room for everyone.

It was a beautiful experience. The entire Whitefield was lit up, there were floral decorations everywhere and between all that, there were statues of Buddha. Baba gave a wonderful speech about Buddha and because I was so lucky to have a very good place in the front, I could see Baba clearly at His pulpit. It was very nice to attend. The celebrations lasted for three days.

I was with Baba for only two weeks this time, because I was aware that he would not be travelling to Puttaparthi during the time I was there. Only in Puttaparthi in Prasanthi Nilayam, I feel at home; it always has been like that. However, another reason was the huge number of people. So I left Whitefield and went to Bangalore, where I got a hotel room. The next day I would go to Air India. I had an unusually pleasant experience, the last night I was in Bangalore, before I went to Delhi, to move on to Benares. There I experienced the Indian culture and hospitality, which they are so well known for. It is wonderful to experience that.

I had dinner at my hotel and went for a short walk to look at the vibrant Indian life that is everywhere in the streets. It is a very picturesque neighbourhood, I live in. It is typically Indian with sacred cows walking in the streets and a small temple for the God Ganesh with incense clouds around it so that you can smell it from a long distance away.

As I walked in the midst of this Indian atmosphere, I heard some beautiful music; it sounded as if it was a large orchestra that was playing. I approached where it came from and it turned out to be a large celebration room. I stood for a while looking at a wonderful large fountain, in all colours of the rainbow, which was arranged in front while people arrived, all dressed up.

There were women in beautiful saris, many with their babies in their arms. The children were beautifully dressed in frills and lace, with flowers in their hair, Hindu marks on the forehead, and, of course, with both arm and ankle bells, even the very small babies, which was so adorable. And just as often, it was the men who carried the baby. They all poured into the place in festive mood.

Now a friendly Indian man approached me and said, "Come in Madame."

"What are they celebrating?" I asked.

"It is an Indian wedding," he said.

"Well, I cannot participate in that," I said.

"Yes, you can; it will please the bridal couple. They are sitting there receiving good wishes from family and friends. However, it is for everyone else who wants to share in their joy and pay tribute to them on their wedding day. It is very festive with wonderful music, and Indian TV is also there, so please join in," he said.

His enthusiasm and kindness did, of course, mean that I went inside and participated in the festivities for the newly married couple.

I came into a large ballroom, crowded with happy people. A large orchestra played, a TV station was visiting and multiple photographers' cameras were flashing. It was all very festive. There were rows of chairs like in a theatre and I was guided to a seat in the first row.

Up on the stage the bridal couple was sitting in some wonderful armchairs. The bride's sari was of thick silk in a sea of colours and she wore a diadem in her hair. The groom's costume was a long cape also of thick silk, in beige, with trousers of the same colour. They looked beautiful. They did not passively sit on the stage being admired by the crowd. They were surrounded by family and friends who endlessly came up on the stage to congratulate them. Often they stood up and spoke to various people, sat down for a while and then others came up to congratulate them. Also, some ordinary Indian families went up to congratulate them. Everyone participated in their wedding.

I was deeply impressed by the whole thing. It was something I had never experienced before. Suddenly, a young Indian man came and gave me a red rose and then suddenly he was gone again. He was just pleased and it seemed obvious that I should have a red rose. There I was, sitting with the rose, while I listened to the wonderful music.

Once again, I was impressed by India's hospitality and culture, and I felt in tune with it.

At one time, a female member of the family of the bridal couple came down to me, asking if I would come up on at the stage to greet them. It turned out to be the bride's sister. I was reluctant at first. But when she said that it would please them, I went up, and congratulated them. Then the groom called up the closest family, and we were lined up for some photographers. I was placed by the bride's side with her sister next to me. There were about twenty family members. Then the photographers were clicking away and everyone was happy, including me. It was a sweet and warm experience.

The bride's sister brought me a small bag and thanked me for participating in her sister's wedding. "It has been a very nice experience," I said. I wished the bridal couple good luck and left the party. When I came up to my room, I placed the rose in a glass of water on my night stand and opened the small bag. In it there were two palm leaves, two small citrus fruits and a small bag with red powder. The powder is considered sacred in India and is called kumkuma. It is customary in India that you never to leave an Indian party without having enjoyed something.

All of this I had been invited to, even though I was a total stranger, and without asking for as much as a single rupee from me. On the contrary, it was they who showed a hospitality beyond all limits, that we do not usually encounter in the West, and they were happy that I should participate in it. It is so typically Indian and above all authentic. It was my last night in Bangalore. The next day I went on to Delhi.

In Benares in 1999

I had always wanted to see Benares at the Ganges river, but it had never turned out to be. Benares is considered to be India's holiest city and the River Ganges likewise. I felt that here was the opportunity to visit Benares. I had read some Indian books about gurus who had lived their lives by the Ganges and it had always fascinated me, so I felt that it had to be now. I stayed for a couple of days with Baba until I got His blessing to travel. The monsoon started. The last afternoon after darshan I walked home in the pouring rain. I was actually travelling from the monsoon in South India and onto Benares where it was the Indian Summer with temperatures of over 40 degrees Celsius. It was a bit of a change. One must be in good health to travel in India.

I arrived in Benares, also known as Varanasi, the old name for Benares which many Indians still use. As I said I arrived to more than 40 degrees Celsius. It was terrible and came as a complete surprise to me because I had experienced a little decrease in temperature when the monsoon started in Bangalore. There was only one thing to do: get a hotel room with air conditioning as soon as possible and that was what I immediately did.

When one comes to Benares, there is immediately a guide who makes himself available for an amount per hour. I got myself a guide as well. There are so many tourists visiting Benares, among other things, to see the Holy Ganges, as it is documented everywhere, and the cremation of bodies on its banks. Of course, I had to see it too.

I felt, now that I had finally come to Benares, that it was not entirely as I had expected. I had a little difficulty spotting the holiness. The whole thing seemed a little staged, no matter where we moved and everything was ultimately about money.

Since I, like everyone else, would like to sail on the Ganges at sunset, viewing the pyres, My illusions of the Holy Ganges were shattered. The River Ganges was so incredibly dirty, even though I had read a lot about how pure and Holy it was, but it was just not the impression I got. A bath in the Ganges; no thank you! The bodies that were burned did not receive any special treatment. I saw no relatives nor any kind of celebration, just a big pile of firewood and a man who quite routinely kept the fires going.

I was told that three fires were burning day and night: One for the rich, one for the poor and one for children. Ah yes, even when one has to leave this world, it is about money.

I said to my guide, "It seems to me that the whole thing is a big show for the tourists. It was centuries ago when Benares on the Ganges was holy. The only holy on this Earth today is Satya Sai Baba." It was obvious that he didn't know how to respond, and many Indians might not feel the same as I. I can only speak for myself.

I went back to Delhi, where it turned out to be even warmer, but I've experienced it before. It cannot be avoided after travelling for twenty years in India. Many years earlier, I had been in Delhi during the worst monsoon I had ever experienced. My son was with me and he believed he was about to die or perhaps rather drown in the downpour.

I was going to visit a public office about some important papers, that would allow me to get out of India. We had been in India for several months. Finally, I got a taxi that came straight up to the hotel. I was not aware of how bad the weather really was, but as we drove quite slowly from the hotel, I got a minor shock as I saw that the streets had become large rivers. The taxi driver had to park far away from the office, since it was impossible to continue due to water in the streets. "What on Earth do we do?" I thought and send a silent prayer to Baba. We had to get out of the taxi, but my son refused. He became almost hysterical when he was aware that there was nothing else to do. He had to take off his socks and shoes and roll his jeans up to the knees. He had never experienced such weather before, so he thought his last hour had come. I had to carry the bag and shoes in one hand and the umbrella in the other, and now it was out into the water, which reached almost to the knees. Very slowly, we moved forward through the water.

At the same time, it was a funny sight that met us. Everywhere we saw elegant business people with their striped trousers rolled up to the knees, shoes in one hand and the briefcase and an umbrella in the other hand. We were amused, for all the time we fought through the water.

At last, we reached the office, and felt almost saved. It took its time, as it does in all offices in India, I think it took about two hours, but for once it was okay. Our clothes dried out before we had to go out again in what looked like rivers flowing in the streets.

Indeed, to my great surprise, I saw the taxi driver come running toward us. He had waited for two hours, even though we had not made any agreement. I was happy to see him and at the same time deeply grateful for the kindness he had showed us. It was impossible to get a taxi and it was a long way to our hotel. So if he had not been there, I would not really know how else we would get back to the hotel. I have never forgotten him for this quite unusual to experience.

It reminds me of a similar experience a few years back. It was at Bombay airport, and it rained vigorously, however, not as badly as in Delhi. I had to find a specific bus to a hotel, where I would be staying. I asked a man on the road. "It stops right over there," he said.

I walked in the rain, but there was no bus. I asked another person, whether he knew where the bus stops. He sent me in the opposite direction and I walked back in the rain. Bombay airport is very large and I was completely soaked. I must have been walking around for half an hour, getting different messages and none of it helped me.

Finally, I said to myself, "Baba, Baba, what should I do?" And suddenly, in the middle of the rain, a car came towards me and stopped a little ahead of me. I saw something quite unbelievable. On the windscreen was a large sign, "Sai Service."

I looked and went closer to the car. Immediately, a friendly Indian man jumped out of the car and came to my rescue. We drove up and down different roads, I had never seen before. Finally, he stopped and said, "Here your bus will arrive in five minutes, Madame."

I thanked him and asked what I owed him. "You owe me nothing; it was a pleasure for me that I could help you," he said and drew away. I stood and marvelled, but of course, it was Sai Service. The same may perhaps be the case in Delhi?

Only Baba knows.

I travelled from Delhi to Benares, as described, and had now come back to Delhi. It was an organiser, a holiday planner as they are called in Delhi, who had planned my trip to Benares. We had many conversations in his office. Not so much because of my trip to Benares, it was something else he was interested in that had us talking so much. It was obviously Baba.

I was, once again, sitting in his office where we continued our talk.

"How did Baba really come into your life?" he asked.

I began telling him about my relationship with Baba over twenty years, how Baba comes to me in dreams and visions and guides me in everything, and that He was the only reason why I came to India. He was deeply impressed.

"Do you have a small picture of Sai Baba for my altar at home?" he asked.

I looked in my wallet and found a small picture of Baba. "Here I have a picture of Baba. You can have it for your altar," I said and handed him the picture.

He looked at it for a long time and I could tell that he was very happy about it. "By the way, I have another small picture here that you must have too," I said.

"Oh, I am so happy. This one is for my office!" he said, and put it under the glass on his desk.

"Next time Sai Baba comes to Delhi, I will go to His lecture. I will never ever forget that you have brought Sai Baba into my life. Every time you come to Delhi, you must come to me and let me help you with tickets and so on. What you have told me about your relationship with Sai Baba has fascinated me deeply," he said.

"I am glad to hear that," I said, as I left him.

I really should have returned to Denmark, but did not go right away. The next day I went back to his office and we continued our talk. He told me about his home town, which was located a few hours drive from Kashmir. "Oh yes, I have often thought of visiting Kashmir, and stay on a houseboat, but have never got there," I said.

"Why not do it now that you are in India? I will plan the entire trip for you; by train to Jammu, and from there you get a car with a driver who will drive you to Kashmir. It is a beautiful drive through the mountains. I will order the stay on a houseboat for you. The car and driver will be available throughout the ten days you stay there; the same goes for the trip back to Jammu, as well as the ticket for the train, which will get you to Delhi the day before the trip to Denmark. And I will give you a good price," he said.

"No, no, I do not intend to go to Kashmir this time," I said.

"Well, so maybe next time you come to India," he said. "Yes, I want to think about it," I said and left his office once again.

However, later that day, I thought a lot of Kashmir and got more and more keen to end my stay in India in Kashmir on a houseboat. "It must surely be peaceful and just what I need before I head back to Denmark," I thought. In the end, I was in no doubt that I was going to Kashmir.

The next day I was back at his office, saying, "I am going to Kashmir, and you may plan my trip."

"It is a good idea that you can look forward to. I will immediately begin to plan your journey in every detail, so you can travel within a few days. I'll call you when everything is ready," he said. He called in the evening, and had planned my whole trip to Kashmir and back to Delhi and all for an incredibly reasonable price. He even accompanied me to the train.

"Great trip, we will meet again," he said. I was on the road to Kashmir and marveled, because it was not something I had planned. But it turned out there was obviously a meaning to it.

On a houseboat in Kashmir

I was on my way to Jammu on the night train and would be there the following morning. I expected a driver and car would be at my disposal when I arrived, and that would take me to Kashmir. I was certainly hoping that he would be there, as agreed, otherwise I would have quite a problem.

To travel by train in India is a special experience. I had a seat with curtains so I could be completely by myself. When sleeping, an extra seat can be pulled down so it becomes a bed, complete with a bed lamp. At the same time, you get handed a rug, a pillow and two sheets. When I was ready to sleep, I pulled the curtains and turned off the lamp. I had a great sleep. When I got the morning coffee and a kind of Indian bun, the train was just entering Jammu station. I was curious to see what would happen; hopefully, what had been agreed on in Delhi.

I got off the train and looked around. There was confusion: no car, and no driver. The carrier who had my suitcase on his head showed me to an office with taxi rental. The man who ran the office looked at my order form that confirmed that everything was paid for and ordered. But no, they knew nothing about it and could not help, although there were eventually at least ten people involved. I was stuck. A wise man said, "Go to the station, where there is a small office with police, and show them your papers so that they can see that you have paid for a car and a driver from here to Kashmir."

"Thank you, I will do that," I said.

My carrier was gradually becoming grumpy. He trudged behind me with my baggage on his head in around the 30 degree heat, so that was understandable. We had to go back to the station area. Finally, we found a small office and, indeed, the police. But of course, there was not a soul. I sat waiting for a while, and really did not know what to think. Suddenly, out of thin air, appeared a smiling little Indian and put up a large in front of me with my name on. I was happy and so was the coolie. It was my driver. Soon I was on my way to Kashmir.

We drove up into the mountains, where the road curled up, higher and higher, so I got quite dizzy. At the same time, there was an absolutely wonderful view and we drove through many small mountain towns. We had probably been driving for an hour when we were stopped by the police. There was a war going on in the area. The old dispute between India and Pakistan over Kashmir had turned violent at the time, and there were police everywhere.

"Well," I thought, "what now?" But it proved to be a friendly policeman who cheerfully asked me, "Are you happy?"

More than surprised at the question, I replied, "Oh yes, I am." He explained that because of the war, two of his colleagues were heading for an important meeting. He asked if they could come along for a couple of hours, because there was no car at their disposal; they would be very happy. I had plenty of space in the car, because there were two seats behind in, so I said, "Yes, of course they can." They thanked me and got in.

It proved to be a father and his son. The son sat in the back of the car in the seat opposite me and the first thing he said was, "We are Christians."

He said this with such conviction, as though Christianity was the only religion in the world that had significance. "Yes, it is good for you," I said, without further comments.

We had been driving for a while when he asked, "Do you have family or friends in India?"

"No, I have not," I replied.

"Well, you are perhaps a tourist?" he asked again.

"No, I have been a follower of Sathya Sai Baba for 20 years; that is why I am in India. I am just using the opportunity of my latest visit in India to stay on a houseboat in Kashmir," I replied.

He was a little surprised to hear that I came from a country where the population is mainly "Christian", but that I preferred Sathya Sai Baba. His family, who lived in India, where most people are Hindus, were Christian. He was interested in hearing about my relationship with Baba and about how Baba had come into my life. "It is a long story," I said. But he continued to ask about my relationship with Baba, so I began to tell my story.

I told about how Baba had called me 20 years ago, how He comes to me in dreams and visions, and how He completely guides me on an internal level, sometimes to the smallest detail. I was referring to my first book, *With Sai Baba by my Side*. "I could never for a second live

216

without His guidance," I said. Moreover, I explained that all religions come to Baba and that He says that all religions lead to the same God.

Quite fascinated, he had been listening to everything I had said and was looking at a photograph showing me standing next to Baba. It was taken during an interview in Puttaparthi many years ago. Baba asked one of his disciples to take the picture. And of course, this is an image I am very, very pleased to have.

He said, "Everything you say about your relationship with Sai Baba is incredible. Now I understand how he means everything to you. I will visit him in Puttaparthi when I get the time, and the next time you come to India, we will all be happy if you come visit my family. I am glad you gave us this ride so I was allowed to hear about Sai Baba; I will never forget it." The time had now come for them to leave the car, and they warmly said goodbye.

We drove further on along the beautiful mountain road. My driver spoke Hindi with only a few phrases of English, so there was not much to talk about. I put on my headphones and listened to some beautiful classical music while enjoying the view. But the peace did not last for long. We hadn't been driving more than half an hour when we had to stop again. We passed a car that had broken down. It was a Muslim family that was heading for Kashmir. Two of the men approached us and asked if I had room for two of their women, who were sick. They were feeling unwell because of the dizzying heights and would be very grateful if they could come along.

"Yes, of course, I have plenty of room," I said. Then not two, but four, women got into the car, two of whom were very sick. One was so sick that we had to stop every ten minutes, for her to vomit. We drove for a few hours but didn't get very far. I had a very patient driver who took it all in good spirit, as did I. They were, after all, sick people, but we had many hours of driving ahead of us.

When we finally came to the border of Kashmir, we were once again stopped by the police. They asked me my business in Kashmir. I explained it briefly, and that was okay, but then they, in a sharp voice, asked me and the driver what the four Muslim women were doing in the car. Everyone was talking at the same time. The women began to cry and were not able to reply because there were speaking different languages. The policemen were Indians and spoke both Hindi and English. I do not know what dialect the women spoke. We could not talk because I only spoke English and my chauffeur spoke, as I said, only Hindi with a few phrases of English. In the end, I left the negotiations to the driver. He explained the situation to the police in Hindi. They were furious with the women because they were Pakistanis while they were Indians and there was a border war going on. We were at the Kashmir border, where Indians and Pakistanis argue about Kashmir, so it obviously had something to do with that. I sat there without intervening, while the women wept and the police and my chauffeur argued. Finally, the policemen slammed the door with a bang, sent raging glares at the women and nodded briefly to me. We drew across the border into Kashmir. Here the women almost fell to their knees and thanked me. In fact, I do not know what I was involved in, but at least we all came unharmed to Kashmir, and I breathed a sigh of relief.

We had been much delayed due to all the controversy, but finally, at about ten in the evening we reached the river with all the houseboats. It was completely dark, but a beautiful sight with the lights from the boats. We all got out of the car, because we had been driving for about 12 hours. I was sick and tired, but my driver had a great smile and helped everyone; he was simply outstanding. The women and the rest of the family, which had been driving behind us in another car, came and thanked me. Everyone was happy and now they seem quite refreshed, as everyone had arrived in Kashmir unharmed.

My driver explained to me that I had to sail in a rowing boat to get over to the houseboat that lay on the other side of the river. "Well, whatever next?" I thought. He got hold of a rowing boat, took my luggage, helped me down into it, and said, "I'll be here every day when you want to go out and look at the different sights we have in Kashmir."

"It is nice that I'll see you again," I said, and sailed off into the darkness.

I reached the houseboat, a beautiful sight, and the family received me on the completely illuminated terrace, which had flowers everywhere. I got something to eat, since I had not had anything all day apart from mineral water and some biscuits. It was a Muslim family who owned the boat. We sat and talked while I ate. Then they showed me my room, which was very beautiful; everything was handmade out of wood. Before long, I was in a large, beautiful bed with the most beautiful carved patterns; I think it was sandalwood. I fell fast asleep.

The next morning breakfast was served on the houseboat's terrace.

It was a rather special experience. All the time I sat and enjoyed my breakfast, one rowing boat after another came toward the houseboat where I was staying to offer their goods. One after another they came onto the terrace and showed me everything from genuine Kashmir carpets to precious stones. They showed incredible patience, although after a while they found out that I would not buy anything because I had no needs. I had a nice chat with them all, however.

I had a casual relationship with everyone on the houseboat and before long they began to ask whether I had family in India and so on. "No, I do not. I am in India because I have been a follower of Sathya Sai Baba for 20 years and I have the pleasure of relaxing on a houseboat in Kashmir for my last week in India," I said once again.

They found it interesting and, of course, they had all heard about Sai Baba, but were not followers. In Kashmir almost everyone is a Muslim. As far as I know, there are only a small number of Hindus. I did not know that in advance, but quickly found out because all the time I was in Kashmir, I lived among Muslims.

I frequently had to talk about my relationship with Baba but I, of course, did not mind. Everyone thought it was exciting to hear about.

On the houseboat, there were two women who made the meals, a young man who assisted in the kitchen, another who did the cleaning and a third who worked as a guide. Then, there was the owner of the houseboat and his family.

Every day, the guide was with me for sightseeing. We sailed in a small rowing boat to the mainland. Then my guide found my driver who stayed in a specific location. We drove around visiting various sites. It was a little of everything. One day, my guide asked me whether I had a desire to see how a genuine Kashmir rug was woven. "Yes, I would like to," I replied, and we decided to spend the day on it.

After a while, we stopped in front of a beautiful white marble building that almost looked like a temple. When we went in, an Indian gentleman presented himself. It was the director himself and he offered to show me around the factory.

We started in the weaving sector and I saw how the beautiful Kashmir carpets were made. He told me how long it took to weave a rug, depending on its size and pattern. It was impressive to see. "You have to visit our sales department, to see some of our finished carpets," he said.

I could, of course, not decline after the tour, and said, "Yes, I want to."

We went up to an impressive room of white marble, with a dark red carpet from wall to wall. The room was circular, and all the way around there was a white marble bench and the walls were obviously white marble shelfs with genuine Kashmir carpets, which hopefully would be sold. For a moment, I thought, "How do I get out of this, except with a rug under my arm?" He believed and hoped, of course, that I was a potential buyer. I absolutely was not, but at the time, I could not just leave.

We sat down on the bench and he sent an order for some genuine Kashmir tea, served in small, fine cups. Not one, but three salespeople came with an unrivalled precision, and rolled out one carpet after another in front of me. One was more magnificent than the other even though they were all beautiful, each in its own right, both in size and pattern. Finally, I believe there were twenty carpets in front of me and I could only admire them. While we drank tea, he politely asked whether I would have a genuine Kashmir carpet. In the end, I said, "I am sorry for all the trouble I have done, but I don't need a carpet, and your salespeople should not show me any more. I did not come to buy a carpet."

But he did not give up straight away, although he did send the salespeople out. He stopped praising the carpets and the atmosphere was a little more relaxed. He asked, "Is this your first trip to India and do you have family or friends here?"

"No, none of the sort," I replied.

"You may be a tourist, who likes to visit other countries with a foreign culture," he said.

"No, I will tell you why I am in India," I said.

"I am here because I am a follower of Sathya Sai Baba and have been for twenty years now. I go to Him twice a year; the only reason I am in India. I have been using this stay in India as an opportunity to stay on a houseboat in Kashmir for the last eight days, to relax a little before I return to Denmark."

He was really interested in hearing how I had come to know Baba and immediately said, "Forget about the carpets and tell me about your relationship with Sai Baba. I have, of course, heard of Sai Baba, but I have never visited Him."

For the fourth or fifth time on this trip, I began to talk about my relationship with Baba. I told about how Baba called me twenty years ago when only a few in Denmark knew him. I told about some of the dreams and visions in which Baba had come to me, and all the time he asked for more tea. "I have written a book, which has just been translated into English, about my relationship with Him. And I am about to write book number two. It is Sai Baba himself, who is the author. He delivers the manuscript. I am merely His instrument and I am happy to be. I would never be able to live without His guidance," I said.

He sat in his own thoughts for a while, then he said, "This is wonderful, what you've told me about your relationship with Sai Baba. I think Sai Baba has sent you to me; I am quite sure. May I invite you to dinner one evening and afterwards, you can see how beautifully I live. I have a beautiful house by the lake, with a wonderful view."

"No, I am now not quite so sure that it is Baba's wish, but perhaps it is Baba's wish that you may have him in your life. You should visit him in Puttaparthi. I believe that no one who has visited Sai Baba can leave unaffected, this may be why I am telling you about Sai Baba," I said.

"Maybe you are right. I think I will go to Puttaparthi and visit him one day. It has been incredibly inspirational, what you said." Then I said goodbye. Yet again the conversation had come to be about Baba.

On another day the owner of the houseboat said, "You must certainly take to the resort, (I do not remember the name). This is a well-known place by a major river, with magnificent scenery around it. It takes a few hours to drive up there, but we can make it a picnic trip and take food and blankets. It will take a whole day, but it will be nice." "Yes, let's do it tomorrow; it sounds exciting," I said.

Somewhat later, my guide came and asked me if the two women who worked for the household and made the meal every day, could join the picnic. "Of course, there's plenty of room in the car," I said.

So the next day there were six of us in the car that drove to the picnic: My guide, the owner's son of 12, the two women, my driver and me. We were all excited about the trip.

During the long drive, I had, once again, to talk about my relationship with Baba. The two women did not understand much English, but my guide translated, and it seemed they thought it was exciting even though they were not followers of Baba. They were all Muslims, but respected it as I, obviously, respect their faith. The weather was brilliant and it was a beautiful drive. After a few hours, we arrived at the spot where we could see the river, which was foaming down from high up; it was a very beautiful view.

We all got out of the car, and found a beautiful location by the river where we would eat our food. The women laid the blankets on the ground and each one got a plate and I got a spoon as well. I did not eat with my fingers. Westerners are not accustomed to that, but it seems quite natural when the Indians do it. The food was poured; it was rice and dahl, which is India's national dish. The women had asked the day before, what I wanted to eat. "Just a light potato meal or something with rice; it doesn't matter," I said. They had made the beautiful potato meal for me and we all enjoyed the food and the beautiful scenery.

When we had finished eating, everything was packed up and we went down to the river, where we sat for a long time, enjoying the beautiful views and the whole surrounding that was so lush for such a large river. We walked around in the beautiful surroundings and were exercising a little all along. We had a three-to-four hour stay before we headed back.

On the way home, we visited some mosques, since the others, as I said, were Muslims. I went with them into the mosques and wrapped my shawl around my head, as is customary in a mosque, in respect to their religion, just as they followed me into Hindu temples and bowed before Krishna. It was a beautiful way to get Baba's message through. We all know what Baba says, "All religions lead to the same God."

It had been a very nice day, when we talked about both Hinduism and Islam. But the two religions are not compatible; it is sad. During the drive, I was reminded how strange it was that I would be on a picnic with Muslims, but it went perfectly.

Eventually it was time for me to go home. My train would be leaving from Jammu for Delhi at about 8pm. so I set off from Kashmir at around 8am. I said goodbye to everyone on the houseboat. We had all had a nice time together.

222

For the last time, my guide rowed me to the other side of the river, where my driver was waiting in the car to drive me one last time. We were ready to drive but were obviously waiting for some reason. I said to my guide, "What we are waiting for?"

"We are waiting for permission from the police in Jammu. Due to the war between Pakistan and India, we cannot drive before we have permission," he said.

Finally, the permission came and he was searching for a pen, but apparently had none. He had to sign the authorisation that I should have, before we drove from Jammu. "I have a pen here," I said and handed him a pen with a picture of Baba.

He looked at it and said, "Sai Baba." It was the last name that was said before we drew off.

Baba, Baba, Baba.

Some strange events

It is at the end of September that I write these lines; I am sitting at a street café in Malaga in southern Spain. There is a festival in the city which is filled with happy rhythms and the joy of life everywhere. The city is decorated with flowers everywhere and the weather is glorious, 28 degrees Celsius. One cannot but be inspired by all this. For my part, I was inspired to write; in this case, about my stay in Kashmir. So wherever I linger in the world Baba is by my side. Three weeks after I had come home from Kashmir, He came to me in a dream.

Dream on 6 July, 1999

I was standing on a balcony, looking at a beautiful river. A single rowing boat approached and docked at the quay. There was only one person on board, now stepping ashore. To my great joy, I saw that it was Baba. As he stood on the quay, He waved, smiled warmly up to me and signalled that I should go down and follow him. I could tell that He would tell me something gratifying. I rushed down, but unfortunately I woke up so I didn't, at the time, know what He would tell me.

The fact that Baba was in a rowing boat showed me that He was referring to my stay in Kashmir, living on a houseboat, when, I sailed in a rowing boat to get ashore, on the other side of the river every day,. All this is described in the previous chapter. Three days later, Baba came to me in a dream.

Dream on 9 July, 1999

Baba was giving me a birthday party. There were many people celebrating with me. Baba came into the hall and up to me. He looked very lovingly at me, gave me His hand and said, "Happy birthday." Then he asked me to come with him in front of the party. There I was, stood at Baba's side while they all sang *Happy Birthday To You*. It was very beautiful, and I was very touched.

Baba went out and came back about a moment later, hugged me lovingly, said 'happy birthday' once again and gave me a birthday present. I opened it and saw, to my surprise, a small beautiful lighter in gold. I looked at Baba and He smiled, teasing me. He could see that I wondered about this strange gift because I had not been a smoker for

224

many years. Then I remembered a lesson Baba had given me many years earlier about my cigarettes, described in my first book. Now I understood. Baba smiled at me, and said, "Tomorrow we will have a nice picnic."

Immediately, when I woke up, I wrote down the dream. Then I looked in my book and saw, to my great surprise, that the lesson Baba gave me about my cigarettes was in the year 1979; now it was 1999; exactly twenty years later.

That was the birthday that Baba celebrated for me, and gave me a lighter in gold to remind me that it was twenty years since I had smoked my last cigarette. There is always a deep sense in what Baba is doing.

Thank you for the beautiful present, Baba.

I was, as I said, with Baba at the end of May 1999, when I ended my stay with a week in Kashmir. I was home again at the end of June. In July, I travelled with a female friend, who was also a follower of Baba, to Turkey. It was a very particular city we visited, and it turned out that it was not by chance that this town was the goal for the holiday.

The previous time I was with Baba was at Christmas and New Year 1999. I was at the usual travel agency which had arranged my travels to India for many years. They had a new employee, a young man and I enjoyed a cup of tea, while waiting for my ticket and talked about travelling in general. I said, "When I come home from Baba, I am always physically tired and often take a small vacation. I must say that it is always wonderful to be with Baba. To be in his physical presence is something special, but it is also hard work and I am not getting younger. Each morning we are up at four o'clock and then we sit in long rows, waiting to be let in to the temple square, where Baba gives his first darshan at about 6:30. By that time, one has already been sitting for two to three hours on a pillow with legs crossed. The same is repeated in the afternoon. Of course, I have long since become accustomed to it, but it is, nevertheless, a hard programme, but I would never do without it. This is why I need to relax when I come home from visiting Baba and since I have retired, it can be done and it is wonderful.

The young man said, "Where do you want to take a holiday this time?"

"In Greece or Turkey," I said.

225

"I know where you could go. You must visit a small, wonderful town in Turkey, called Kahs. It is located next to the sea, surrounded by the beauty of nature. It is five hours by bus from the airport. It is just something for you," he said and gave me a note with the name of the city.

"It is nice to tell me where I should take a holiday. I will consider it when I come back from visiting Baba. Thank you for the good advice; you never know how it will turn out," I said.

While we were talking, a customer came in and joined the conversation. He travelled a lot, I gathered. He said to me, "Why not travel to Malaga in southern Spain; Andalusia is beautiful, it takes just four hours by air, and is not very expensive."

"There are, of course, many possibilities," I said. Then I got my ticket to India, said goodbye and went without knowing that I would go to both Kahs in Turkey and to Malaga in Southern Spain, but that was the way it turned out.

The stay in Turkey confirmed that Baba controls everything. Never have I experienced something so incredibly funny as what happened in Kahs in Turkey. Baba's mood is without equal. Later, it would prove that it was not by chance that I came to Malaga in Spain, so I didn't have to bother making plans; Baba was doing that for me.

Back to my stay in Turkey. When we landed at the airport, we sat down and looked at a map to find the small town we had to visit. We found it quickly, but at the same time, we saw something else on the map that led us to look again. Just above the city was the text "Noel Baba" marked with a small man dressed in red. This amused us tremendously. After recovering from this incident, we went on a bus that would take us to Kahs. When we finally approached the town, we turned to the right.

My friend pushed me in the side, "Look up at the sign." I looked up at a large road sign, "Kahs, road to Baba." This amused us again, and I said, "We are apparently on our way to Baba."

Finally, we reached Kahs; a fairy-tale town by the Mediterranean Sea with wonderful scenery. In the old town there was a rich culture with restaurants and cafés everywhere, and here and there small hotels were built into the rocks. We found a small hotel and later we went out to dine. We were quite impressed by the town with all its charm where new and old were completely united. After we had had a nice dinner, we would find a café to get a cup of coffee. We went down to the yachting harbour, which was the town centre; it was very beautiful and filled with life. We were aiming for a particular café, which we had seen from a distance. It was the most beautiful of all the cafés located right next to the sea, and had a view of the yachting harbour with all the beautiful boats, all with lights, and palms everywhere. It was the place where everyone met in the evening: both the local Turks and the tourists. We came to the café, and walked around to find a table. At one point, we end up in front of the café, looking up at a large, beautiful sign with the café's name. And what do you think, dear reader, the café was called? I hardly need to say that it was called "Baba". We got a table in the Café Baba, and enjoyed our coffee, as we did all the following evenings. We always said, "We will end the day by Baba."

Absolutely wonderful!

Every day, we sailed on a small fishing boat to a very idyllic area with a wonderful beach, where we enjoyed the sun and the sea. Of course, there was a fishing boat called Baba, and on large beautiful boxes filled with chocolates it also says "Baba".

We were told that a great Saint lived in this area many hundred years ago, and the Turks commemorate him at a specific time every year. They call him "Noel Baba". Baba means father, but for us, it meant Baba. It was a wonderful vacation where we came across the name Baba all the time. It was incredibly inspiring. So it gave meaning to the fact that the young man in the travel agent had said to me, "You must visit this place; it is something for you." And he was right. When I was home and would later purchase my ticket to Malaga, of course I went to see him, but he was not working for the agent any more.

I had been home for a couple of months and the summer was almost at its end. One day, I sat at a pavement café, talking with a woman. We talked about a number of things. She told me that she did not live in Denmark more. "I live in Malaga in Southern Spain, and have lived there for the last twenty years. I only visit Denmark once a year."

I said, "Well, I have been travelling a lot to India over the last twenty years. In fact, twice each year."

"Oh, that sounds exciting."

"Do you have family in India?" she asked.

"No, I am a supporter of a great Indian master named Satya Sai Baba," I said. Now, she was very interested and wanted to know more, so I told a little about my relationship with Baba. She was very thrilled to hear about it.

We left the café and walked together until we would part. I wanted to visit a shop so I said, "I will shop here so I will say goodbye now."

She said, "You must surely visit me if you ever come to Malaga. Here is my phone number." I gave her my small notebook so she could write her name and phone number.

At the exact moment that she was about to write her telephone number, an elderly gentleman stood in front of me. He was well dressed, as we rarely see nowadays, and had a beautiful walking stick with a silver handle. I could not avoid seeing this. He broke into the conversation, but in a very civilised way. He addressed me, saying, "I am sorry, can you tell me where to find a shop selling women's and men's clothing, it should be located around here, with three steps down to the shop." I shop there a lot and had actually been there just before I visited the café.

I thought for a moment; then I said, "I know that shop. You must go straight up to the corner there; the shop will be on your left hand side."

"Thank you very much," he said and left us. The woman gave me back the notebook with her telephone number and we agreed that we would meet again. We said goodbye and went our separate ways.

Some days later, the man who had been in the travel agent, came to my mind. While the young man was about to tell me that I had to visit Kahs in Turkey, the man just intervened in the conversation, "Why not go to Malaga in Southern Spain; Andalusia is wonderful."

I replied: "Yes, there are many opportunities." In that moment I got my ticket to India, not thinking more of either Kahs in Turkey or Malaga in Spain.

All of that I have come to think about now. The Danish woman I had met, who lives in Malaga, had said, "You must surely come to Malaga, to visit me." And the vacation in Turkey, which was fresh in my mind, I had also been invited to visit.

Suddenly I knew with certainty that I must go to Malaga in Spain and ordered a ticket. Then something very strange happened. Two days before I was supposed to travel to Malaga, I was visiting the same shop that the elderly gentleman had asked for, just at the moment the contact with Malaga had been created. In the shop, right in front of me was the most beautiful Spanish blouse in pitch black silk. Spread across the chest were Spanish fans and Spanish newspapers, and in between all that Spanish, lovely orange roses. They had only this one, and it was of course in my size. It was hanging there as if it was waiting for me. I bought it and it was not even expensive.

As I left the shop I thought, "Now you are dressed up to go to Spain. How funny. And what about the elderly gentleman who interrupted the conversation; what about him? It all seems to fit together in one way or another, but how, only Baba knows. Mysteries are wonderful, but inexplicable."

As described, the stay in Malaga was fantastic. The festival was held in the city of Torremolinos. It is located twenty minutes drive from Malaga, by the sea. It was here I stayed.

I felt Baba had sent me there, at the exact moment for the festival, to give me a real inspirational boost for my writing. It seemed quite unbelievable. I was told that the festival was held at the same time each year. Just the time I was there: not the week before or the week after.

Baba sent me to Malaga, as He had sent me to Kashmir and Turkey. All of this was His will, and therefore it becomes so.

In about a month, I would be travelling to Baba again. I had to be with Him at Christmas and New Year and be there when we go into the year 2000. What can we look forward to?

Only Baba knows.

Year 2000

It was the end of January 2000. I had just returned from Baba. It was a wonderful and very intensive stay. There were so many people that I would think that almost every country was represented. That meant that we had to get up at three every morning. Baba gave darshan at about six and Bhajans at nine. We then just had time to get to our rooms to get a hot bath and do a few other things. At noon, it was back to the hall and at 12:30, we stood in line if we wanted to attend darshan which was, after all, why we were with Baba. There was no time for anything like lunch. It was a very hard programme. One has to be absolutely at the top, in order to do it. I would, as I said, only be there for three weeks; that was the limit for me. However, just to be in the presence of Baba made me capable of doing it.

Baba gave me a warm welcome and, in general, a lot of attention during the first two weeks and that meant that I was in a constant good mood and in balance. But in the last week that changed. He simply made it clear to me that it was not the physical Baba which was important for me but the inner Baba. He did it in so many ways and extremely effectively. From that day, attention from Him ended. I sat further and further back in the rows. And at the end, he was only an orange dot in the distance. But it did not bother me, because I understood it completely.

In the afternoon of 24 December, there is always a Christmas arrangement; and it was the same this year. A large choir sang and played for Baba. He sat in his chair on the patios enjoying the whole thing. After a while Baba signalled for them to finish. Then he went up to the conductor, clapped him on the shoulder and suddenly Baba materialised a large, thick, long gold chain for him. He fell at Baba's feet and it seemed as the applause would never end. It was breathtaking to experience.

The next day, Baba gave his Christmas speech. He also held a New Year's speech, on the morning of 1 January, 2000. I was very lucky to get a good seat for both.

Moreover, among other things Baba said in his New Year's speech, "There will be many floods around the world in January, February and March." A professor who gave a New Year's speech just before Baba, said, "The new technology that gets more and more ground in the world is not good for the human race."

I left just after Baba's New Year's speech, fully clarified in my relationship with Him and, at the same time, deeply grateful for the personal guidance Baba gives me, and has done for twenty years.

The last night of the old year, I got a rather unusual and symbolic dream. It is told here.

The dream

I was driving in my car with my son. We had to catch a train and were in a hurry. Suddenly, it came to me that I had forgotten the tickets. I was driving back and Birger, a close friend of mine, handed me the tickets.

Then we saw that in Kenneth's left temple was a small vertical cut, of about five centimetres. I was choked and said to Birger, "He must be hospitalised immediately; it must be stitched."

Suddenly, a man showed up and knowledgeably said, "No, it is not necessary to go the hospital. As you can see, there's no bleeding and it has started to heal. I made the small cut with my diamond ring. It is all as it should be." And just as suddenly as he had appeared, he was gone again. I looked at Kenneth and realised that it was true; the small cut was gone.

Then I said goodbye to Birger and drove quickly, this time with the tickets, to catch the train.

The time now was five minutes to twelve and I understand that we only had a few minutes, to catch the train. In the real world, the time is five minutes to twelve as well. Tomorrow was the last day of the year. Then it would be the year 2000.

Then the traffic lights were red and we had to wait. We were obviously not meant to be on that train; therefore, we were stopped by the red light. Then I woke up.

I saw the dream in the sense that Kenneth would perhaps begin to develop more and I will continue to work for Baba. Each of us has our work to do. However, we will never know anything with certainty.

Only Baba knows.

All religions lead to the same god

As stated earlier, I left Baba just after His New Year's speech which He held in the morning on 1 January, 2000. It was a nice goodbye to the old year but, at the same time, I was very tired, because I had been up at three o'clock in the morning for three weeks in a row. I arrived in Bangalore just after dinner, and I quickly got a room at the hotel I usually stayed in. The only thing I had in mind was to go to bed, which I did and fell immediately asleep.

In the evening I went down to the restaurant. I looked at the menu and was pretty hungry as I had not had anything since breakfast in Puttaparthi. The restaurant was about half full. A little later a gentleman, a Westerner came in. He looked around to find a table. Once he had made his decision he steered towards a table behind me. I registered all this while I studied the menu. When he passed me, he stopped and looked casually at me. He stopped, waited a little and then asked very politely, "Where are you from?"

"I am from Denmark," I said. "Well, I am from Canada," he said.

He was now about to sit down at the table behind me, but suddenly he said, "Have you been on a Christmas holiday with family or friends here in India?"

"No, I am a follower of Sathya Sai Baba and have spent Christmas and New Year with him in Puttaparthi. I left just after His New Year's speech this morning and will continue to Trivandrum," I said.

Suddenly, he was very interested and asked, "May I be allowed to sit at your table?"

I considered a short while, and then I said, "Yes, you're welcome."

After being seated, the first thing he asked was, "Who is the person you mentioned?"

"Do you not know Sathya Sai Baba?" I asked.

"I have never heard of Him," he said.

Then I began to tell him about Sai Baba, what Baba stands for, His mission, His message, His birth, His miracles and so forth. I also told him a little about my own relationship with Baba.

After only a few minutes he said absolutely outraged, "How can you believe in that? This Sai Baba is nobody. There is only one master who has significance to humanity and that is the Master Jesus, who walked on Earth 2000 years ago. Believe me, he is the only master who has ever been on Earth."

I thought for a moment about what he had said, and said to myself, "Well, now I am challenged." I could not listen to that without replying: I said, "No, there you're mistaken. The Master Jesus is not the only one who has been on Earth. He was undoubtedly a great master, but He was just one of them. Many great masters have lived on Earth and Sai Baba lives on Earth today. He is a great master and at the same time a spiritual mentor for thousands of humans. You should really visit Him. It would probably change your views on the matter."

He looked at me as if I was insane and said, "How can you compare an ordinary man who calls himself divine and who performs miracles, with the Master Jesus? Anyone can call themselves divine and magicians have been doing miracles for years. It is terrible that you have been deceived to believe in this. Please wait a moment; I'll fetch a book from my room. There is something I must read for you. I'll be right back."

I thought for a moment, about how to end this insane debate, but felt that I could not stop here, although it certainly would be the easiest, but perhaps not the right thing, to do.

A little later he returned with the Bible. I was not the slightest surprised. He was so excited that he must have thought, "This must convince her." He sat down, found something he thought was important for me to hear and began reading aloud.

I listened for a little while and said in a kind voice, "You must stop. I think most of us know a little about that and it doesn't change my relationship with Sai Baba, so it's wasted words. Keep them to yourself. It is your way." We had been speaking quietly the whole time, but had kept to our own opinion.

He stopped, but was deeply shaken. Then he said, "I believe the Master Jesus has sent me to you because you have gone astray and I have to get you on the right path again."

Now I was amused, and said to him, "Hold on, I think it is Sai Baba, who sent you to me because, for some reason, you have become fanatical and walk around with the Bible under your arm, preaching to people without thinking that others might have a different belief. It is very wrong."

He looked at me as if he had the greatest sympathy for me, and felt redeemed. Then the dinner was served, and we ate in peace and quiet; all the while I was thinking, "What should all this mean?"

Then I said in a relaxed tone, "It's nice for you, that you feel so much a Christian and believe in that religion, but do not think it is the only religion which is right. The major religions such as Hinduism and Buddhism are just as right as Christianity. All religions lead to the same God. It is just different cultures, taking different ways. That is the only difference. Respect all religions; that is what Sai Baba preaches every day and has done for years. He not only performs miracles, but shows his followers the way back to God. It is his greatest miracle."

He listened politely and then began to tell a little about his life, "I am from a wealthy family. My parents are divorced and I live alone with my father in a large house. I'm a businessman, have had many businesses with slot machines and earned a lot of money. Furthermore, I have had many female partners, but have never wanted to marry. They are only interested in sex and money and I was finally sick and tired of the whole thing. Everything was completely insignificant. I could not find the meaning of my life."

"I understand you very well. I think unfortunately a lot of people have it that way today. Everything must happen so quickly. It is only materialism that counts, and the humanism disappears more and more. Technology soon controls everything and everyone and makes people totally confused. It will not be better in the future. Evolution cannot stop. Each one must find one's own belief and live as they want. We have our free will. With regard to faith and religion, we see today more and more Westerners looking to India and other Eastern countries because the Eastern religions are more appealing. It is indeed very interesting," I replied.

He thought deeply about what I had said, but would not or could not understand. He had completely lost his distinction ability, and could no longer reconcile things.

It is the hardest hurdle to cross after starting on the spiritual path. I know about that myself. It is extremely difficult.

"Now you go back to Canada and have to make your life work. Where will you start? Of course, you have to earn a living. We all have to." I asked.

"Yes, I know. I am thinking of it, but right now I don't have the

234

overview, but I'm a businessman, so I'll figure it out," he said.

A little teasingly, I told him, "If you still want people to work for you, I will give you this piece of advice: Don't show up with the Bible and begin preaching or you'll never get anyone to work for you. People won't have anything pulled down over their heads. Everyone must believe in what they want. It's a private matter. Something quite different is if people ask you. Only then, one can tell somebody about their beliefs, otherwise not." We were both amused.

"Yes, I'll remember that when I have come to that point, but I do not understand why people don't want to hear about Jesus. I have so much to tell and I like to take the time and effort to tell them," he said.

"I don't doubt you, but no one is interested in hearing about it. Keep the divinity you have experienced to yourself. It is your experience and not others'," I said.

He sat a little in his own thoughts. Then he said in a beautiful way, "You are a very holy woman."

"That's not how I see myself," I said.

He ended, however, by saying, "You should forget Sai Baba, and instead put your faith in Jesus."

"No, it is not my way," I said.

"The world is becoming increasingly cold to live in. It is as you said. There is no room for the human more. It is terrible," he said.

"Tell me," I asked, "why are you actually in India?"

"By chance I heard a talk about the Master Jesus and was deeply impressed. I sold my business and went to India," he said.

"Yes, but I still do not understand: Why in Western India? Here, of course, Hinduism is in the majority and not Christianity, even though all religions are represented in India," I said.

He replied, "I speak with many people every day and many have told me that in Southern India, in the State of Kerala, there are many Christians. I therefore decided to go to India, to Trivandrum in Kerala. I have just been there and it was wonderful. I have been to Church every day and there were many of them. Now I am going back to Canada, but India is a very sacred land and I will return."

"It sounds nice. You really got something from your stay in India, which you can take home. It might make your life more content. I hope that for you. However, it is really strange: In my country, almost all churches are empty. A lot of people want them closed and used for other purposes because they don't think about Christianity anymore. Most only visit a church four times in their lives: First time when they are baptised, then when they are confirmed and many young girls get a trip from their parents instead of the confirmation party. Then the wedding and finally, when your body must be buried. This is how most people use the Church. Of course, there are also Christians and I hope they live their lives as Christians should do, but it's only a minority of the population," I said.

"It is terrible that not more think of Jesus Christ, but only focus on materialism."

Here I interjected. "But you have been doing the same until recently."

"Yes, it is true, but I do not any more. I will continue to go to Church and live as a Christian, no matter what others say. Even though I'll be called a fanatic," he said.

I would, as I have said, gone to Trivandrum in Southern India in the State of Kerala. I had intended to spend a week at a spa there, which is associated with an Ayurveda clinic, where I would get an Ayurveda massage each day. These treatments with Ayurveda oils should bring mind, body and spirit in balance and are based on more knowledge dating back more than 5,000 years. Kerala is known for its many Ayurveda clinics.

The next day I went to the station to buy a ticket to Trivandrum. I was standing amongst hundreds of Indians, looking around, quite confused. I soon learned that in India it's more complicated than just going to a ticket office and buying a ticket. The last time I went by train from Delhi to Benares, everything was done for me at a tourist bureau. Now it proved that everything was done for me this time as well. Fortunately, I had my passport on me, as I needed to use it to get the ticket. I didn't know that, in fact, two different kinds of forms must be completed.

Suddenly, a friendly Indian man came to me, and said, "Can I help you with something?"

"Yes, thanks, I need a ticket to Trivandrum. There are long rows at all ticket hatches, but nowhere that says Trivandrum," I said.

"You must first fill out a form. I will just get it for you," he said and was quickly back. "May I borrow your passport? I must use it, so I can fill out the form."

"Yes, I have it here," I said and gave him my passport. When he had completed it, I just had to sign it. I gave him some rupees, he went off to buy a ticket for me and a little later, he was back.

"Thank you, very much, it was kind of you," I said and expected that everything was done. I would leave on a night train that evening, and there were just a few things I had to attend to before that.

I was already on the way out of the station when he said, "Your ticket is not okay yet. You must address a second office in another department. It is located in the building next door. Now I'll lead you there."

"What do I need that for? I have got my ticket and paid for it." I said.

"Yes, but it's not enough. It must be confirmed and stamped okay." he said.

I thought, "Unbelievable, all this hassle just to buy a train ticket." However, I followed him, and I was of course delighted with his help.

When we finally entered the second office, it turned out that it opened at ten o'clock, and it was no more than nine. He said, "There is an hour and waiting here may not be worthwhile. Have you got any breakfast? I have not had anything yet."

"Yes, I had breakfast in my hotel," I said.

"There is a nice restaurant on the corner serving breakfast. We can stay there until the office opens. I can eat my breakfast and you can just have a cup of tea or coffee."

"Yes, that's okay," I said. Everything was said in a very friendly tone. He was not the least bit importunate, but simply helpful.

We went to the restaurant; a wonderful place where some Indians were having their breakfast. My companion ordered breakfast and I was content with Indian tea. While we were sitting there, came the usual questions. He asked, "Do you have family or friends here in India, or are you just on vacation?"

"Neither, I am a follower of Sathya Sai Baba and have spent Christmas and New Year with him," I said.

Immediately, there was a reaction from him, which completely surprised me. He said, "You can't be serious, believing in the man. Sai Baba is not the least divine. He admittedly does miracles, but so do magicians and they do not claim to be divine. What Sai Baba does is to take money from the wealthy Westerners, from which he has built universities, schools and an expensive hospital. Those who have contributed will then, in turn, benefit in one way or another and Sai Baba himself has become a very powerful person. It's something everyone knows. It has nothing to do with the divine. You must definitely not believe in Him."

I was deeply shocked and utterly in awe, and said nothing at first. It showed that he didn't know Baba's divinity and grandeur. He spoke only about everything external, which is just a part of Baba's mission. He knew nothing about the universal Baba, the internal Baba, who is omnipresent and paramount. What he does on the internal level goes far beyond time and space. I need only to think of my own relationship with Baba.

I sipped my tea and had no idea what I should do or say, but I had to reply once again. I clearly had in mind the conversation with the man from Canada the night before. He did not believe in Baba either, but certainly tried to convert me to become a Christian. "Forget Sai Baba," he had said. He was, after all a Westerner, and knew nothing of Baba, so it was easier to understand. But here I had an Indian who had downgraded Baba and almost felt disgust for Him. I had never been exposed to that before. "It will be a heavy discussion," I thought and felt the urge to leave but I couldn't. My companion sat quietly eating his breakfast, while looking at me. Of course, he was waiting a response from me.

Finally, I said, "You are completely wrong. You don't know Sai Baba. You're only talking about everything external, as is known to everyone. The universal Baba, which is ubiquitous, you do not know. He is definitely divine. He comes to many of his followers in dreams. He has shown thousands of people the meaning of their lives. He has healed countless humans from deadly diseases and most of it is documented. Baba can be in several places at once, which is described in many books. He knows people's thoughts and He knows the future. Everything He wants is happening here and now because He is divine. He often helps His supporters, no matter where in the world they are,

238

and often in different guises. Baba is working for his followers around the clock because he loves them and nothing else. You come with the nonsense about the money He receives. He uses the money only for good purposes and never for Himself. Of course, the money comes from wealthy supporters; where else would it come from? It is humans that give an amount to His organisation, because they know it is used for a good cause. Just as people give an amount for anti-cancer organisations, because they feel that it is used for a good cause. I know all these things with certainty, because Sai Baba has guided me directly for twenty years. He comes to me in dreams and often shows me the smallest detail. He gives me beautiful visions, but also many hardships because of the homework I have to learn. He is everything to me. I could never do without His guidance. It is most definitely not because I am wealthy. I have never given a single penny to His organisation because it is not within my reach. You see everything from a completely wrong point of view. You do not at all understand what the whole thing is about and I feel sad for you."

He looked surprised, but said, slightly arrogantly, but politely, "All this sounds very interesting, but don't believe in the dreams. My father died last year and he comes to me in my dreams. When one thinks of a person, he or she often comes in a dream. It is quite common. Also, there are many who can read other people's thoughts. There are also many other people in the world who heal people miraculously and none of them call themselves divine. So it does not change my views on Sai Baba. Can we not stop the conversation about Sai Baba? I do not like Him. I believe in the universal God. He leads everyone and is everywhere. It is the only truth."

What he believed in was just as true. It was just that he had not seen Baba's divinity. So faced with the allegation, I said no more. There was simply nothing more to say. It would be a waste of time and effort and anyone must, after all, believe in what is right for them.

When we had finished our breakfast we went back to the office, which was now open. My ticket was stamped okay, but our conversation was over. Neither Baba nor God was mentioned, but the man was still polite and helpful and finally he said, "I have a computer company in Delhi, so when you come to Delhi on your way home to Denmark, you must call me if there is anything I can do for you. Here's my business card with both my telephone numbers: for my office and my private residence."

"Thank you," I said, and took his business card. Then we said fare-well.

When I was back in my hotel room, I thought of what he had said and what I had said. I got quite tired at the thought that it looked as if I constantly had to tell people about what Baba stands for. I will gladly do that, if people want to hear about him, but I could really do without meeting two people, two days in a row, both of whom tried to get me to give up my relationship with Baba, and at the same time spoke very negatively about Him. I prayed, "Baba, Baba, spare me, let me not meet more of this kind of people. I really don't have the strength."

Finally, I was on the train to Trivandrum. I pulled my curtains and made myself as comfortable as possible for the night. I read a bit of my book, but quickly turned off the light because I was tired and immediately fell asleep. In the morning I woke up and was wonderfully rest-ed. On the train one could buy tea, coffee and various Indian breads for breakfast. I ate a couple of rolls with a cup of tea and they tasted very good. We drove through a rich landscape and the sun shone from a cloudless sky. I came from Bangalore, where it is normally cool in January but very cold, especially at night, to Southern India, where it is significantly warmer at this time of year. I had to change into slightly lighter clothing, but I had it ready because I was on the way to Kerala in Southern India.

At that time there were probably five to six people in the compart-ment, as some had got off and others had got on at the various stations. It was a long journey, and we would not be in Trivandrum until the afternoon. At one point, an older Indian couple came into the compart-ment and took a seat opposite mine, where I was sitting, reading my book. We greeted each other briefly as they came in but then I returned to my book. The other people greeted them as well, and the older mar-ried couples spoke quietly with each other so everything was peaceful and calm.

At some point I had laid down the book, and was looking out of the window. Suddenly, the older man said to me, "Are you on Christmas and New Year's holidays in India, Madame?"

I was pulled out of my thoughts, and answered like so many times before, "Yes, you can, in a sense, say that. I have spent Christmas and New Year in India, but that is not why I am here. I am a follower of Satya Sai Baba and have spent Christmas and New Year with him, like

240

so many times before. I have been a fan of Him for many years."

Immediately, he said very solemnly and slightly provocatively, "We are Christians and have just celebrated Jesus' birth. It was 2,000 years ago now since He was on Earth."

It was as if to be Christians was the only right thing, even if they were Indians. However, even though there are many Christians in India, the majority are, after all, Hindus.

I thought, "No Baba, not again." I took my book and was about to continue reading, to show him that I had no desire to continue the conversation. But no, it was not going to be that easy.

He said again, a little uncomprehending, "Everything cannot be only about Sai Baba. What about Jesus Christ?"

I had to put the book away again. There was no way out of it. Yet another provocation. I could not simply let the question be unanswered and said quite calmly, "Now I must tell you something. Do you, as an Indian, not know that Sai Baba is a divine incarnation who is here on Earth today, preaches every day, and has done so for years? Namely: that all religions lead to the same God. There are just different cultures and therefore different paths. All religions are represented by Sai Baba and people come to him from all over the world. You're mistaken if you think that because you are a Christian, you are better than a Hindu."

He looked at me in awe, but did not say a word. I continued, "Every Christmas, Christians from all over the world visit Sai Baba, but there are just as many Hindus from India and from other countries, who celebrate Christmas with Him. At Christmas, Sai Baba gives a talk about the birth of Jesus, on Krishna's birthday, he lectures about Krishna, and on Buddha's birthday, he lectures about Buddha. What can Sai Baba really do more than respect all religions?"

Everyone in the compartment had been listening to my lecture, but no one said anything. It was certainly not something I had wanted or planned, but had almost been forced to. We then made a stop at a station, where the older married couples had to get off. They quickly collected their luggage and left the compartment without a word. I returned to my book. You would almost believe, that because we had just entered the year 2000, and therefore had celebrated Jesus' birth, it had gone to everyone's head. I felt it that way.

Ayurveda treatment

There were only a few hours before we would be in Trivandrum. There were only two of us in the compartment now: a nice young Indian girl and myself. We had some small talk. She was from Trivandrum and had been in Bangalore celebrating the New Year 2000. She said, "You must be on holiday in Trivandrum."

"You could say that, but actually, it is more to find a good Ayurveda clinic that is part of a nice hotel, where I intend to spend a week or so, having a few Ayurveda massages, and Kerala in South India known for that," I said.

"It is a good idea," she said.

"Now, as you are from Trivandrum, you may be able to recommend a good place," I asked.

"Yes, I can. I will give you the address of a large tourist bureau. They can help you with everything."

"Well, that sounds lovely," I said.

"It's important not just to pick a place. There are indeed many Ayurveda clinics here in Kerala, but many of them do not know enough about Ayurveda treatment, and not all the clinics are careful with hygiene. They just take the money out of the tourists' pockets, so one should preferably know a little about it in advance, or be lucky. Visit the tourist bureau, and ask for (here she mentions an Indian name). She knows everything, and will be keen to help you," she said. Then she gave me a business card with a name and address.

"Thank you very much. Now I know a little more about the whole thing, and have something to go on," I said.

The train then arrived at the station. She rushed out, waving to me and she was gone. I went outside and got hold of a taxi, and drove to the address she had given me. It proved to be a very big tourist bureau. I went in and asked one of the employees, where I could find the lady whose name the young girl had given me. It was indeed an Indian name. I was instantly shown up to the first floor, and into a beautiful office where the Indian woman, who no doubt had a responsible position, was sitting. I sensed that immediately. She spoke on the phone, and gave an order. I sat down and waited.

She was now finished and asked politely, "How can I help you?"

"I would ask if you could recommend a good hotel with an Ayurveda clinic; I am in Trivandrum for the first time, and I have come to Kerala to get Ayurveda massages. There should be many around here," I said.

She looked at me for a little while and then asked, "Where do you come from and who sent you here for me?"

"I come from Denmark, but have been travelling in India for many years. On the train, I met a sweet young girl who gave me your name and address. She assured me that you would find the perfect place for me, as I have understood, there are some places that are pretty poor. So here I am," I said.

Before she could answer, a young girl entered the office very casually. She went directly to the woman, gave her a kiss on the cheek and said, "Hello mother." I looked at the young girl, and she at me, and somewhat surprised I realised that it was the young girl I had met on the train.

"Hello again," she said happily to me.

"Tell me, is it your mother, I am sitting here talking to?" I asked.

"Yes, it is my mother," she said and smiled, while the woman, who was her mother, watched us with surprise.

Then she said, "Do you know each other?"

"Yes, mother, we met on the train," she said.

"Well, it was my daughter who sent you to me," she said.

"Yes, obviously," I answered. Her daughter left us again quickly. She had just come in to say hello to her mother after returning from Bangalore.

When the girl had left us, we looked at each other and were a little amused. There was now a completely different atmosphere, not the normal business-like feeling, there always is when one enters a place as a customer. We chatted for a bit, then she said to me, "Now I need to find a really nice place for you, which also gives the right Ayurveda treatment." She called on the phone, and I could understand that she got a room for me, including full meals and Ayurveda treatment. I even got a large reduction in the price, as it was at the end of the season.

"Everything is taken care of now. I will immediately order a taxi for you; it takes close to an hour to get there."

"I thank you very much for your help. I apparently came to the right place. It was probably fortunate that I met your daughter on the train, which meant that I ended up here with you," I said.

"Yes, we can say so. When you return from the stay, you must visit me. I would like to know if everything was in order, and in fact, you must purchase your train ticket back to Bangalore now. One of the staff will ensure that on the floor below. I hope you will enjoy your stay. Here you have my business card," she said, and we said goodbye. When I put her business card in my wallet, I saw that she was the director. I was sent directly to her, due to sitting with her daughter in the train amongst hundreds of passengers. I could only think:

Baba, Baba, nothing is by chance.

At last I was in a taxi, heading for a health resort with an Ayurveda clinic. It was early evening and the sky was starting to become dark. We had been driving for a long time and I could see that we were driving into a forest. It looked totally enchanting, with the road winding in and out. We could only see the light from the car that shone on the tree trunks. It really looked like a magic forest. We drove further and further, and I thought, "Where will I end up?"

At last, I could see a lot of small lamps. The closer we got, I could see some very beautiful bungalows spread out over a large area. A stream winding through the area, and here and there, small Japanese bridges were linking it all together. I could see waterfalls, gushing down over magnificent stone outcrops into small lotus lakes. The climate was tropical. There were giant palm trees everywhere and wonderful vegetation. Everything was illuminated by small lights.

When I got out of the taxi, I immediately sensed a wonderful serene atmosphere. The only things I heard were the cicadas, the frogs and waterfalls.

When I got inside, a woman at the front desk welcomed me. I was given a small bungalow, adorable and stylishly arranged. The bathroom was quite wonderful, with a large palm tree in one corner, growing straight up in the air. Everything was very beautiful. "Is it satisfactory?" she asked.

"Oh yes, absolutely," I replied. "Is it possible to get something to eat at this time?"

"Yes, we have a nice restaurant. I'll show you," she said.

We went over a few small bridges, and passed some lotus lakes where the water was foaming down. Then we stood in front of a beautiful restaurant. She said to me, "Tomorrow, our Ayurveda doctor will come and greet you and together you'll determine what Ayurveda treatment you should have."

"Thank you! I will go in and get something to eat," I said.

The restaurant was very special with a glass pyramid without a roof in the middle with tropical plants, and the outer walls were of solid glass, so we could look at the scenery outside. It looked most of all, like an adventure park. "Here it must be possible to have the mind, body and spirit brought into balance," I said to myself.

I paid and the food was, of course, impeccable, just like everything else in this place. Later, when I left the restaurant and was slowly heading for my bungalow, it was a tropical night, and I thought, "Baba, Baba, is this perhaps the Garden of Paradise you've sent me to?"

Ayurveda is a 5,000 year-old natural medical health system that originates from India, and the very word Ayurveda simply means "knowledge of life".

There are various reasons why people choose an Ayurveda treatment. Some have a disease for which they only want Ayurveda treatment. The treatment will be based on the person's individual body type and the disease with different oils and so on. Then there are others who regularly get treatments, simply because it strengthens the body. Ayurveda treatments also prevent diseases, which is important for all people. It may also be a question of faith. Some believe in one thing, and others believe in completely other methods. It is up to the individual.

In our busy world, especially in the West, there is more focusing on the body, and we use a lot of time and money on that effort. Unfortunately, it is not that kind of awareness of the body that makes the mind, body and spirit, brought into balance.

The next morning the Ayurveda doctor came and welcomed me. She measured my blood pressure; it was in order. "Are there any special diseases, we must take into account in the treatment?" she asked.

"No, but I'm not very young anymore, and one's body, of course, over time, becomes worn. This applies to organs, muscles, tissues and so on, but that is natural for all people," I said.

"You are quite right, but we can do a little ourselves. Among other things, the right diet, a bit of exercise, and of course, no cigarettes and alcohol should be taken in moderation. This may well sound a little boring, but in the long run it is best for the body and life is, after all, much more than that. To destroy one's body through the wrong lifestyle, is the dumbest thing anyone can do. It is unavoidable that there will be disease, but you have the right attitude," she said.

"Yes, I suppose. First of all, I am a vegetarian, and I have not been smoking for the last twenty years. I do not drink spirits, but I could perhaps do a little more exercise, and now that I'm in India, I thought that I would have a little Ayurveda treatment. It will undoubtedly be good for my body. It is not done in Denmark, where I come from. And as you say: one may well do a little, in order to strengthen one's body," I said.

"You are absolutely right. Now I know what treatment we will give you, and we'll start tomorrow morning at ten," she said.

"I'll look forward to that," I replied.

The next morning I went to the Ayurveda clinic. I was met by a smell of incense and the sweet Ayurveda oils. I greeted the masseuse, who would give me the treatment together with the Ayurveda doctor. The masseuse showed me into a changing room to change. I put my glasses and jewellery in a drawer. I had been given a small piece of white cotton cloth, which worked like a small pair of panties, they fastened on each side; it was the only thing I wore. Now I was ready for Ayurveda treatment.

"Oh, you've forgotten your earrings," the masseuse said. I took them off and then the treatment began supervised by the Ayurveda doctor. First, I sat on a small stool, getting oil massaged into the scalp and hair very thoroughly. Then I lay on a massage couch and was massaged with various oils everywhere. Some oils were warm and they all smelt different. I was constantly being turned, so I finally was one with the massage couch, and all the time under the supervision of the Ayurveda doctor.

The masseuse was adorably dressed in a blue sari and very professional. She had done this before, I could tell, and she did not hold back. It was really a wonderful feeling. The whole thing lasted an hour, and then they helped me up, led me out into the bathroom and sat me on a stool. Here I was covered in something thick, quite hot oil, which reminded me a bit of mud in texture, but it was not because of its very nice smell. Eventually, I was washed with warm water, and the masseuse washed my hair, while indulged in some small talk. Later, I was standing in the locker room, dressed myself and combed my hair, that really was in a mess. Then I was finished.

I felt absolutely wonderful, not a single thought in my head and in total balance. I just went out of the clinic, into the beautiful nature. Suddenly, I heard someone calling. It was the Ayurveda doctor, and I went right back. She smiled and said, "You're not quite finished yet; come to my office." Both the masseuse and I went in, and we both laughed a little as it turned out that I had forgotten both my jewellery and my glasses. I had forgotten all about them.

After I had received both the jewellery and the glasses, we sat and talked for a while. I got an appointment for the next day and the doctor gave me two different kinds of Ayurveda medicine, which would strengthen my body. The treatment took an hour and a half. I then went to my bungalow and spent some time on the porch, looking at the large lake that surrounded the whole area, that was why it felt like a tropical climate. On the lake there were some young Indian men in some beautiful rush boats. Now and then they plunged into the lake diving to the bottom. I don't know what they were diving for; maybe mussels? The whole scenery seemed very peaceful and harmonious.

In the night, I became ill. I got severe diarrhoea and vomiting. I was constantly on the toilet. In the morning, I was completely exhausted but it is the kind of thing that can happen when you travel in India. "You may have given me a cleansing, Baba," I thought. In the morning, I put on my kaftan and went to the clinic, to say that I could not attend the appointed treatment. The only thing I could do was to lie in my bed.

"You're definitely not looking good," the doctor said when she saw me.

"I have had diarrhoea and, at the same time, thrown up all night, so I am totally exhausted and cannot get the treatment today," I said.

"I'll follow you back. The treatment must wait and so I'll come with some medicine for you," she said. I was then, again, in my bed. And a bit later she came with two different kinds of medicine that I should drink. It tasted dreadful and I threw up again. I could not keep it down: I was, of course, dehydrated and was very weak. She got some boiled water with added salt and sugar, as one always must take in such a situation, but it didn't help. Finally, I asked them to send for a doctor.

"I must have a drip with glucose water. It is necessary; it's the only thing to do now," I said. After having travelled so many years in India, I have tried this before.

"We'll call the doctor right away. There is a hospital, only three kilometres from here, so it's no problem," she said. A little later she came back, "We have called the hospital and talked to the doctor; he'll come within an hour."

"Thank you," I said.

Less than an hour later the doctor arrived with his assistant, a tripod for the bags with glucose water, medicines, syringes and so on. Above all, he was smiling and friendly, as is typical for Indians, "Hello Madame, I'll see to it that you will be fresh again tomorrow." He measured my blood pressure, touched me on the forehead and looked in my throat. "It's an infection. You must have two bottles of glucose water and my assistant will give you two injections, one for the fever and one for the infection. In addition, you'll get two different kinds of tablets against diarrhoea and vomiting," he said.

He now put the others to work. The Ayurveda doctor boiled water because I must not drink cold water and he gave her instructions regarding the various tablets. His assistant fixed the bags to the stand and I got the needle in my hand.

While this was happening, different people had entered my room. The manager came and greeted me and was sorry that it had happened now, under these circumstances. Then came the reception manager, who had called the doctor, and at the same time the masseuse. The Ayurveda doctor was already there. So there were six people in my room.

It was, fortunately, a double room, so there was enough space. They were apparently all interested to see how bad I was. There were two beds which were separated. I was in one and the doctor was sitting on the other. Since he had now set things in motion, he was sitting, chatting with me. It was not that I had a high fever, so I could take part in a conversation, and that's what happened, completely automatically.

First, he asked, "Are you touring in India?"

"Not quite. I am a follower of Sathya Sai Baba, and have been for twenty years now. I have spent Christmas and New Year with him," I replied.

He was obviously very interested, likewise, the others who were present in my room, so he asked again, "Yes, but how did you come to know of Sai Baba in a country that is so far from India? You say that you've been a supporter for 20 years."

"Well, I have to do it again, Baba," I thought.

"It is a long story," I said. However, they all wanted to hear about how I had got in touch with Baba, so I began to tell them about my relationship with Him and how He called me twenty years ago. I also told them about different dreams and visions, and how He guides me in everything. They all listened with great interest and deep respect for Sai Baba and his mission.

I think I talked for an hour. Finally, the doctor said, "It has been fantastic to hear about your experiences with Him. I am a Muslim, but have great respect for Sai Baba. You are indeed very blessed to have this close relationship with Him."

"Yes, I could not live without Him today. He is certainly the reference point in my life," I said.

"Yes, it is understandable. Now I must thank you very much for everything we've heard about Sai Baba and your relationship with Him. It has been funny and at the same time incredibly exciting. We will not disturb you anymore. You must rest and then I will come and see you tomorrow," he said.

They all wished me well and left my room except the Ayurveda doctor, she was with me the whole day and I felt much better. Once again, it was Baba who had been the main character, who else could it be?!

The next morning I woke up and felt all right. The Ayurveda doctor visited me. "Yes, I am quite well again now," I said.

"Yes, I can see that, but you cannot get a treatment today. You should relax and you must take the rest of your pills. The doctor will come one more time to check up on you. You should not be swimming in the pool today, but tomorrow you can get both a treatment and swim again," she said.

"I'll do what you say," I said.

"I'll call the restaurant and order some breakfast for you," she said.

"Thank you, I feel a little hungry," I replied.

Shortly after, a waiter came with breakfast, and an hour later the doctor and his assistant arrived. "Can you see it was just as I said: Tomorrow you'll be well and I can see that you are. You'll get a final injection, take the rest of your pills today and preferably relax," he said.

"Yes, I've been told that, so I'll do so. And thank you for coming. I am very pleased. At the same time, I would like to pay what I owe you," I said.

"Yes, thank you."

I paid and got a last injection. "Now I wish you a fast recovery and if anything comes up, you must call me. Goodbye, goodbye," he said.

I took it easy throughout the day. I read a little, listened to some good music and went for a walk in the wonderful park before I went to the restaurant to have my lunch. I could feel that I was a bit tired, so in the evening when I had had my dinner, the Ayurveda doctor paid me a visit.

"I can see that you've recovered, so tomorrow we'll continue the Ayurveda treatment. Come at ten o'clock. Now I wish you a good night. You'll hopefully sleep well," she said. That I definitely did.

The next morning, I continued the treatments. So the days went, in a wonderful, peaceful way, where I really felt that, my body, mind and spirit were totally in balance.

On the last day I had a treatment called Dhara. I got a ribbon tied around my forehead and then I lay down on the massage couch. My head was placed in a kind of small support, to bend it a little back. Behind me, the doctor was stirring a pot on a small fire. It was the hot oil, a very special oil, which she had ordered the day before. It is the last treatment you get before you leave.

The warm oil began to flow from my forehead and spread slowly around my entire head. It was almost like getting my hair washed in warm oil. While the oil was spilt over my forehead, the doctor applied a special massage. Her index finger slid endlessly from side to side in certain movements while the masseuse kept pouring the warm oil over me. It was a very intense feeling. Finally, it almost seemed as if I did not know who I was or where I was. I was totally balanced. It lasted about half an hour. Then they helped me to slowly sit up and led me out into the bathroom.

"How do you feel?" the doctor asked with a smile.

"I'm feeling very good," I replied. I simply could not find anything else to say. It was as if there were no thoughts in my head and I did not want to make an effort to get them started. My mind was completely quiet; nothing could disturb me.

The masseuse poured warm water over me, and said, "You have finished now and you can go home and relax."

"Yes, I'll do that," I replied. Then she followed me into the locker room. I was undressed, almost in slow motion, and felt wonderful within myself. I combed my hair and remembered both my glasses and jewellery this time. I went to the doctor in her office and, for one last time, we sat and talked a little, all three of us. "Now I'll go home and rest and tomorrow I'll say goodbye to you, before I leave," I said, and they replied, "We indeed hope you'll do just that.

Then I went very, very slowly home. Over the Japanese bridges, past the lotus lakes and the waterfall, which was pouring down. All the while, the sun was shining in addition to this magnificent nature and this wonderful tropical climate and I thought to myself, "There is really a place on Earth, such as this, even in our confused world where technology will soon control everything."

It was at the end of the season and there were only a few visitors, so everything was so intense that one felt the silence in soul and body.

It was for the same reason that I had received a large reduction in the price; otherwise I would not have stayed in such an expensive place. But it happened to me and I was glad.

When I got home, I laid down on the bed and immediately fell into a deep sleep. When I woke up, I felt extremely comfortable. I went to the restaurant and had a late lunch. In the afternoon I was at the swimming pool and enjoyed it.

The next day I went to the Ayurveda clinic, to say goodbye to the two lovely Indian women who had given me Ayurveda treatment each day for a week. "Thank you for all the treatments you have been giving me every day. It has been a fantastic experience and, without doubt, been good for my body. Perhaps we will meet again. I will never forget you and your lovely mood. Goodbye, goodbye," I said. The cab was waiting for me. I turned for one last time, and waved. Then I was on my way back to Trivandrum.

It should just be added that the director said to me, "Because you have been sick for two days, I will give you two days free here, also with Ayurveda treatment. We do not have so many guests now, at the end of the season."

"Thank you very much, I would very much like to," I said. It was a nice gesture. So it was, therefore, a total of nine days I stayed there.

I drove directly to the tourist bureau where I got my train ticket to Bangalore. In India, there are no return tickets when you travel by train. At the same time, I visited the Indian woman who had arranged the whole stay for me. "How have you been? Has it all been satisfactory?" she asked.

"Oh, yes, it has been a fantastic stay. I have been very pleased," said I.

"Have you got your train ticket?" she asked.

"Yes. And the last week that I have left here in Trivandrum, I'll spend at the beach before I head back to Bangalore," I said.

"It sounds nice. If you are ready to go, I'll call a taxi for you. I hope we see you again," she said.

"Yes, you never know," I replied. Then she called a taxi.

I was on the way to Kovalam Beach, a well-known resort in Kerala. After an hour's drive, I was there. I found a lovely small hotel, owned by an Indian family, situated only five minutes from the beach. I could clearly feel the difference from the fine quiet atmosphere around the Ayurveda clinic and this place, full of noisy tourists. However, that is the way it is today, but when I land in Denmark, in about ten days, I'll come home to the cold and snow; so I enjoyed the sun and the sea in my last week in India.

Before I knew it, I was on my way to Trivandrum and had reserved my seat in the train back to Bangalore.

I may have been eaten something that my stomach apparently could not tolerate, because I felt a little uncomfortable and also had a light fever. In the last week at the beach, I had been eating at several different locations and it does not take much to get a small infection when you travel in India. We had left Trivandrum at nine in the morning and would not arrive in Bangalore before the afternoon of the next day. I had not eaten anything for lunch, for I had no appetite. However, I had neither the diarrhoea nor had been vomiting, as I did the last time, fortunately.

I had pulled the curtains and laid on the bed, relaxing. Unfortunately, I had no tablets against fever, but I thought "It will probably be gone by tomorrow, if I can get a good night's sleep." However, when we arrived in Bangalore the next day, I was still uncomfortable and had a light fever. I drove directly to the hotel and got a room. At the same time, I got a little to eat, and bought two litres of mineral water, because I knew from experience that one should drink a lot, and went up to my room. I went to bed, since it was all I wanted to. Just before I fell asleep, I thought, "I'll buy some tablets in the morning.

I only had a day left in Bangalore where, among other things, I visited Air India, made a few last purchases and got the tablets. I had, after all, two days back in India and a long journey ahead of me. Although I was not seriously ill, I would like to be completely fresh, before the journey home. It is always difficult to travel that far. In the night, Baba came to me in a dream.

Dream in January 2000

I stood in front of my house, waiting for something; I don't know what. Suddenly, I saw a nice car coming which stopped in front of the house next to mine. A person, most definitely Baba, stepped out, this time, as a female doctor in the beautiful white coat. She looked fantastic. Her face was exactly Baba's, but her hair was longer. She was a beautiful woman to look at. I just stood and looked at her, deeply fascinated. She walked confidently up to her house. When she passed me, she nodded and smiled, then unlocked the door, went into her home and closed the door. I woke up.

A heady scent

It was, as I said, my final day in Bangalore. I started by doing the different things I needed done. Firstly, I went to Air India to have my ticket stamped OK. Then I visited my hairdresser. After that, I saw my tailor. The whole family had been followers of Baba for many years. We spoke a little, of course, about Baba before I left. The last thing he said was, "He is a teacher for all of us."

I could only agree. They were some fine words to hear about Baba, just before I left Bangalore, when I think of the Jesus fanatics I'd met, just after I had left Baba's New Year's speech in Puttaparthi, where all three had spoken only negatively about Baba. Two of them were even Indians. The third was from Canada and he felt that it was Jesus who had sent him to me, so I would understand that I had to leave Baba. It is incredible that one must hear this kind of thing when one travels to India.

After the tailor, it was time to get a bit to eat. After my lunch, I went to a pharmacy to buy some tablets for the fever. I was still a little tired and uncomfortable. It was the last errand I had. A saleswoman came up to me.

"I just need to have some tablets against fever and I had better get some tablets against diarrhoea at the same time," I said.

She solemnly told me, "It is better for you to go to the doctor."

It was nonsense. If I had been seriously ill, I would long since have gone to the doctor, but not for a little fever. In addition, I have been travelling in India for many years and on many occasions have received tablets for fever and diarrhoea. Please give me the tablets I ask for," I said.

She looked confused at me, but then the phone rang, and she went and answered it. Immediately, an attendant came up to me and said, "How may I help you?"

I reiterated, "I just need to have some tablets against diarrhoea and some against fever."

Immediately, he went onto a shelf, took a package of tablets, a second package from another shelf, and soon he was back and said, "These tablets are for diarrhoea and the others are for fever."

"Thank you," I said, paid and left.

I stood for a moment, waiting to get a rickshaw and just like lightning from a clear sky, the fever and the fatigue disappeared, and I was completely fresh again. "That's strange," I thought, "and I have not yet taken any of the tablets."

Then I remembered the dream from the night before, where Baba had come to me as a female doctor. The saleswoman had been quite right when she said, "You should go to the doctor." Of course, it was the doctor of all doctors who had made me well, and not the tablets; which I did not need. Despite this, I must always act, and never take anything for granted.

Incredible!

I arrived back at the hotel in a good mood, and could only think, "Baba, Baba." It was late in the afternoon, and I had been in a hurry, with the last things I had to do before I travelled to Delhi the next day. I laid on the bed to relax a little before I went down for dinner. I wore my headphones and was listening to a wonderful violin concerto. I had been lying a while, and was totally relaxed. Then suddenly I was surrounded by a heady, wonderful fragrance. It became more and more intense, but I could not really define it. It was neither jasmine nor rose fragrance. I finally came to the conclusion that it was the fragrance from a fine perfume which completely encircled me. It continued for a while, then it wore off a bit, but then the smell came back again with full strength. I almost felt, as if I was in seventh heaven. This wonderful music and at the same time this heady fragrance, which completely surrounded me. It can certainly not be described.

I was so moved and the tears ran down my cheeks. It was such a beautiful experience and I cannot put words to it. The smell just kept flowing around me as if it would take no end. The music had stopped, and now the smell slowly died out; then it completely disappeared. It lasted approximately half an hour. I was absolutely elated when I finally went down for my dinner.

Baba gives and gives. He gives each of us what we need.
Thank you, Baba.

The next day, I was on my way to Delhi, where I would spend my last night before going back to Denmark. I arrived in the early evening. I have never spent much time in Delhi and therefore had no specific hotel I use or know, so when we arrived in Delhi, I went directly to the tourist information office in the airport. "It must be the easiest way, when it only involves one night," I thought.

An employee immediately came and asked how he could help me.

"I need to have a hotel room for a night, and I'll not pay more than 600 rupees. It must just be neat and clean," I said.

"Yes, I need to fetch our book of hotels," he said and came back with a large book. We looked in the book for a while and he proposed some different hotels.

Suddenly, he said quite convincingly, "Here is a hotel I would recommend to you. It is a small hotel, neat and clean, and it costs 500 rupees per night.

"It's okay, I'll take that one," I said. I paid a deposit, and he followed me to a taxi.

I was on my way to a hotel for the last time in this trip. I expected, of course, it would be a small, clean and nice hotel I would arrive at, because it had been pointed out by the tourist office. We drove for quite a while and eventually we were a long way from the centre and had come to a desolate area. It was not very appealing.

"Tell me, do you think it is the right way we're driving? It looks a little strange here. It is not a place I'd like to stay," I said.

"Of course, the hotel is close by," the taxi driver said, quite calmly.

I looked around and it was awful. It was an excruciatingly remote place, with old, ugly worn buildings. It looked like an old abandoned factory headquarters.

Then the driver said, "Yes, it is right here."

"I can't see any hotel, only an old property without light. So I think you're wrong. I would never stay in such a place," I said.

"Yes, but, it is the right place. Can you not see the sign over there? You must go through the gate and up a staircase," he said.

I looked out; everything was dim. The only thing I saw was an old ugly property, with a small sign that was swinging. I was very annoyed when I saw it, but the taxi driver was not to blame. He had brought me to the correct address so I paid him, got my luggage and he left. A young Indian arrived and carried my luggage up a wobbly staircase.

It reminded me of a hostel; absolutely nothing for me. At the front desk was an older man. I went directly to him and said, "This must be a misunderstanding. I have been travelling in India for many years and have stayed in many different hotels, but I have never seen anything similar to this, and it was even the Tourist Office, which sent me to you. I simply cannot stay here."

He listened to me without replying. Then he said quietly, "Yes, it is true. I cooperate with the Tourist Association and they send many tourists out to me. If you do not want to stay here, I will call the Tourist Office and you'll get your deposit back."

"Yes, please, if you would be so kind," I said.

He called the Tourism Office and talked with the man who had sent me out to his hotel. Then I spoke with him and almost nagged him for several minutes. I do not remember everything I said because, unfortunately, my temper once again took over me. Finally, we agreed that the hotel owner would pay me my deposit. After having paid me, he asked kindly, "Where will you stay?"

"If you would be so friendly,to call a taxi, I'll find somewhere myself," I replied.

"Yes, I'll call immediately," he said.

I said goodbye and left.

I was back in a taxi, on my way to a hotel. It was exactly what I would have wanted to avoid by using the Tourist Association. I was very annoyed.

"Where will you go?" the taxi driver asked.

"You just drive until I say stop. I need to find a decent hotel," I said, probably not very polite.

He then drove back toward the centre. I stopped several times at different hotels, but they were either too busy or too expensive, so we drove on.

Finally, I said to him, "Please drive down this street. It seems that there are some hotels there."

He did so and we drove for a short time until I said, "I think you should stop here for a little while. I will go out and look at the different hotels."

"I'll wait here," he said kindly.

As soon as I had got out of the car and walked a few metres, I was suddenly in front of a beautiful hotel and the name was clear in front of me. It was illuminated in red neon, flashing without interruption, "Baba Baba". I just stood there looking at it: Baba Baba, Baba Baba. Again, I was deeply moved, understanding everything. A hint from Baba. I need it all. Not just sweet fragrances, beautiful dreams and visions, but also trails.

When I had recovered, I went inside asking for a room, but everything was booked up. I went out continuing down the street. Then a young Indian man came running from the hotel, "Madame, we have a room for you." I followed him inside and it turned out to be true. It was located across the street from "Baba Baba". It was in another small, charming hotel in white marble, it was called Hotel Rama.

I got a beautiful room for 500 rupees per night and I was happy. From my window, I could see the name "Baba Baba", flashing without interruption, as if to remind me that

Baba controls everything.

The next day I went home to Denmark with Air India. We took off at the scheduled time and were in Copenhagen in the late afternoon, Danish time. It was 23 January, 2000. As I said, I came home to winter: snow and cold. After I had been home for a few weeks, I thought, "I want to travel south, down to the sun. There I'll be more inspired to get started with the writing." I had not got a pad and a pencil yet. Although I knew that is what Baba expected of me.

About three weeks after I had come home, Baba gave me a vision. Now I really was inspired beyond measure to write and so I finally got the pad and pencil.

The vision is described here.

A vision on 18 February, 2000

I was with some friends in a house by the sea. There was the most lovely view one could think of. As far as the eye could see, there was only the white sandy beach and the blue sea. It was completely silent. The sun had just set, which gave the whole thing an enchanting glow. Here I stood looking out of the window at this wonderful sunset.

Suddenly, I saw something quite amazing. A large, colourful parade was approaching very slowly from the right. It was a wonderful view as it moved along the white sand beach alongside the calm sea. It was exactly like a caravan in the desert, with the difference that in the desert, there is the only sand, sand and more sand.

Now I could see an elephant at the front of the parade. Just after the elephant, I could see a car. After the car, several people were riding on camels. It was really a breathtaking sight. The whole cavalcade had now reached the front of the house where I stood, absolutely astonished and I looked at it all, as if it were a fairy tale.

To my surprise, it was Baba with all his entourages. I could hardly believe it, but then Baba waved to me. It was Baba's elephant, Gita, in full regalia, which led the parade. Then Baba came in a wonderful open car, completely covered with flowers. Also the camels were decorated, as were all of the participants.

I said to my friends, "Hurry, come and see something quite fantastic. Baba is here, with a great entourage." Immediately everyone came running, but before they had reached the window, I was out of the house and down with Baba.

He opened the door and said, "Come and sit a little while," after which he welcomed me lovingly.

"As you can see, we are on a long journey," he said, while we left the car. He gave the cavalcade the order to stop.

I said, "You can spend the night at my friend's house, Baba, there are many rooms and we would be pleased." Baba was thinking a little about my offer.

Now my friends arrived and Baba welcomed them warmly. We talked a bit about the accommodation and finally Baba agreed. My friends were full of enthusiasm and so was I. Baba now told everyone to camp for the night. Gita laid down and relaxed, as did all the camels and all the participants. They had travelled far and were tired.

Finally, my friends asked Baba if they could take a picture of this magnificent vision, as a keepsake. Baba agreed.

I stood next to Baba, in the midst of the colourful parade, while the picture was taken. Sadly, I cannot show you the image, so you must be content with my story. However, at the same time this fantastic experience ended for me as well. I woke up to my everyday life. The whole can and must be connected. It is the most important of all, but not always easy.

Baba, Baba. What will be my next experience?

The next experience Baba gave me, came on 9 August, when He once again materialised some vibhuti in my little bowl. Marvellous! On 13 August, I'll once again travel to India. I have long thought about getting an apartment in Bangalore, so I have an Indian home. It is in India that I feel at home; both in heart and soul.

Now I would look at the possibilities of getting an apartment in Bangalore. At the same time, I certainly hope that if I got an apartment

it would be with Baba's blessings.

Throughout the years in which Baba had come to me in dreams and visions, He had often alluded to an apartment, but I had always thought, "Well, time will tell," but when I travelled to India in August to explore the possibility of getting an apartment in Bangalore, it proved to be possible. So now I have a nice apartment.

"Now I have an Indian home only four hours drive from Baba, and it is absolutely perfect for me," I thought. At the same time, I began, with friends' help, to fill it with everything you need in a home. As things took shape, I looked around at my new apartment and I really thought that it was a beautiful Indian home.

I was now ready to go to Baba in Puttaparthi. I was curious to know whether He would comment on it. He did, but just not in a way that I had expected.

In recent years, many foreigners have either bought or rented an apartment in Puttaparthi, but I had never done it. I had actually been quite satisfied with staying at a hotel as I was never with Baba for more than a month at a time. There are so very many people today and life in the ashram is very strenuous. Also for this reason, I got an apartment in Bangalore. "This is the right thing for me," I thought, but I was wrong about what surprised me. What I believe is one thing, another is what Baba says. I had completely forgotten to take that into account, so I had to work that out once again.

All the time I stayed in Bangalore decorating my home, I only thought of one thing, namely to go to Baba in Puttaparthi. It was almost as if everything else was completely insignificant. Finally, I was ready to go to Him.

I arrived just at the god Ganesh's birthday. It is a large religious celebration for the Hindus and Baba celebrates it every year. When I arrived, Prasanthi Nilayam was all decorated for the celebrations as was Puttaparthi. Never had I felt more at home. The celebrations lasted for seven days and in that week, Baba changed my entire future. He gave me so much attention and made it quite clear to me that it was here with Him in Puttaparthi I belonged and not in Bangalore. I felled deeply in my heart that it was only here I belonged and never had I felt more at home in Puttaparthi than this time, so I had to find an apartment here and sell my apartment in Bangalore. I was completely convinced of that and one day when I walked down the main street of Puttaparthi, Baba came driving in his car. When He passed me, He waved and smiled warmly to me. In that moment, I felt very happy and knew with certainty what I had to do.

Baba rules everything.

My Indian home

I began to look for a suitable apartment. However, it was not that straightforward. They were either too expensive or they were somewhere I never wanted to live. I was about to give up when something happened. I went for a walk passing a beautiful white building with oval balconies. It was being built and there were craftsmen everywhere. I noticed that it was located in a very quiet area. I stopped and looked at the busy workmen. Next door, was a private house with an open door leading into an office. An Indian man came out from the office and I asked, "Is it your property that is currently being built here?"

"Yes, it is; come inside," he said kindly.

When in his office, he said, "The property has four floors. We have the first and second floors finished and they are rented out. The third and fourth floors will be finished in the beginning of December. Do you want to see the apartments?"

"Yes, I would like that," I said, and we went into the building. He rang the doorbell of a few of the residents and asked if I could see the apartments. They were Indian families and they were very kind to show their apartments to me. They were all followers of Baba. They turned out to be some very beautiful apartments. In every apartment, there was a living room, a bedroom, a kitchen, and a bathroom and the rent were absolutely reasonable. I thanked them for their kindness and said to the owner, "I would like to see an apartment on the fourth floor."

"Yes, we only have one. We'll have a look at it. It is only half-finished, but they are all the same, although you can look at the lovely view," he said.

"Yes, it would be exciting to see the view," I replied.

We came up to the half-finished apartment on the fourth floor. The view was wonderful. I looked over Puttaparthi city and mountains and rice fields as far as the eye could see. However, the most beautiful aspect of the whole thing was, that from my small balcony, I looked straight at Baba's balcony. I was in no doubt. I wanted to live here! I went out onto the small balcony. Baba's balcony was part of His private residence. However, I could not see His house, although I was happy and felt warm hearted.

"I'll take this apartment, from 1 December. It coincides nicely with the termination of my apartment in Bangalore," I said.

"I am glad to hear that. We'll talk about it in my office," he said. We did so, I paid a deposit, got a receipt and the address of my apartment. A little later his wife came into the office with a glass of juice. They asked about my relationship with Baba and I told them a little about how Baba had led me for almost 22 years, through dreams and visions. It seemed they were very excited to hear about it and it turned out that they were also old followers of Baba. They were around my age.

The man said to me, "I was born in a small village not far from Puttaparthi and I am happy that I have lived all my life so close to Puttaparthi where Sai Baba was born."

"I understand," I said.

"Would you like to see our house altar?" his wife asked."

"Yes, please," I said.

I followed her into a beautiful room and in a niche, they had a very beautiful house altar. The whole wall was covered with a very large, beautiful picture of Baba. A board was covered with wonderfully thick orange silk, a candle was lit, incense was burning and there was a small bowl of vibhuti. She gave me a little vibhuti and left me to let me be alone with my thoughts. In whom my thoughts were directed to at this moment, no one could be in any doubt.

After a little while, I went out to her and I followed her to her husband, who was sitting in the office. We talked for a little while about some practical things concerning the apartment.

"I'll be leaving in a few days, but I'll come in to say goodbye, before that," I said.

"Yes, we will meet again," they replied."

A little later I went down the main street of Puttaparthi and - good God - Baba came driving towards me. I rushed to the wayside, along with a number of others, waiting for Baba's car to pass. When his car approached where I was standing, He stopped for a moment, waved and smiled at me. I waved back. The others also began waving, which one does not normally do and suddenly, we were all quite close to Baba's car. We touched the windows, and Baba waved to us all. We felt completely elated. It is indeed very rare that Baba stops His car to wave to the crowds, so it was a very special darshan. Slowly, the car began to move again. What I felt at that moment, cannot be described.

Now there were only two days left before I had to go to Bangalore, so I took care of the last practical things. I also visited a good friend of many years, to say goodbye. She had been a great help to me, especially this time, and supported me in everything, when I had to take such a big decision about the apartment. On many occasions she cooked for both of us, so I did not need to be in the long queue in Baba's canteen, which was crowded because of the festivities. She had lived with Baba for about twenty years, and made food for herself every day. We had a good talk about the old days with Baba.

In the evening before travelling the next day, I had to go and say goodbye to the apartment owner. He received me in a friendly manner as he took both of my hands, smiled warmly and said, "Goodbye, see you in November, Sai Ram."

The next morning I went to an Indian café, to get my morning coffee. As I was walking, immersed in my own thoughts, I saw Baba's car in the distance. "Baba, Baba, one last hello," I thought. Once again, I stepped at the roadside, with all the others, and was waiting for Baba to pass. When his car passed me, he looked very intensely at me for a moment. It felt very affirmed and beautiful. Happily, I left for Bangalore.

What I was not so pleased about, was that I had to cancel the lease of my apartment in Bangalore. I had only lived there for a few months. It was a new house I had moved into as well and the owner and his deputy had done so much for me. So when everything was neat and complete, I came back from Baba, only to move out; but that was that.

The owner had, of course, long heard of my long-standing relationship with Baba and had great respect for Sai Baba, although he was not a follower of Baba; he was Muslim, although he was a very good and helpful man.

When I arrived at my apartment at noon, he stood outside his office, in the house next to where I lived. It was some of his relatives, who lived there. When he saw me, he approached me and said with a smile "How are you?"

"Thank you, I'm fine, but do you have a moment, I would like to talk with you," I said, feeling a little uneasy.

"Yes, please came in," he said kindly.

We sat down and he looked invitingly at me. I had prepared myself and said, "Well, you see; I have to quit my apartment from 1 December, unfortunately for you, but it's a beautiful apartment, so I am sure it will be rented out quickly. I will not be living in Bangalore."

He looked confused. I could clearly see that it came as a surprise. It had actually surprised myself that Baba had wanted me to live in Puttaparthi. However, of course, I had long been aware that was how it should be.

He sat for a little while looking at me. Then he said, "May I ask why?"

"As you know, I have been a follower of Sai Baba for many years and He is, and remains, the most important person in my life, and that is how it will always be. Sai Baba wants me to live with Him in Puttaparthi, not in Bangalore, and I've got a beautiful apartment in Puttaparthi from 1 December. It's also a new house and I am very happy," I said.

He said then, "I respect that of course. I will get my deputy to assist with anything."

"Thank you very much," I said, and with my heart relieved, I went into my apartment. I looked around. Everything should now be packed up once again. I could start over.

A little later the owner and his deputy came and we talked about the practical things. The deputy would get some boxes so that we could start packing because I would go to Denmark for a few days, later staying there for a couple of months, before returning in the middle of November for Baba's birthday. My new apartment should be finished by the end of November. The intention was that when Baba's birthday party was over, I would go back to Bangalore, but only to move my things. Everything should be ready to be loaded onto a truck.

The deputy and I got busy. He came with some boxes and we began to pack. The next day we were finished and everything was moved into the guest room, so I had only to think about the journey. I said goodbye to the owner and the various people I, for a brief moment, had come to know.

Finally, after a long and difficult journey, I was back in my home in Denmark. I relaxed for the first couple of days. There was so much to think about. Baba had, of course, totally changed my plans regarding where I stay when I was in India. At the same time, I was very happy that Baba wanted me to live in his presence. It was not what I had planned, but apparently Baba had. He confirmed that later. About two weeks after coming home, he came to me in a dream.

Dream on 21 October, 2000

Baba was driving in his car in Puttaparthi. He got out and walked towards me. He stopped in front of me, and I said, "Baba, I will leave tomorrow."

Slightly teasingly, He said, "Well, you do? But where do you live?"

"I live in an old house, Baba," I replied.

"Oh no, you don't live in an old house," Baba said.

"When I come next time, I'll move into a new house in Puttaparthi, Baba," I said.

Baba took both my hands, smiled warmly at me, and said, "Yes, you move into a new house here with me in Puttaparthi. This is where you belong."

He embraced me lovingly and left.

Baba had taken both my hands, just as the owner had done when he parted with me, and I had to travel to Bangalore and said, "Goodbye, see you in November, Sai Ram."

Baba is all knowing. He is everywhere. He is divine.

It was now the beginning of November 2000, and I would be travelling to Baba in a few days. He would be 75 years old on 23 November and I wanted to celebrate Him.

Once again, Baba:
Thank you for all you are to me.
SAI RAM.

Illustration index

All vignettes were made in 1980.

The small colour painting of Krishna on the inside of the back cover and in gray on page 81, and the drawings of the lotus flowers on page 7 to 9, are created by Lise Jersing.

The End

I hope you have enjoyed the book. Please take a moment to leave a
short review at your favourite retailer site.
Thanks!
Marguerite Jalving